READERS AND READING

LONGMAN CRITICAL READERS

General Editor
STAN SMITH, Professor of English, University of Dundee

READERS AND READING

Edited and Introduced by

ANDREW BENNETT

LONGMAN
LONDON AND NEW YORK

Longman Group Limited,
Longman House, Burnt Mill,
Harlow, Essex CM20 2JE, England
and Associated Companies throughout the world.

Published in the United States of America
by Longman Publishing, New York

First published 1995

ISBN 0–582–21289–8 CSD
ISBN 0–582–21290–1 PPR

British Library Cataloguing-in-Publication Data

A catalogue record for this book is
available from the British Library

Library of Congress Cataloging-in-Publication Data

Readers and reading / edited and introduced by Andrew Bennett.
    p. cm. – (Longman critical readers)
    Includes bibliographical reference (p.) and index.
    ISBN 0–582–21289–8. – ISBN 0–582–21290–1 (pbk.)
    1. Reader-response criticism. 2. Authors and readers. 3. Books
    and reading. I. Bennett, Andrew, 1960– . II. Series.
PN98. R38R424 1995
028–dc20   94-27865
                                                    CIP

Set by 5K in 9/11.5 pt Palatino
Produced by Longman Singapore Publishers (Pte) Ltd.
Printed in Singapore

Contents

General Editors' Preface

The outlines of contemporary critical theory are now often taught as a standard feature of a degree in literary studies. The development of particular theories has seen a thorough transformation of literary criticism. For example, Marxist and Foucauldian theories have revolutionised Shakespeare studies, and 'deconstruction' has led to a complete reassessment of Romantic poetry. Feminist criticism has left scarcely any period of literature unaffected by its searching critiques. Teachers of literary studies can no longer fall back on a standardised, received, methodology.

Lecturers and teachers are now urgently looking for guidance in a rapidly changing critical environment. They need help in understanding the latest revisions in literary theory, and especially in grasping the practical effects of the new theories in the form of theoretically sensitised new readings. A number of volumes in the series anthologise important essays on particular theories. However, in order to grasp the full implications and possible uses of particular theories it is essential to see them put to work. This series provides substantial volumes of new readings, presented in an accessible form and with a significant amount of editorial guidance.

Each volume includes a substantial introduction which explores the theoretical issues and conflicts embodied in the essays selected and locates areas of disagreement between positions. The pluralism of theories has to be put on the agenda of literary studies. We can no longer pretend that we all tacitly accept the same practices in literary studies. Neither is a *laissez-faire* attitude any longer tenable. Literature departments need to go beyond the mere toleration of theoretical differences: it is not enough merely to agree to differ; they need actually to 'stage' the differences openly. The volumes in this series all attempt to dramatise the differences, not necessarily with a view to resolving them but in order to foreground the choices presented by different theories or to argue for a particular route through the impasses the differences present.

The theory 'revolution' has had real effects. It has loosened the grip of traditional empiricist and romantic assumptions about language and literature. It is not always clear what is being proposed as the new agenda for literature studies, and indeed the very notion of 'literature' is questioned by the post-structuralist strain in theory. However, the uncertainties and obscurities of contemporary theories appear much less worrying when we see what the best critics have been able to do with them in practice. This series aims to disseminate the best of recent criticism and to show that it is possible to re-read the canonical texts of literature in new and challenging ways.

RAMAN SELDEN AND STAN SMITH

The Publishers and fellow Series Editor regret to record that Raman Selden died after a short illness in May 1991 at the age of fifty-three. Ray Selden was a fine scholar and a lovely man. All those he has worked with will remember him with much affection and respect.

Acknowledgements

We are grateful to the following for permission to reproduce copyright material:

Columbia University Press for 'An Unnecessary Maze of Sign-Reading' from *Reading Woman: Essays in Feminist Criticism* by Mary Jacobus. Copyright © 1986 Columbia University Press, New York, for extracts from the chapters 'Reader-Response Criticism' and 'Literary Structuralism and Semiotics' from *American Literary Criticism from the Thirties to the Eighties* by Vincent B. Leitch, pp. 211–37, 424–5, 252–9, 426. Copyright © 1988 Columbia University Press, New York, and for the chapter 'Reading Unreadability: de Man' from *The Ethics of Reading: Kant, de Man, Trollope, James, and Benjamin* by J. Hillis Miller. Copyright © 1987 Columbia University Press, New York; Duke University Press for the article 'Feminism, New Historicism and the Reader' by Wai-Chee Dimock from *American Literature*, **63** (4): 601–22. Copyright 1991, Duke University Press; Harvard University Press for the chapter 'Renewing the Practice of Reading, or Freud's Unprecedented Lesson' from *Jacques Lacan and the Adventure of Insight: Psychoanalysis in Contemporary Culture* by Shoshana Felman. Copyright © 1987 by the President and Fellows of Harvard College; The Johns Hopkins University Press for the article 'Labourers and Voyagers: From the Text to the Reader' by Roger Chartier from *Diacritics*, **22**: 2 (summer 1992): 49–61, and for extracts from 'Reading Ourselves: Toward a Feminist Theory of Reading' by Patrocinio P. Schweickart from *Gender and Reading: Essays on Readers, Texts, and Contexts*, ed. Elizabeth A. Flynn and Patrocinio P. Schweickart (1986); Princeton University Press for 'Interaction between Text and Reader' by Wolfgang Iser from *The Reader in the Text: Essays on Audience and Interpretation* by Susan R. Suleiman and Inge Crosman. Copyright © 1988 by Princeton University Press; Routledge, Inc. for the essay 'Wilde's Hard Labour and the Birth of Gay Reading' by Wayne Koestenbaum from *Engendering Men: The Question of Male Feminist Criticism*, ed. Joseph A. Boone and Michael Cadden (1990); Station Hill Press for 'Reading' from *The Gaze of Orpheus and Other Literary Essays* by Maurice Blanchot, trans. Lydia Davis (1981); University of California Press for the chapter 'Reading as Poaching' from *The Practice of Everyday Life* by Michel de Certeau, trans. Steven Rendall. Copyright © 1984 The Regents of the University of California; The University of Chicago Press and the author, Professor Yves Bonnefoy, for the article 'Lifting Our Eyes from the Page', trans. John Naughton from

Critical Inquiry, **16** (1990): 794–806; Yale French Studies for an extract from the essay 'The Resistance to Theory' by Paul de Man from *Yale French Studies*, **63** (1982).

Introduction

The reader! You, dogged, uninsultable, print-oriented bastard, it's you
I'm addressing, who else, from inside this monstrous fiction. You've
read me this far, then? Even this far? For what discreditable motive?
How is it you don't go to a movie, watch TV, stare at the wall, play
tennis with a friend, make amorous advances to the person who
comes to your mind when I speak of amorous advances? Can nothing
surfeit, saturate you, turn you off? Where's your shame?[1]

The reader has been the object of a long and distinguished history of
abuse. From Laurence Sterne's provocative teasing of readers in
Tristram Shandy, through Baudelaire's and then T. S. Eliot's 'You!
hypocrite lecteur! – mon semblable, – mon frère!' ('You! hypocrite
reader! – my double – my brother'), to, more recently, the postmodern
antagonisms of John Barth's 'Life-Story', this is a tradition of what
might be called the 'mocked reader'. Thus Barth's address
characterizes the reader in terms of shame and desire, collusion and
voyeurism, illegitimacy and suspect motivation, violence and
abjection, monstrosity and insatiable lust. The joke is, of course, that
no reader will identify with this 'reader', with 'you': the reader is
uninsultable, not you. Who, then, is the reader? Where is she? And
what is she doing?

Who reads? What is reading?

'The illusion is endlessly reborn', comments Paul Ricoeur, 'that the text is
a structure in itself and for itself and that reading happens to the text as
some extrinsic and contingent event.'[2] Much of the work in criticism and
theory in recent years has been concerned to question the seductions of
this endless illusion. Indeed, it has become clear that the double question
'who reads?' and 'what is reading?' is fundamental to many different
aspects of criticism and theory. In the work of such critics as
Wolfgang Iser, Stanley Fish, Michael Riffaterre, Jonathan Culler,

Steven Mailloux, Judith Fetterley, Mary Jacobus and Paul de Man, there has been an explicit concentration on readers and reading. More generally, however, no aspect of literary criticism has remained immune to reading theory.

The two questions which this collection asks – Who reads? What is reading? – may be subdivided into a number of discrete problems: what do readers do when they read? Is reading determined by the text, by the reader's subjective responses, by social, cultural and economic factors, by conventions of reading, or by a combination of these? Is there such a thing as a true or correct reading? And if so, can we determine which reading is right? How do texts affect readers? Is there an ethics of reading? How might we describe the identity of the reader? Does such an identity change in reading or after reading? How is reading gendered? What would constitute a history of reading? What is the significance of rereading? And of misreading? This collection presents some of the ways in which recent reading theory has engaged with such questions.

The question of the identity of the reader has been answered in a confusingly large number of different ways. But this abundance of identities may itself suggest something about readers and reading: as Wai-Chee Dimock comments in an essay reprinted below, rather than a 'unified entity', the reader should be understood as a figure who is 'traversed by time and dispersed in time, making its staggered appearances in a variety of stages, in its residual, established, and emergent forms, and through its inflections by class, gender, and race'.[3] The fact that the question 'Who reads?' has been answered in so many ways, then, may be indicative of the instability or mobility of what we call 'the reader'. Before going on to consider the consequences of such variety it might be useful briefly to list a few examples of the ways that critics have described readers in recent theory:

- the reader is a hypothetical construct with all possible knowledge and interpretive skills at his or her disposal (Riffaterre);
- the reader is an individual subject and reading is determined by his or her 'identity theme' (Holland);
- the reader is not an individual but a community of readers functioning through the reading strategies employed by a particular member of that community (Fish);
- the reader is a series of moves or responses more or less predetermined by the language of the text itself but 'concretized' in the act of reading (Iser);
- the reader is an individual in a particular historical and social situation whose responses are available to empirical investigation through written records (Chartier);

– the reader is a woman, a gay man, the member of an ethnic minority or other marginalized person whose responses involve a certain resistance produced by ethnic, sexual or social difference (Fetterley).

Together with various other descriptions, these have all been offered as models of 'the reader' or have been emphasized as the focus of reading theory. Similarly, readers have been variously named by these and other critics: in *The Return of the Reader*, for example, Elizabeth Freund lists 'the mock reader (Gibson), the implied reader (Booth, Iser), the model reader (Eco), the super-reader (Riffaterre), the inscribed or encoded reader (Brooke-Rose), the narratee (Prince), the ideal reader (Culler), the literant (Holland), the actual reader (Jauss), the informed reader or the interpretive community (Fish)'[4] – and we might add the virtual reader and the real reader (Prince), the resisting reader (Fetterley), the actual, authorial and narrative audience (Rabinowitz), the embedded reader (Chambers), the Lacanian reader (Felman), the female reader (Schweickart, Flint), the gay or lesbian reader (Koestenbaum), and even the mind reader (Royle).

Reader-response criticism

The best-known and most influential attempts to describe readers and reading in recent years have gone under the general heading of 'reader-response criticism' or 'reader-oriented criticism', particularly associated with critics such as Stanley Fish, Wolfgang Iser, Norman Holland and Michael Riffaterre. The high point of reader-response criticism may be said to have occurred around the year 1980, when two important collections of essays in reader-response criticism were published: Jane Tompkins's *Reader Response Criticism: From Formalism to Post-Structuralism*, a collection of representative essays from the 1970s and earlier, and Susan Suleiman and Inge Crosman's *The Reader in the Text: Essays on Audience and Interpretation*, a collection of original essays. In the same year Stanley Fish published his influential book *Is There a Text in this Class? The Authority of Interpretive Communities*.

Various forms of reader-response criticism are explored in detail by Vincent B. Leitch in the second chapter of this collection: here, we shall simply indicate one or two general questions raised by such reading theory. The simplest way to approach reader-response criticism may be to think about the question of the *location* of textual meaning. The central question for reader-response criticism in this respect is: 'Who makes meaning?' or 'Where is meaning made?' As Stanley Fish asks, 'Is the

3

reader or the text the source of meaning?'[5] The different answers to this question may be reduced to three major variants which map the limits of reader-response criticism. Firstly, there are those critics, most influentially Norman Holland and David Bleich, who approach the problem from the perspective of American Ego Psychology. The focus for these critics is the particular response pattern of the individual reader, what Holland calls his or her 'identity theme'. Secondly, there are critics such as Michael Riffaterre whose work develops a structuralist approach to emphasize ways in which texts themselves direct, coerce or 'compel' reading: for Riffaterre, it is above all the text itself that controls the production of meaning. Finally, there are critics such as Wolfgang Iser, who attempt to negotiate between text and reader, to elaborate the interactive space of reading. Despite their other differences, reader-response critics do agree, however, that it is the task of reading theory to decide on the location of authority for interpretation.

This assumption has been questioned from a number of perspectives. Thus, for example, Stanley Fish himself has argued that reading theory should consider reading as an experience rather than simply in terms of the elucidation of textual meaning.[6] Deconstructive critics such as Paul de Man also argue against the kind of hermeneutic criticism proposed by reader-response critics, suggesting that such work attempts to 'do away with reading altogether' by making reading a 'means toward an end' – the end of 'a hermeneutically successful reading'.[7] In de Man's work, reading is itself the problem, not a means toward a solution. Finally, reader-response criticism has also come under attack from critics for whom any reader and any reading is necessarily positioned by particular social, political, historical and economic contexts: in the work of, for example, Schweickart and Koestenbaum, the tendency of reader-response criticism to describe a universal 'reader' is seen to ignore the differences of reading produced by women, gay or lesbian readers, or readers from ethnic minorities.

The present collection, then, demonstrates that during the 1980s and early 1990s reading theory has developed primarily in two directions. The first direction has been towards the recognition that readers are historically or socially constructed, rather than abstract and eternal essences. This has necessitated a recognition of the politics and history of reading: once it is established that readers are *different*, that no single identity can be demanded of or imposed on readers, then questions of social, economic, gender and ethnic differences become inescapable in reading theory. The second direction has involved a problematization of the very concept of 'reading' and 'the reader', a recognition not only that readers are different from one another, but that any individual reader is multiple, and that any reading is determined by difference.

The politics of reading

To talk about the politics of reading might appear to be a contradiction in terms. The conventional view is summarized by the psychologist Alan Kennedy: 'Reading is a solitary affair, involving one person and a book.'[8] Reading is widely represented in paintings, books, films, and so on, as embowered, secluded, abstracted. Reading, in the modern, post-enlightenment era, characteristically involves a dissolution of the world and of the reader's self into the book – as in Wallace Stevens's poem 'The House Was Quiet and the World Was Calm': 'The reader became the book; and summer night/Was like the conscious being of the book.'[9] Reading is seen as an escape – a removal of the self from the world, or, as here, a dissolution of the borders of self, world and book. The reader is characteristically seen as isolated, and political questions – concerned with social relationships and intersubjective structures of power – are understood to be arbitrary interruptions of a private activity.

In recent years, however, the very privacy with which reading is often thought to begin has been described within a historical context as part of a specific discursive regime. Privacy has been redescribed as a historically specific result of a certain construction of personal identity (briefly, privacy depends on an enlightenment notion of the autonomous subject, which in turn is understood to be a product of liberal humanism or bourgeois individualism).[10] In this respect, reading as an isolated, silent activity can be put into historical context, and decisions about what to read, where to read, when to read, and how to read can be understood to be determined by social, religious or political restraints and codes.

A number of critics have recently begun to develop theories of the politics of reading. A brief account of the work of three of these critics, Steven Mailloux, Ross Chambers and Tony Bennett, will provide a sense of what might be involved in such a political rereading of reading. Steven Mailloux argues for a 'rhetorical hermeneutics' in which such 'foundational' theoretical problems as the identity of the reader, reading and meaning are suspended to make way for an analysis of the historical circumstances of particular acts of reading. Mailloux suggests that a pragmatist theory and practice of criticism would focus on the 'argumentative forces at work within the particular historical contexts in which interpretive knowledge emerges'. For Mailloux, the search for a general theory of reading or a final clarification of the relation between text and reader such as those proposed by reader-response critics are 'simply the wrong questions to ask'.[11]

In *Story and Situation: Narrative Seduction and the Power of Fiction* (1984) and, more recently, *Room for Maneuver: Reading (the) Oppositional (in) Narrative* (1991), Ross Chambers has developed a theory of oppositional

reading. Chambers argues that desire is fundamental to the act of
reading and that reading necessarily involves a *change* in desire.
'Reading', Chambers suggests, 'is the name of the practice that has the
power of producing shifts in desire.' The political dimension in such an
alteration is indicated when Chambers argues that 'to change what
people desire is, in the long run, the way to change without violence the
way things are'.[12] Chambers develops his theory with the help of
Michel de Certeau's concept of oppositionality – represented in the
present collection by de Certeau's essay on reading – whereby the
subordinate elements in a system 'appropriate' and disturb the
dominant elements, producing an alteration in the system without
challenging it as such (factory workers will appropriate or customize for
their own use the materials, functions, or conditions of work in their
environment; readers will appropriate the text for their own purposes).
Developing such a model of appropriation, Chambers argues that both
the identity of the reader and of the text are shifted by or in reading by
what he calls the irony of a certain (mis-)reading.

Finally, Tony Bennett has developed the notion of the 'reading
formation' in order to describe ways in which texts produce 'reading
effects' within cultural, political and institutional contexts. Reading
formations – the particular strategies of reading determined by a specific
historical and political context – are constantly changing, rather than
absolute or eternal, they are 'constantly *rewritten* into a variety of
material, social, institutional, and ideological contexts': 'The Text',
declares Bennett, 'has no meaning effects that can be constituted outside
such reading relationships.'[13]

The most influential politics of reading to have emerged in the 1980s
and 1990s, however, has been that produced by feminism. In work by
Judith Fetterley, Elaine Showalter, Nina Baym, Annette Kolodny,
Mary Jacobus and others, women readers or readers as women have
become crucial for both feminism and reading theory. In her pioneering
study of the position of women in the reading of nineteenth-century
American fiction, for example, Judith Fetterley suggests that the female
reader of classic American fiction is subject to a process of *immasculation*
whereby she is taught 'perforce to identify as male', to read as a man,
and to suffer 'the powerlessness which results from the endless division
of self against self'.[14] Fetterley proposes a resisting (female) reader, who
would attempt to 'disrupt the process of immasculation by exposing it to
consciousness'.[15] Fetterley's work has been widely influential, and has
been developed by various critics in the 1980s and 1990s. But it is also
exemplary in the problems it raises concerning the identity of women
readers or feminist reading: in a recent essay, Pamela Caughie has
argued that the identity of the reader constitutes an important site of
conflict in feminist reading theory. Caughie suggests that such work as

Fetterley's and that represented in Flynn and Schweickart's important collection from 1986, *Gender and Reading* (see, for example, Schweickart's essay below pp. 67–94), appear to agree on 'the *point* of reading literature' as 'self-definition or self-awareness', as a certain resistance to male hegemony, to 'androcentric' reading, through an assertion of female identity. By contrast, Caughie argues, the work of post-structuralist feminist critics such as Mary Jacobus, Naomi Schor and Barbara Johnson tends to question such an identity: for them, 'Reading as a woman . . . involves *constructing* a gender identity in relation to the text', rather than *'finding* oneself'.[16] Thus, while Judith Fetterley argues that, for women readers, reading women's writing can produce a 'knowledge of the self . . . putting us in contact with our real selves',[17] Caughie suggests that such a model of reading may simply invert the androcentric model of reading that Fetterley wishes to subvert. As Caughie explains, the point of 'reading as a woman' in the work of Jacobus, Schor and Johnson is 'to challenge masculine appeals to legitimate (textual) meanings and legitimate (sexual) identities . . . Not identity (sameness, symmetry) but difference (heterogeneity, ambiguity) is the goal of women's readings.'[18] Feminist reading theory, then – its conflicts as well as its resolutions – indicates the importance of attending to ways in which reading identities are constructed in a social and political context. This debate is exemplified in the essays by Schweickart, Jacobus and Dimock reprinted in the present collection.

Histories of reading

At first sight, like the 'politics' of reading, the notion of a social history of reading may seem to be paradoxical: how can there be a social history of an activity which is so intangible and elusive, a process enclosed within the uncertain space of consciousness? Nevertheless, in the last few years a number of critics and historians have begun to trace the historical determinants of reading. As the influential historian Robert Darnton remarks, it is a simple fact that 'Reading has a history. It was not always and everywhere the same.' By virtue of the fact that reading is an interpretive activity of which records remain, reading can be 'historicized', because, Darnton suggests, 'Interpretive schemes belong to cultural configurations, which have varied enormously over time.'[19] And in an essay which reviews recent developments in the field, Roger Chartier describes three 'macroscopic oppositions' governing such a study: in the first place, there is an opposition between reading aloud and silent reading; secondly, between reading in public and reading in solitude; and thirdly, between educated and 'popular' reading.[20]

A history of reading would need to take account of work in the histories of literacy, book production, printing and publishing, libraries, education, population, reviewing and even such factors as architecture and clothing.[21] Robert Darnton has described five possible paths that such a history might take: firstly, it is possible to study the 'ideals and assumptions underlying reading in the past' by examining such documents as eighteenth-century anti-novel tracts and texts on the 'art of reading', religious manuals of study and worship, advertisements and prospectuses for books, reports of censors, and so on.[22] Secondly, in order to study how 'ordinary readers' have gone about the business of reading, it is necessary to study the history of education and literacy. Thirdly, it is possible to study the records which certain individuals have left of their reading habits – diaries, autobiographies, notebooks, marginal notes and so on – and to reconstruct the processes and strategies of particular readers. Fourthly, Darnton suggests a collaboration between literary theory and the history of reading, pointing out that a text by a writer such as Ernest Hemingway makes very different demands of its readers than does one by, say, Jane Austen, and that reader-response criticism has already developed methodologies for discussing such differences but that these should be combined with more specifically historical research on how contemporary audiences did actually read and respond.[23] Finally, Darnton points to the fact that the physical appearances of books themselves are suggestive for a history of reading – factors such as binding, typographical design, layout, paragraphing, punctuation, and so on, hold clues to historical developments in reading.

With Cathy N. Davidson's books *Revolution and the Word* (1986) and *Reading in America* (1989), and with James L. Machor's recent collection of essays *Readers in History* (1993), critics of American literature have also begun to explore the possibilities for a historical analysis of reading. Davidson and Machor, in fact, represent two separate strands in recent studies of the history of readers and reading. On the one hand, influenced by the work of Robert Darnton and Roger Chartier (see Chartier's essay below, pp. 134–50), there are studies such as Cathy Davidson's analysis of readers of early American novels. On the other hand, more directly in a line from classic reader-response criticism, is the collection edited by James Machor. Machor himself remarks on the difference between the essays in his book and the work exemplified by Davidson and Darnton which, Machor suggests, fails to engage with questions of '*how* people read', with 'the process of response and the dynamics of audience engagement in earlier periods'. Machor summarizes the concerns of his collection of essays in two parts: '(1) the exploration of reading as a product of the relationship among particular interpretive strategies, epistemic frames, ideological imperatives, and social orientations of readers as members of historically specific – and historiographically specified – interpretive communities; and (2) the analysis of the way literary texts construct the reader's role through strategies necessitated and even produced by particular historical conditions.'[24] Disappointingly, however, once the contributors in Machor's collection get down to specific examples, rather than studying the wealth of potential materials listed in Darnton's five categories summarized above, they often confine themselves to reviews in literary or popular periodicals. Blurring the distinction between conventions of book-reviewing on the one hand and those of reading itself on the other, many of the essays overlook the fact that what they are discussing is a form of writing, one with its own specific ideological and historically determined constraints, presuppositions and conventions.

Another recent history of reading, which also engages with feminist criticism and questions of the 'woman reader', is Kate Flint's *The Woman Reader, 1837–1914* (1993). Flint's book discusses the construction of the woman reader – what she calls the 'topos of the woman reader'[25] – in nineteenth- and early twentieth-century discourses. By examining such texts as medical and psychological works, advice manuals, books and essays on education and articles in newspapers, magazines, journals, as well as letters, diaries, biographies, novels, poetry, paintings, photographs, and so on, Flint's book graphically indicates ways in which reading theories and practices were 'frequently used to uphold and reinforce dominant patriarchal structures'. As Flint comments, reading 'involves . . . a fulcrum: the meeting-place of discourses of subjectivity and socialization'.[26] Flint's wide-ranging survey of this field will no doubt be developed in the future through rereadings of literary and other texts, as well as by way of more rigorously theorized analysis of readers and reading – particularly women readers – in nineteenth-century discourse.

Stop making sense

For some theorists, attempts by reader-response criticism to 'locate' meaning on the one hand, and attempts to specify a politics or history of reading on the other, will necessarily elide a number of fundamental difficulties in any theory of reading. In this respect, the most sustained and influential elaboration of the problematics of reading in the early 1980s must be the work of Paul de Man. Briefly summarized, de Man is concerned to examine the moment in which a text presents readers with a choice between two interpretations, neither of which can be given priority: in each case there is a conflict between grammar and rhetoric, between constative and performative usage, or between literal and figurative language. These conflicts produce what de Man terms the 'impossibility' of reading, an impossibility, unreadability, or undecidability entailed by 'a set of assertions that radically exclude each other', assertions which 'compel us to choose while destroying the foundations of any choice'.[27] For de Man, it is within the impossible space of such an aporia or contradiction that reading may be most fully explored and, indeed, constituted.

More generally, deconstruction has been concerned to emphasize ways in which conventional descriptions of reading appear to resist reading itself – ways in which such descriptions involve a 'systematic avoidance of the problem of reading'.[28] In *Of Grammatology*, Jacques Derrida points to a 'powerful, systematic, and irrepressible desire for . . . a signified', which results in what he terms '*transcendent* reading'.[29] In a recent interview, Derrida glosses the word 'transcendent' in this phrase as 'going beyond interest for the signifier, the form, the language . . . in the direction of the meaning or referent'. The work of de Man, Derrida and others is precisely an attempt to 'do a nontranscendent reading', to focus on the resistance of reading to itself.[30] In this respect, as de Man says, 'Reading has to begin in [an] unstable commixture of literalism and suspicion.'[31] It is not simply that 'transcendent' reading (reading 'for meaning') should be or can be excluded – as Derrida comments, 'a text cannot by itself avoid lending itself to a "transcendent" reading' – rather, such transcendence must be 'suspended'.[32] While 'absolute resistance' to a transcendent reading 'would purely and simply destroy the trace of the text', Derrida insists that 'without annulling either meaning or reference' a literary text 'does something with this resistance'.[33] And what it does, for Derrida, is called reading.

It might be useful to sketch briefly a number of problems – moments or sites of resistance in reading – implied in or produced by deconstruction. The following summary is an attempt to bring together ways in which the work of Derrida and others would question the possibility of a single, unified configuration of readers and reading.

(1) With respect to what Derrida refers to as 'that impulse of identification which is indispensable for reading',[34] reading is, above all, a question of impossible identity. Readers must both identify with the text and at the same time open a space of reading, distance themselves or differ in reading. 'If [reading] succeeds it fails', remarks Samuel Weber, 'betraying the text by excess of fidelity, as it were, usurping the latter's prerogatives, taking its place or presenting itself as the double of writing; but if it fails, this too would condemn it to the very difference it seeks to efface; reading would fall short of its goal, its telos, the re-presentation of the text itself'.[35]

(2) 'By definition the reader does not exist':[36] the reader is produced in reading. The reader, as Shoshana Felman puts it, is a 'reading effect'.[37] At the same time, however, the work does not exist before the reader, it is produced in reading. In this respect, the priority, the originary locus and even the temporal primacy of text and reader are uncertain.

(3) Reading appears to involve a conflict between the singular and the general. On the one hand, each reading is different, inaugural, originary. On the other hand, as Derek Attridge puts it, 'readability ... however subject to change across the particular instances of reading and interpretation, implies a repetition, a law, an ideality of some type'.[38] As J. Hillis Miller comments, reading 'occurs in a certain spot to a certain person in a certain historical, personal, institutional and political situation, but it always exceeds what was predictable from those circumstances'.[39] Reading is both a repetition and an origin.

(4) Whose is any particular reading? Paul de Man points out that a reading is 'not "our" reading, since it uses only the linguistic elements provided by the text itself'.[40] On the other hand, it is the task of reading to introduce meanings which do not 'belong' to the text but are conditioned by a specific reading event.

(5) Elaborating a theory of reading based on Lacanian psychoanalysis, Shoshana Felman suggests, in an essay reprinted below (pp. 182–8), that 'analytic reading' is 'the reading of a difference that inhabits language, a kind of mapping in the subject's discourse of its points of disagreement with, or difference from, itself'.[41] If interpretation involves a displacement and an articulation of a text's differences from itself, then the possibility of defining the location and identity of reading is disturbed. How can we read that which is different from itself? How could we possibly be 'true' to a text or read it right?

(6) As Werner Hamarcher comments, while the justification for reading would be that 'it can successfully restore the meaning inherent in the sign', at the same time, the 'fundamental contingency of the relation between sign and meaning condemns its efforts to failure'.[42] Language itself, it would seem, resists reading.

Such resistances to reading within reading put into question the possibility of reading as 'communication' and call for a reappraisal of conventional models such as those proposed by reader-response criticism. The demand inhabiting the deconstruction of reading, rather than 'make sense', is to stop making sense. The action by which communication is produced – reading – is necessarily inhabited by its other, by its own resistance. While in most forms of writing, writers and readers would seek to avoid the interruption, disturbance or dissolution of communication in reading, as Yves Bonnefoy argues in an essay reprinted below (pp. 224–35), it is precisely such a disruption of 'communication' which may be said to constitute the literariness of a literary text.[43] An alternative tradition of critical engagement with questions of readers and reading, then, understands communication to be just *one element* in literary reading. Writing in the 1950s, the French writer and critic Maurice Blanchot rejects the interpretive or communicative model of reading and questions the identity of the reader. In a two-part essay from *The Space of Literature*, 'Communication and the Work' (the first part of which is reprinted below, pp. 189–96), Blanchot comments that 'What most threatens reading . . . is the reader's reality, his personality, his immodesty, his stubborn insistence upon remaining himself in the face of what he reads – a man who knows in general how to read'.[44] Concerned to elaborate the literariness of literary texts – the 'space' of literature – Blanchot rejects the conventional view of reading as an exchange between two pre-established, fixed identities, the reader and the text. Far from attempting to establish identities for readers or for reading, Blanchot sees such identifications as barriers to reading: 'What most threatens reading' is knowing how to read. Paradoxically, it seems, 'knowing' how to read is, precisely, *not* knowing how to read.

The trance of reading

'Reading', Derrida declares, 'is transformational'.[45] Reading may be understood in terms of what we might call the 'trance of reading' – 'trance' as in transition or transit, transference, transposition, translation, transformation, transgression and, finally, entrancement. In the trance of reading, the identity of the reading subject is itself unstable, yet to be determined or constituted in the 'experience' of reading. In its most extreme form, the trance of reading would involve forgetting one's surroundings, being 'lost in a book' – in what Blanchot calls the 'fascination' of reading and what Derrida refers to, in a portmanteau neologism, as *delireium*.[46] As William Ray comments, glossing Georges Poulet's theory of reading, 'For the reader thus absorbed, a trance-like state ensues, in which the active intending of a meaning effaces, rather than constitutes, personal identity.'[47]

In his lucid discussion of readers and reading in *On Deconstruction*, Jonathan Culler points out that, by and large, reading theory, whether psychoanalytic, feminist, Iserian or Fishean, has appealed to the 'experience' of the reader. But as the notions of the trance, fascination, or delirium of reading would indicate, such 'experience' is by no means beyond question because 'it proves no easier to say what is in *the* reader's or *a* reader's experience than what is in the text: "experience" is divided and deferred – already behind us as something to be recovered, yet still before us as something to be produced'.[48] In this sense, reading might be defined as an event which is *not yet* an experience. Similarly, in *Reading Woman*, Mary Jacobus argues that an 'appeal to "experience" . . . creates an illusory wholeness or identity, denying the internal division which simultaneously produces the gendered subject and the reading subject'.[49] Strangely, apparently paradoxically or 'counter-intuitively' (but intuition is also put in question by this reading of reading), reading is not, in any straightforward, unmediated sense, an experience.

This point may be demonstrated by a consideration of the temporality of reading. The classic questions of reader-response criticism –'who or what is reading?' – might be understood to disguise an even more fundamental problem: '*When* is reading?' This question is often answered by an appeal to a first reading as originary. By such an account, criticism is understood to be a distortion of the original experience of reading a text, an artificial, supplementary, or even parasitic defacement of reading. But there are a number of ways in which the time of such reading is disrupted. The time involved in reading any particular text varies from one reader to another and from one reading to the next. Indeed, the relation between the text and the experiential time of reading may be said to be constituted by a series of slippages. Even – or especially – in the most concentrated reading, the action of reading a text is subject to minute blockages, fits and starts, interruptions, speeding up and slowing down of the flow of the text. Furthermore, reading is constituted by movements forwards and backwards in the text, by the progressive and retroactive construction of meaning. Characteristically, reading a narrative involves an anticipation of future events (the end, the solution to the mystery, the consummation of love, the death of the protagonist, and so on), together with a retroactive reconstruction of prior events as reading proceeds.[50] The experience of reading a detective novel, for example, includes our knowledge of the solution to the mystery. But with this knowledge comes a fundamental alteration in our understanding and experience of the text up to the moment of revelation: with the revelation of the truth of the murder comes a reinterpretation of the whole text by which such experience is split in two, doubled or folded. To the extent that any narrative is determined by its own end, reading cannot take place until after it has finished.

The temporality of reading and the possibility of an originary, pure or unmediated experience of reading is further questioned by the notion of rereading. Rereading has itself recently become the subject for a richly provocative book by Matei Calinescu entitled *Rereading* (1993), as well as a chapter in Marcel Cornis-Pope's recent book *Hermeneutic Desire and*

Critical Rewriting (1992). Calinescu suggests that 'under certain circumstances the first reading of a work can in fact be a *double* reading' consisting of 'the sequential temporal movement of the reader's mind . . . along the horizontal or syntagmatic axis of the work' together with an attempt to '"construct" . . . the text under perusal, or to perceive it as a construction'.[51] As both Calinescu and Cornis-Pope note, forms of rereading have, in fact, been central to the work of certain theorists of reading. Michael Riffaterre, for example, develops a two-stage model – a first 'heuristic' linear reading and a second 'hermeneutic' or retroactive reading attending to the underlying 'matrix' or 'hypogram'.[52] Summarizing the various figurations of rereading in the work of, for example, Roland Barthes, Umberto Eco and Vincent Leitch, Cornis-Pope has suggested that in each case, a 'first reading depends primarily on the expectation of pleasure (of a vicarious or hermeneutic kind)' while 'rereading draws on a critical (self)awareness'.[53] J. Hillis Miller even argues that reading, 'if it is really reading is always, even the first time, a matter of re-reading or re-vision' because such 'real' reading involves not only 'a knowledge of what the text says' but also 'of what the text represents or allegorizes'.[54] Rather differently, as Cornis-Pope points out, it would be possible to argue that an 'active feminist reading' (and, by extension, we might say, any oppositional reading, whether determined by class, gender or race, which reads against the hegemonic grain) is 'always *re-reading*' because of the way in which it is produced in opposition to – and therefore necessarily 'after' – that of phallogocentric readings.[55] In this respect, an originary or first reading would be an ideological construct concerned to confirm what Derrida calls the 'metaphysics of presence'.[56] Finally, Pierre Bourdieu has pointed to the way in which reading seems inevitably to slide into a theorization of reading, rereading as meta-reading, when he asks 'Can you read a text without wondering what reading is?'[57] Reading as rereading opens up a temporal space of reading, an irreducible difference in the time that we take to read.

The trance of reading, *delireium*, may also be understood in terms of the cognition of reading. What might it mean to 'understand' a text? Even in conventional discussions of reading, 'understanding' has a curious status. In *Critical Understanding*, Wayne Booth states that understanding 'is the goal, process and result whenever one mind succeeds in entering another mind or, what is the same thing, whenever one mind succeeds in incorporating any part of another mind'.[58] Not only would this description seem to involve a form of telepathic transference – one aspect of what we have termed the 'trance of reading' – but it also immediately suggests the problem of identity: the understanding mind is that which is, at least in part, other to itself. This is what William Ray calls the 'schizophrenic cognitive activity of the reader', the way in which the mind's contents in reading are split or doubled, our thoughts not our thoughts.[59]

In this respect, reading involves a necessary otherness or alterity – as is suggested, in particular, in essays by Blanchot and de Certeau reprinted below. Paul Ricoeur makes this point in a recent interview: 'When a reader applies a text to himself, as is the case in literature, he recognizes himself in certain possibilities of existence – according to the model offered by a hero, or a character – but, at the same time, he is transformed; the becoming other in the act of reading is as important as is the recognition of self.'[60] Paradoxically, as we have seen, those critical discourses which attempt to reinscribe sexual and political difference in reading often rely for their work of political transformation on a coherent and stable identity for the reader. As Wayne Koestenbaum points out (below, pp. 166–81) in attempting to construct an identity for reading based, for example, on sexual orientation or race or gender, one risks 'submitting to a dangerously comfortable essentialism'.[61] The alternative tradition which 'begins' with Blanchot, attempts to hold in suspense the possibility of any such identity.[62] In reading, Poulet declares, I read 'the thoughts of another, and yet it is I who am their subject' – reading is 'a way of giving way not only to a host of alien words, images, ideas, but also to the very alien principle which utters them and shelters them'.[63] We are possessed, inhabited by other thoughts and others' thoughts, words, language – reading ourselves not ourselves, reading not reading.

Notes

For their careful readings of and comments on earlier versions of this Introduction, I would like to thank Anna-Maria Hämäläinen-Bennett, James Giles, Nicholas Royle and Tiina Sarisalmi,.

1. JOHN BARTH, 'Life Story' from *Lost in the Funhouse: Fiction for Print, Tape, Live Voice* (New York: Doubleday, 1969), p. 123.

2. PAUL RICOEUR, *Time and Narrative*, vol. 3, trans. Kathleen Blamey and David Pellauer (Illinois: University of Chicago Press, 1988), p. 164.

3. DIMOCK, 'Feminism, New Historicism, and the Reader', p. 122.

4. ELIZABETH FREUND, *The Return of the Reader: Reader-Response Criticism* (London: Methuen, 1987), p. 7; for brief descriptions of these terms, see the 'Key Concepts' section below (pp. 236–41).

5. See *Is There a Text in This Class: The Authority of Interpretive Communities* (Cambridge, Mass: Harvard University Press, 1980), p. 1.

6. See, for example, STANLEY FISH, 'Literature in the Reader: Affective Stylistics', in *Is There a Text in This Class*, pp. 21–67.

7. PAUL DE MAN, 'Introduction', in HANS ROBERT JAUSS, *Toward an Aesthetic of Reception*, trans. Timothy Bahti (Brighton: Harvester Press, 1982), p. ix.

8. ALAN KENNEDY, *The Psychology of Reading* (London: Methuen, 1984), p. 140.

9. *The Collected Poems of Wallace Stevens* (New York: Alfred A. Knopf, 1954), p. 358.

10. See PHILIPPE ARIÈS and GEORGES DUBY (eds), *A History of Private Life*, 4 vols (Cambridge, Mass: Harvard University Press, 1987–91); on the privatization of reading in pre-revolutionary France and in Europe more generally, see ROGER CHARTIER, 'The Practical Impact of Writing', in Chartier (ed.), *Passions of the Renaissance*, trans. Arthur Goldhammer (Cambridge, Mass.: Harvard University Press, 1989), (vol. 3 in *A History of Private Life*); see also CHARTIER, *The Cultural Uses of Print in Early Modern France*, trans. Lydia G. Cochrane (New Jersey: Princeton University Press, 1987), pp. 219–25.

11. STEVEN MAILLOUX, 'Power, Rhetoric, and Theory: Reading American Texts', in Gerhard Hoffmann (ed.), *Making Sense: The Role of the Reader in Contemporary American Fiction* (Munich: Wilhelm Fink Verlag, 1989), pp. 117, 118; and see his *Rhetorical Power* (Ithaca: Cornell University Press, 1989).

12. ROSS CHAMBERS, *Room for Maneuver: Reading (the) Oppositional (in) Narrative* (Illinois: University of Chicago Press, 1991), p. xii; see also EDWARD W. SAID, *Culture and Imperialism* (New York: Alfred A. Knopf, 1993), p. 66, on 'Contrapuntal reading' which would 'take account of both . . . imperialism and . . . resistance to it'.

13. TONY BENNETT, 'Text, Readers, Reading Formations', in Philip Rice and Patricia Waugh (eds), *Modern Literary Theory: A Reader* (London: Edward Arnold, 1989), pp. 218, 219.

14. JUDITH FETTERLEY *The Resisting Reader: A Feminist Approach to American Fiction* (Bloomington: Indiana University Press, 1978), pp. xii, xiii.

15. PATROCINIO SCHWEICKART, 'Reading Ourselves', p. 74, below.

16. PAMELA L. CAUGHIE, 'Women Reading/Reading Women: A Review of Some Recent Books on Gender and Reading', *Papers on Language and Literature* **24** (1988): 322, 326 (my italics).

17. Quoted in ibid., p. 322.

18. Ibid., pp. 326–7. Compare SHOSHANA FELMAN's comment in *What Does a Woman Want? Reading and Sexual Difference* (Baltimore: The Johns Hopkins University Press, 1993), that 'The danger with becoming a "resisting reader" is that we end up, in effect, *resisting reading*' (p. 6).

19. DARNTON, 'First Steps Toward a History of Reading', in *The Kiss of Lamourette: Reflections in Cultural History* (London: Faber & Faber, 1990), p. 187.

20. ROGER CHARTIER, 'Frenchness in the History of the Book: From the History of Publishing to the History of Reading', *Proceedings of the American Antiquarian Society* **97**: 2 (1988): 322–4; on the development of silent, private reading as 'undeniably one of the major cultural developments' of the early modern period, see CHARTIER, 'The Practical Impact of Writing', p. 125.

21. On the relevance of the latter, see DARNTON, 'First Steps', pp. 167–8; see also ROGER CHARTIER, *The Cultural Uses of Print*, p. 221, and 'The Practical Impact of Writing', especially pp. 134–47.

22. DARNTON, 'First Steps', p. 171; for Darnton's five 'steps', see pp. 171–87. See PETER DE BOLLA, *The Discourse of the Sublime: Readings in History, Aesthetics, and*

the Subject (Oxford: Basil Blackwell, 1989), Chapter 10, and FRIEDRICH A. KITTLER, *Discourse Networks 1800/1900*, trans. Michael Metteer (California: Stanford University Press, 1990), for examples of the use of such materials.

23. See DAVIDSON 'Introduction: Toward a History of Texts', in *Revolution and the Word: The Rise of the Novel in America* (Oxford: Oxford University Press, 1986), for a similar argument for a cross-fertilization of historical research with reader-response criticism; see also JAUSS, *Toward an Aesthetic of Reception*.

24. JAMES L. MACHOR, 'Introduction: Readers/Texts/Contexts', in Machor (ed.), *Readers in History: Nineteenth-Century American Literature and the Contexts of Response* (Baltimore: The Johns Hopkins University Press, 1993), pp. x, xi.

25. FLINT, *The Woman Reader, 1837–1914* (Oxford: Oxford University Press, 1993), p. viii.

26. Ibid., pp. 10, 43.

27. DE MAN, *Allegories of Reading: Figural Language in Rousseau, Nietzsche, Rilke, and Proust* (New Haven: Yale University Press, 1979), p. 245.

28. PAUL DE MAN, *Blindness and Insight: Essays in the Rhetoric of Contemporary Criticism*, 2nd edn (London: Methuen, 1983), p. 282.

29. JACQUES DERRIDA, *Of Grammatology*, trans. Gayatri Chakravorty Spivak (Baltimore: The Johns Hopkins University Press, 1976), pp. 49, 160.

30. JACQUES DERRIDA, *Acts of Literature*, ed. Derek Attridge (London: Routledge, 1992), p. 44.

31. DE MAN, *Allegories of Reading*, p. 58.

32. DERRIDA, *Acts*, pp. 45, 48.

33. DERRIDA, *Acts*, p. 47. The work of Derrida generally may be understood as a meditation on – as well as a practice of – not least, reading. Despite the fact that to talk about the elaboration of a Derridean 'method' of reading would be an oxymoron, Derrida does, in a section of *Of Grammatology* entitled 'The Exorbitant Question of Method', present what he terms 'my principles of reading', which, it turns out, involves a 'justification . . . entirely negative' (*Of Grammatology*, p. 158).

34. Quoted in DEREK ATTRIDGE, 'Introduction' in *Acts*, p. 5.

35. SAMUEL WEBER, *Institution and Interpretation* (Minneapolis: University of Minnesota Press, 1987), p. 92.

36. DERRIDA, *Acts*, p. 74.

37. SHOSHANA FELMAN, 'Turning the Screw of Interpretation', *Yale French Studies* **55/56** (1977): 124.

38. ATTRIDGE, 'Introduction', p. 15; see also DERRIDA, *Acts*, pp. 69–70.

39. J. HILLIS MILLER, *Versions of Pygmalion* (Cambridge, Mass.: Harvard University Press, 1990), p. 22.

40. DE MAN, *Allegories of Reading*, p. 17.

41. FELMAN, 'Renewing the Practice of Reading', pp. 184–5.

42. WERNER HAMACHER, 'LECTIO: de Man's Imperative', in Lindsay Waters and Wlad Godzich (eds), *Reading de Man Reading* (Minneapolis: University of Minnesota Press, 1989), p. 178.

43. For more on this point, see my essay, 'On Not Reading' in Andrew Bennett (ed.), *Reading Reading* (Tampere, Finland: University of Tampere, 1993), pp. 221–37.

44. MAURICE BLANCHOT, *The Space of Literature*, trans. Ann Smock (Lincoln: University of Nebraska Press, 1982), p. 198.

45. JACQUES DERRIDA, *Positions*, trans. Alan Bass (Illinois: University of Chicago Press, 1981), p. 63.

46. On Blanchot and fascination, see TIMOTHY CLARK, *Derrida, Heidegger, Blanchot: Sources of Derrida's Notion and Practice of Literature* (Cambridge: Cambridge University Press, 1992), p. 138; for Derrida on *delireium*, see 'Living On', in HAROLD BLOOM et al., *Deconstruction and Criticism* (New York: Seabury Press, 1979), p. 94, and *La Carte postale: de Socrate à Freud et au-delà* (Paris: Flammarion, 1980), p. 22 ('délirer'), and see TEMMA F. BERG, '*La Carte Postale*: Reading (Derrida) Reading', *Criticism*, **28** (1986): 331–2; VICTOR NELL'S study *Lost in a Book: The Psychology of Reading for Pleasure* (New Haven: Yale University Press, 1988), presents an empirical account of such loss of subjectivity or 'consciousness' in reading.

47. WILLIAM RAY, *Literary Meaning: from Phenomenology to Deconstruction* (Oxford: Basil Blackwell, 1984), p. 11. Poulet's work presents an intense theoretical engagement with the entrancements of reading – see, in particular, GEORGES POULET, 'Criticism and the Experience of Interiority', in Tompkins (ed.), *Reader-Response Criticism*, pp. 41–9.

48. JONATHAN CULLER, *On Deconstruction: Theory and Criticism After Structuralism* (London: Routledge & Kegan Paul, 1983), p. 82; see also pp. 63, 68–9. For a critique of Culler's critique of experience and the experience of reading (as a woman), see SCHOLES, 'Reading Like a Man', in Alice Jardine and Paul Smith (eds), *Men in Feminism* (New York: Methuen, 1987), pp. 204–18.

49. MARY JACOBUS, *Reading Woman: Essays in Feminist Criticism* (London: Methuen, 1986), p. 5.

50. See RICOEUR, *Time and Narrative*, for a detailed elaboration of the phenomenology of the temporality of reading: see also ROBERT SCHOLES, *Protocols of Reading* (New Haven: Yale University Press, 1989), p. 8.

51. MATEI CALINESCU, *Rereading* (New Haven: Yale University Press, 1993), pp. 18–19.

52. See VINCENT LEITCH, 'Reader-Response Criticism', p. 58 below.

53. MARCEL CORNIS-POPE, *Hermeneutic Desire and Critical Rewriting: Narrative Interpretation in the Wake of Post-structuralism* (London: Macmillan, 1992), p. 22.

54. J. HILLIS MILLER, *The Ethics of Reading: Kant, de Man, Eliot, Trollope, James, and Benjamin* (New York: Columbia University Press, 1987), p. 117.

55. CORNIS-POPE, *Hermeneutic Desire*, p. 133.

56. See CALINESCU, *Rereading*, pp. 35–6, on the presuppositions which lie behind such an ideology of reading.

57. PIERRE BOURDIEU, 'Reading, Readers, the Literate, Literature', in *In Other Words: Essays Towards a Reflexive Sociology*, trans. Matthew Adamson (Cambridge: Polity, 1990), p. 94.

58. Quoted by CULLER, *On Deconstruction*, p. 177; for a similar description, see WOLFGANG ISER, 'The Reading Process', in Tompkins (ed.), *Reader-Response Criticism*, pp. 65–8.

59. WILLIAM RAY, *Literary Meaning*, p. 21. On the relationship between reading and telepathy, see NICHOLAS ROYLE, *Telepathy and Literature: Essays on the Reading Mind* (Oxford: Basil Blackwell, 1991).

60. 'World of the Text, World of the Reader' (an interview with Paul Ricoeur and Joël Roman), in Mario J. Valdés (ed.), *A Ricoeur Reader: Reflection and Imagination* (Hemel Hempstead: Harvester–Wheatsheaf, 1991), pp. 492–3.

61. KOESTENBAUM, 'The Birth of Gay Reading', p. 166.

62. One way in which reader identities might then be multiplied and dissolved is by the construction of a 'typology' of readers, such as that by Roland Barthes in *The Pleasure of the Text* when he describes a psychoanalytic typology which links 'the reading neurosis to the hallucinated form of the text' (BARTHES, *The Pleasure of the Text*, trans. Richard Miller (New York: Farrar, Straus & Giroux, 1975), p. 63).

63. POULET, 'Criticism and the Experience of Interiority', pp. 44–5.

1 Interaction between Text and Reader*

WOLFGANG ISER

Wolfgang Iser's books *The Implied Reader* (1974) and *The Act of Reading* (1978) were arguably the most influential works to emerge from classic reader-response criticism of the 1970s. In the following essay Iser gives a brief account of his phenomenological theory of the way in which reading is interactive, occurring *between* text and reader. For Iser, neither the study of texts nor the study of readers in isolation is likely to produce an adequate account of the literary work. Instead, he argues, the text is 'actualized' by the reader to become a 'virtual' aesthetic work. At the heart of Iser's model of reading is the idea that texts produce uncertainties or gaps in readers' comprehension, and that these gaps spur the reader to produce connections which 'complete' the text. 'Whenever the reader bridges the gaps', Iser declares, 'communication begins.'

There are a number of useful critical overviews of Iser's work: in addition to Vincent Leitch's summary in Chapter 2, below, see William Ray, *Literary Meaning* (1984), Chapters 3 and 4, for an account of Iser in the context of the phenomenological aesthetics of Roman Ingarden; Robert C. Holub, *Reception Theory*, Chapter 3, for an account of Iser in the context of German *Rezeptionsästhetik* (1984); and Elizabeth Freund, *The Return of the Reader* (1987), Chapter 6, for a consideration of Iser's place in reader-response criticism more generally; finally, for a critical account of *The Act of Reading*, see Samuel Weber's essay, 'Caught in the Act of Reading' (1986).

Central to the reading of every literary work is the interaction between its structure and its recipient. This is why the phenomenological theory of art has emphatically drawn attention to the fact that the study of a literary work should concern not only the actual text but also, and in

---

* Reprinted from SUSAN R. SULEIMAN and INGE CROSMAN (eds), *The Reader in the Text: Essays on Audience and Interpretation* (New Jersey: Princeton University Press, 1980), pp. 106–19.

equal measure, the actions involved in responding to that text. The text itself simply offers 'schematized aspects'[1] through which the aesthetic object of the work can be produced.

From this we may conclude that the literary work has two poles, which we might call the artistic and the aesthetic: the artistic pole is the author's text, and the aesthetic is the realization accomplished by the reader. In view of this polarity, it is clear that the work itself cannot be identical with the text or with its actualization but must be situated somewhere between the two. It must inevitably be virtual in character, as it cannot be reduced to the reality of the text or to the subjectivity of the reader, and it is from this virtuality that it derives its dynamism. As the reader passes through the various perspectives offered by the text, and relates the different views and patterns to one another, he sets the work in motion, and so sets himself in motion, too.

If the virtual position of the work is between text and reader, its actualization is clearly the result of an interaction between the two, and so exclusive concentration on either the author's techniques or the reader's psychology will tell us little about the reading process itself. This is not to deny the vital importance of each of the two poles – it is simply that if one loses sight of the relationship, one loses sight of the virtual work. Despite its uses, separate analysis would only be conclusive if the relationship were that of transmitter and receiver, for this would presuppose a common code, ensuring accurate communication since the message would only be traveling one way. In literary works, however, the message is transmitted in two ways, in that the reader 'receives' it by composing it. There is no common code – at best one could say that a common code may arise in the course of the process. Starting out from this assumption, we must search for structures that will enable us to describe basic conditions of interaction, for only then shall we be able to gain some insight into the potential effects inherent in the work.

It is difficult to describe this interaction, not least because literary criticism has very little to go on in the way of guide-lines, and, of course, the two partners in the communication process, namely, the text and the reader, are far easier to analyze than is the event that takes place between them. However, there are discernible conditions that govern interaction generally, and some of these will certainly apply to the special reader–text relationship. The differences and similarities may become clear if we briefly examine types of interaction that have emerged from psychoanalytical research into the structure of communication. The findings of the *Tavistock School* will serve us as a model in order to move the problem into focus.[2]

In assessing interpersonal relationships R.D. Laing writes: 'I may not actually be able to see myself as others see me, but I am constantly supposing them to be seeing me in particular ways, and I am constantly acting in the light of the actual or supposed attitudes, opinions, needs, and so on the other has in respect of me.'[3] Now, the views that others have of me cannot be called 'pure' perception; they are the result of interpretation. And this need for interpretation arises from the structure of interpersonal experience. We have experience of one another insofar as we know one another's conduct; but we have no experience of how others experience us.

In his book, *The Politics of Experience*, Laing pursues this line of thought by saying: '*your experience of me is invisible to me and my experience of you is invisible to you*. I cannot experience your experience. You cannot experience my experience. We are both invisible men. All men are invisible to one another. Experience is man's invisibility to man.'[4] It is this invisibility, however, that forms the basis of interpersonal relations – a basis which Laing calls 'no-thing'.[5] 'That which is really "between" cannot be named by any things that come between. The between is itself no-thing.'[6] In all our interpersonal relations we build upon this 'no-thing', for we react as if we knew how our partners experienced us; we continually form views of their views, and then act as if our views of their views were realities. Contact therefore depends upon our continually filling in a central gap in our experience. Thus, dyadic and dynamic interaction comes about only because we are unable to experience how we experience one another, which in turn proves to be a propellant to interaction. Out of this fact arises the basic need for interpretation, which regulates the whole process of interaction. As we cannot perceive without preconception, each percept, in turn, only makes sense to us if it is processed, for pure perception is quite impossible. Hence dyadic interaction is not given by nature but arises out of an interpretative activity, which will contain a view of others and, unavoidably, an image of ourselves.

An obvious and major difference between reading and all forms of social interaction is the fact that with reading there is no *face-to-face-situation*.[7] A text cannot adapt itself to each reader it comes into contact with. The partners in dyadic interaction can ask each other questions in order to ascertain how far their images have bridged the gap of the inexperienceability of one another's experiences. The reader, however, can never learn from the text how accurate or inaccurate are his views of it. Furthermore, dyadic interaction serves specific purposes, so that the interaction always has a regulative context, which often serves as a *tertium comparationis*. There is no such frame of reference governing the text–reader relationship; on the contrary, the codes which might regulate this interaction are fragmented in the text, and must first be reassembled or, in most cases, restructured before any frame of reference *can* be established. Here, then, in conditions and intention, we find two basic differences between the text–reader relationship and the dyadic interaction between social partners.

Now, it is the very lack of ascertainability and defined intention that brings about the text–reader interaction, and here there is a vital link with dyadic interaction. Social communication, as we have seen, arises out of the fact that people cannot experience how others experience them, and not out of the common situation or out of the conventions that join both partners together. The situations and conventions regulate the manner in which gaps are filled, but the gaps in turn arise out of the inexperienceability and, consequently, function as a basic inducement to communication. Similarly, it is the gaps, the fundamental asymmetry between text and reader, that give rise to communication in the reading process; the lack of a common situation and a common frame of reference corresponds to the 'no-thing', which brings about the interaction between persons. Asymmetry and the 'no-thing' are all different forms of an indeterminate, constitutive blank, which underlies all processes of interaction. With dyadic interaction, the imbalance is removed by the establishment of pragmatic connections resulting in an action, which is why the preconditions are always clearly defined in relation to situations and common frames of reference. The imbalance between text and reader, however, is undefined, and it is this very indeterminacy that increases the variety of communication possible.

Now, if communication between text and reader is to be successful, clearly the reader's activity must also be controlled in some way by the text. The control cannot be as specific as in a *face-to-face-situation*, equally it cannot be as determinate as a social code, which regulates social interaction. However, the guiding devices operative in the reading process have to initiate communication and to control it. This control cannot be understood as a tangible entity occurring independently of the process of communication. Although exercised *by* the text, it is not *in* the text. This is well illustrated by a comment Virginia Woolf made on the novels of Jane Austen:

> Jane Austen is thus a mistress of much deeper emotion than appears upon the surface. She stimulates us to supply what is not there. What she offers is, apparently, a trifle, yet is composed of something that expands in the reader's mind and endows with the most enduring form of life scenes which are outwardly trivial. Always the stress is laid upon character. . . . . The turns and twists of the dialogue keep us on the tenterhooks of suspense. Our attention is half upon the present moment, half upon the future. . . . Here, indeed, in this unfinished and in the main inferior story, are all the elements of Jane Austen's greatness.[8]

What is missing from the apparently trivial scenes, the gaps arising out of the dialogue – this is what stimulates the reader into filling the blanks with projections. He is drawn into the events and made to supply what is meant from what is not said. What is said only appears to take on significance as a reference to what is not said; it is the implications and not the statements that give shape and weight to the meaning. But as the unsaid comes to life in the reader's imagination, so the said 'expands' to take on greater significance than might have been supposed: even trivial scenes can seem surprisingly profound. The 'enduring form of life' which Virginia Woolf speaks of is not manifested on the printed page; it is a product arising out of the interaction between text and reader.

Communication in literature, then, is a process set in motion and regulated, not by a given code, but by a mutually restrictive and magnifying interaction between the explicit and the implicit, between revelation and concealment. What is concealed spurs the reader into action, but this action is also controlled by what is revealed; the explicit in its turn is transformed when the implicit has been brought to light. Whenever the reader bridges the gaps, communication begins. The gaps function as a kind of pivot on which the whole text–reader relationship revolves. Hence, the structured blanks of the text stimulate the process of ideation to be performed by the reader on terms set by the text. There is, however, another place in the textual system where text and reader converge, and that is marked by the various types of negation which arise in the course of the reading. Blanks and negations both control the process of communication in their own different ways: the blanks leave open the connection between textual perspectives, and so spur the reader into coordinating these perspectives and patterns – in other words, they induce the reader to perform basic operations *within* the text. The various types of negation invoke familiar and determinate elements or knowledge only to cancel them out. What is cancelled, however, remains in view, and thus brings about modifications in the reader's attitude toward what is familiar or determinate – in other words, he is guided to adopt a position *in relation* to the text.

In order to spotlight the communication process we shall confine our consideration to how the blanks trigger off and simultaneously control the reader's activity. Blanks indicate that the different segments and patterns of the text are to be connected even though the text itself does not say so. They are the unseen joints of the text, and as they mark off schemata and textual perspectives from one another, they simultaneously prompt acts of ideation on the reader's part. Consequently when the schemata and perspectives have been linked together, the blanks 'disappear'.

If we are to grasp the unseen structure that regulates but does not formulate the connection or even the meaning, we must bear in mind the various forms in which the textual segments are presented to the reader's viewpoint in the reading process. Their most elementary form is to be seen on the level of the story. The threads of the plot are suddenly broken off, or continued in unexpected directions. One narrative section centers on a particular character and is then continued by the abrupt introduction of new characters. These sudden changes are often denoted by new chapters and so are clearly distinguished; the object of this distinction, however, is not separation so much as a tacit invitation to find the missing link. Furthermore, in each articulated reading moment, only segments of textual perspectives are present to the reader's wandering viewpoint.

In order to become fully aware of the implication, we must bear in mind that a narrative text, for instance, is composed of a variety of perspectives, which outline the author's view and also provide access to what the reader is meant to visualize. As a rule, there are four main perspectives in narration: those of the narrator, the characters, the plot, and the fictitious reader. Although these may differ in order of importance, none of them on its own is identical to the meaning of the text, which is to be brought about by their constant intertwining through the reader in the reading process. An increase in the number of blanks is bound to occur through the frequent subdivisions of each of the textual perspectives; thus the narrator's perspective is often split into that of the implied author's set against that of the author as narrator. The hero's perspective may be set against that of the minor characters. The fictitious reader's perspective may be divided between the explicit position ascribed to him and the implicit attitude he must adopt to that position.

As the reader's wandering viewpoint travels between all these segments, its constant switching during the time flow of reading intertwines them, thus bringing forth a network of perspectives, within which each perspective opens a view not only of others, but also of the intended imaginary object. Hence no single textual perspective can be equated with this imaginary object, of which it forms only one aspect. The object itself is a product of interconnection, the structuring of which is to a great extent regulated and controlled by blanks.

In order to explain this operation, we shall first give a schematic description of how the blanks function, and then we shall try to illustrate this function with an example. In the time flow of reading, segments of the various perspectives move into focus and are set off against preceding segments. Thus the segments of characters, narrator, plot, and fictitious reader perspectives are not only marshaled into a graduated sequence but are also transformed into reciprocal reflectors. The blank as an empty space between segments enables them to be joined together, thus constituting a field of vision for the wandering viewpoint. A referential field is always formed when there are at least two positions related to and influencing one another – it is the minimal organizational unit in all processes of comprehension,[9] and it is also the basic organizational unit of the wandering viewpoint.

The first structural quality of the blank, then, is that it makes possible the organization of a referential field of interacting textual segments projecting themselves one upon another. Now, the segments present in the field are structurally of equal value, and the fact that they are brought together highlights their affinities and their differences. This relationship gives rise to a tension that has to be resolved, for, as Arnheim has observed in a more general context: 'It is one of the functions of the third dimension to come to the rescue when things get uncomfortable in the second.'[10] The third dimension comes about when the segments of the referential field are given a common framework, which allows the reader to relate affinities and differences and so to grasp the patterns underlying the connections. But this framework is also a blank, which requires an act of ideation in order to be filled. It is as if the blank in the field of the reader's viewpoint had changed its position. It began as the empty space between perspective segments, indicating their connectability, and so organizing them into projections of reciprocal influence. But with the establishment of this connectability the blank, as the unformulated framework of these interacting segments, now enables the reader to produce a determinate relationship between them. We may infer already from this change in position that the blank exercises significant control over all the operations that occur within the referential field of the wandering viewpoint.

Now we come to the third and most decisive function of the blank. Once the segments have been connected and a determinate relationship established, a referential field is formed which constitutes a particular reading moment, and which in turn has a discernible structure. The grouping of segments within the referential field comes about, as we have seen, by making the viewpoint switch between the perspective segments. The segment on which the viewpoint focuses in each particular moment becomes the theme. The theme of one moment becomes the background against which the next segment takes on its actuality, and so on. Whenever a segment becomes a theme, the previous one must lose its thematic relevance[11] and be turned into a marginal, thematically vacant position, which can be and usually is occupied by the reader so that he may focus on the new thematic segment.

In this connection it might be more appropriate to designate the marginal or horizontal position as a vacancy and not as a blank; blanks refer to suspended connectability in the text, vacancies refer to non-thematic segments within the referential field of the wandering viewpoint. Vacancies, then, are important guiding devices for building up the aesthetic object, because they condition the reader's view of the new theme, which in turn conditions his view of previous themes. These modifications, however, are not formulated in the text – they are to be implemented by the reader's ideational activity. And so these vacancies enable the reader to combine segments into a field by reciprocal modification, to form positions from those fields, and then to adapt each position to its successor and predecessors in a process that ultimately transforms the textual perspectives, through a whole range of alternating themes and background relationships, into the aesthetic object of the text.

Let us turn now to an example in order to illustrate the operations sparked off and governed by the vacancies in the referential field of the wandering viewpoint. For this reason we shall have a brief look at Fielding's *Tom Jones* and again, in particular, at the characters' perspective: that of the hero and that of the minor characters. Fielding's aim of depicting human nature is fulfilled by way of a repertoire that incorporates the prevailing norms of eighteenth-century thought systems and social systems and represents them as governing the conduct of the most important characters. In general, these norms are arranged in more or less explicitly contrasting patterns; Allworthy (*benevolence*) is set against Squire Western (*ruling passion*); the same applies to the two pedagogues, Square (*the eternal fitness of things*) and Thwackum (*the human mind as a sink of iniquity*), who in turn are also contrasted with Allworthy and so forth.

Thus in the individual situations, the hero is linked up with the norms of latitudinarian morality, orthodox theology, deistic philosophy, eighteenth-century anthropology, and eighteenth-century aristocracy. Contrasts and discrepancies within the perspective of the characters give rise to the missing links, which enable the hero and the norms to shed light upon one another, and through which the individual situations may combine into a referential field. The hero's conduct cannot be subsumed under the norms, and through the sequence of situations the norms shrink to a reified manifestation of human nature. This, however, is already an observation which the reader must make for himself, because such syntheses are rarely given in the text, even though they are prefigured in the theme-and-background structure. The discrepancies continually arising between the perspectives of hero and minor characters bring about a series of changing positions, with each theme losing its relevance but remaining in the background to influence and condition its successor. Whenever the hero violates the norms – as he does most of the time – the resultant situation may be judged in one or two different ways: either the norm appears as a drastic reduction of human nature, in which case we view the theme from the standpoint of the hero, or the violation shows the imperfections of human nature, in which case it is the norm that conditions our view.

In both cases, we have the same structure of interacting positions being transformed into a determinate meaning. For those characters that represent a norm – in particular Allworthy, Squire Western, Square, and Thwackum – human nature is defined in terms of one principle, so that all those possibilities which are not in harmony with the principle are given a negative slant. But when the negated possibilities exert their influence upon the course of events, and so show up the limitations of the principle concerned, the norms begin to appear in a different light. The apparently negative aspects of human nature fight back, as it were, against the principle itself and cast doubt upon it in proportion to its limitations.

In this way, the negation of other possibilities by the norm in question gives rise to a virtual diversification of human nature, which takes on a definite form to the extent that the norm is revealed as a restriction on human nature. The reader's attention is now fixed, not upon what the norms represent, but upon what their representation excludes, and so the aesthetic object – which is the whole spectrum of human nature – begins to arise out of what is adumbrated by the negated possibilities. In this way, the function of the norms themselves has changed: they no longer represent the social regulators prevalent in the thought systems of the eighteenth century, but instead they indicate the amount of human experience which they suppress because, as rigid principles, they cannot tolerate any modifications.

Transformations of this kind take place whenever the norms are the foregrounded theme and the perspective of the hero remains the background conditioning the reader's viewpoint. But whenever the hero becomes the theme, and the norms of the minor characters shape the viewpoint, his well-intentioned spontaneity turns into the depravity of an impulsive nature. Thus the position of the hero is also transformed, for it is no longer the standpoint from which we are to judge the norms; instead we see that even the best of intentions may come to nought if they are not guided by *circumspection*, and spontaneity must be controlled by *prudence*[12] if it is to allow a possibility of self-preservation.

The transformations brought about by the theme-and-background interaction are closely connected with the changing position of the vacancy within the referential field. Once a theme has been grasped, conditioned by the marginal position of the preceding segment, a feedback is bound to occur, thus retroactively modifying the shaping influence of the reader's viewpoint. This reciprocal transformation is hermeneutic by nature, even though we may not be aware of the processes of interpretation resulting from the switching and reciprocal conditioning of our viewpoints. In this sense, the vacancy transforms the referential field of the moving viewpoint into a self-regulating structure, which proves to be one of the most important links in the interaction between text and reader, and which prevents the reciprocal transformation of textual segments from being arbitrary.

To sum up, then, the blank in the fictional text induces and guides the reader's constitutive activity. As a suspension of connectability between textual perspective and perspective segments, it marks the need for an equivalence, thus transforming the segments into reciprocal projections, which in turn organize the reader's wandering viewpoint as a referential field. The tension that occurs within the field between heterogeneous perspective segments is resolved by the theme-and-background structure, which makes the viewpoint focus on one segment as the theme, to be grasped from the thematically vacant position now occupied by the reader as his standpoint. Thematically vacant positions remain present in the background against which new themes occur; they condition and influence those themes and are also retroactively influenced by them, for as each theme recedes into the background of its successor, the vacancy shifts, allowing for a reciprocal transformation to take place. As the vacancy is structured by the sequence of positions in the time flow of reading, the reader's viewpoint cannot proceed arbitrarily; the thematically vacant position always acts as the angle from which a selective interpretation is to be made.

Two points need to be emphasized: (1) we have described the structure of the blank in an abstract, somewhat idealized way in order to explain the pivot on which the interaction between text and reader turns; (2) the blank has different structural qualities, which appear to dovetail. The reader fills in the blank in the text, thereby bringing about a referential field; the blank arising in turn out of the referential field is filled in by way of the theme-and-background structure; and the vacancy arising from juxtaposed themes and backgrounds is occupied by the reader's standpoint, from which the various reciprocal transformations lead to the emergence of the aesthetic object. The structural qualities outlined make the blank shift, so that the changing positions of the empty space mark out a definite need for determination, which the constitutive activity of the reader is to fulfill. In this sense, the shifting blank maps out the path along which the wandering viewpoint is to travel, guided by the self-regulatory sequence in which the structural qualities of the blank interlock.

Now we are in a position to qualify more precisely what is actually meant by reader participation in the text. If the blank is largely responsible for the activities described, then participation means that the reader is not simply called upon to 'internalize' the positions given in the text, but he is induced to make them act upon and so transform each other, as a result of which the aesthetic object begins to emerge. The structure of the blank organizes this participation, revealing simultaneously the intimate connection between this structure and the reading subject. This interconnection completely conforms to a remark made by Piaget: 'In a word, the subject is there and alive, because the basic quality of each structure is the structuring process itself.'[13] The blank in the fictional text appears to be a paradigmatic structure; its function consists in initiating structured operations in the reader, the execution of which transmits the reciprocal interaction of textual positions into consciousness. The shifting blank is responsible for a sequence of colliding images, which condition each other in the time flow of reading. The discarded image imprints itself on its successor, even though the latter is meant to resolve the deficiencies of the former. In this respect the images hang together in a sequence, and it is by this sequence that the meaning of the text comes alive in the reader's imagination.

Notes

This essay contains a few ideas which are dealt with more comprehensively in my book *The Act of Reading: A Theory of Aesthetic Response* (The Johns Hopkins University Press: Baltimore, 1978).

1. See ROMAN INGARDEN, *The Literary Work of Art*, trans. George G. Grabowicz (Evanston, Ill., 1973), pp. 276ff.
2. R.D. LAING, H. PHILLIPSON, A.R. LEE, *Interpersonal Perception: A Theory and a Method of Research* (New York, 1966).
3. Ibid., p. 4.
4. LAING, *The Politics of Experience* (Harmondsworth, 1968), p. 16. Laing's italics.
5. Ibid., p. 34.
6. Ibid.
7. See also E. GOFFMAN, *Interaction Ritual: Essays on Face-to-Face Behavior* (New York, 1967).
8. VIRGINIA WOOLF, *The Common Reader: First Series* (London, 1957), p. 174. In this context, it is well worth considering Virginia Woolf's comments on the composition of her own fictional characters. She remarks in her diary:

   I'm thinking furiously about Reading and Writing. I have no time to describe my plans. I should say a good deal about *The Hours* and my discovery: how I dig out beautiful caves behind my characters: I think that gives exactly what I want; humanity, humour, depth. The idea is that the caves shall connect and each comes to daylight at the present moment.

   (A Writer's Diary: Being Extracts from the Diary of Virginia Woolf, ed. Leonard Woolf (London, 1953), p. 60)

   The suggestive effect of the 'beautiful caves' is continued in her work through what she leaves out. On this subject, T.S. Eliot once observed:

Her observation, which operates in a continuous way, implies a vast and sustained work of organization. She does not illumine with sudden bright flashes but diffuses a soft and placid light. Instead of looking for the primitive, she looks rather for the civilized, the highly civilized, where nevertheless something is found to be *left out*. And this something is deliberately left out, by what could be called a moral effort of the will. And, being left out, this something is, in a sense, in a melancholy sense, present.

('T.S. Eliot "Places" Virginia Woolf for French Readers', in Virginia Woolf: The Critical Heritage, ed. Robin Majumdar and Allen McLaurin (London, 1975), p. 192)

9.   See ARON GURWITSCH, *The Field of Consciousness* (Pittsburgh, 1964), pp. 309–75.

10. RUDOLF ARNHEIM, *Toward a Psychology of Art* (Berkeley and Los Angeles, 1967), p. 239.

11. For a discussion of the problem of changing relevance and abandoned thematic relevance, see ALFRED SCHÜTZ, *Das Problem der Relevanz*, trans. A. v. Baeyer (Frankfurt am Main, 1970), pp. 104ff., 145ff.

12. See HENRY FIELDING, *Tom Jones*, III 7 and XVIII, Chapter the Last (London, 1962), pp. 92, 427.

13. JEAN PIAGET, *Der Strukturalismus*, trans. L. Häfliger (Olten, 1973), p. 134.

2 Reader-Response Criticism*

VINCENT B. LEITCH

In this chapter Vincent B. Leitch presents an historical survey of the ideas, the influence, and the implications of reader-response criticism in the United States during the 1970s and the early 1980s. In the course of his discussion, Leitch suggests that Stanley Fish, Norman Holland, David Bleich, Hans Robert Jauss and Wolfgang Iser tend to depoliticize reading by eliding questions of the social and the historical. By contrast, he suggests, the feminism of Judith Fetterley and the Marxism of Mary Louise Pratt provide alternatives to the essentializing, ahistorical theories of classic reader-response criticism. Leitch also considers the work of those that he categorizes as 'structuralist' theorists of reading and readers – Michael Riffaterre, Gerald Prince, Jonathan Culler and Robert Scholes. Leitch suggests that the approaches of such theorists avoid the subjectivity or essentialism of descriptions produced by other reader-response critics, by recognizing that any reading is determined not only by textual but also by cultural constraints. The achievement of such theorists, Leitch suggests, is to allow for a theorization of reading in terms of its connection with 'deep structures in society'.

For a vigorous critique of classic reader-response criticism from a Marxist perspective, see Terry Eagleton, *Literary Theory* (1983), Chapter 2; for other useful surveys of the field, see Elizabeth Freund, *The Return of the Reader* (1987), and Peter Rabinowitz, 'Whirl Without End: Audience-Oriented Criticism' (1989).

The era of the reader

From the Great Depression to the onset of the Space Age, American critics tended primarily to focus either on literary texts, or on the

---

* Reprinted from *American Literary Criticism from the Thirties to the Eighties* (New York: Columbia University Press, 1988), pp. 211–37, 252–9.

historical and cultural contexts of literature, or on both. During the early years of the Space Age, the focus of concern for many leading critics and theorists shifted to the activities of reading and readers. The rise of reader-oriented criticism manifested itself more or less forcefully in numerous and varied critical projects, including those carried out by literary phenomenology, hermeneutics, structuralism, deconstruction, and feminism. While an interest in text reception appeared before World War II in the works of I.A. Richards, Maud Bodkin, D.W. Harding, Kenneth Burke, and Louise Rosenblatt, it was not until the late 1950s and shortly afterwards that a veritable landslide of studies started to concentrate self-consciously on readers and reading, initiating a broad-based movement opposed to earlier text-dominated and context-dominated criticism. Among the many critics in America contributing to the development of a reader-centered criticism were David Bleich, Stephen Booth, Wayne Booth, Jonathan Culler, Paul de Man, Judith Fetterley, Stanley Fish, Norman Holland, Simon Lesser, J. Hillis Miller, Richard Palmer, Mary Louise Pratt, Gerald Prince, Alan Purves, Michael Riffaterre, Walter Slatoff, and William Spanos. Significantly, half of these critics associated themselves with specific schools rather than this broad movement: Wayne Booth with Chicago formalism; de Man and Miller with phenomenology, then with deconstruction; Palmer and Spanos with hermeneutics; Prince and Riffaterre with structuralism; Culler with structuralism, then with deconstruction; Fetterley with feminism; and Pratt with speech-act theory, then with Marxism. As a result, the roster of leading American Reader-Response Critics, established by the peak of the movement's vitality in the late 1970s, was limited arguably to Fish, Holland, and Bleich – listed here in order of their chronological entry into the field and treatment in this chapter.

Whether or not the membership of the movement is construed narrowly or broadly, certain tenets characterized reader-response criticism during its heyday from the late 1960s to the early 1980s. It argued against the text-centered criticism of formalism, advocating instead a reader-oriented approach. It often stressed the temporality of reading, resisting tendencies toward spatial hermeneutics and toward organicist poetics. It pioneered accounts of textual discontinuity over doctrines propounding literary unity. It investigated the epistemological, linguistic, psychological, and sociological constraints on the activity of reading and the labor of readers. It often ignored explicit questions concerning aesthetic value and the role of history. It did not tamper with the canons of scholarly style, and it pushed critical inquiry toward pedagogy, typically locating the text and reader in the classroom. Not surprisingly, it fostered various didactic poetics. It tended toward a politics of liberal pluralism, which advocated the rights of readers against the prescriptions and dogmas of doctrinaire methodologies. Focused tightly on the reader, it developed a rich panoply of types of readers – informed readers, ideal readers, implied readers, actual readers, virtual readers, super-readers, and 'literents'. Like other schools and movements during the Space Age, it cast New Criticism as a scapegoat responsible for many of the ills and errors of contemporary literary criticism. Unlike some other groups, Reader-Response Critics did not constitute a tightly knit cadre or circle of colleagues with access to certain journals, presses, institutes, and universities. Instead, the movement had an increasingly broad geographical and intellectual base – more so than all other schools of American criticism from the thirties to the eighties except feminism and leftist criticism during the Space Age.

Given the wide scope of the movement, reader-response criticism was characterized by numerous differences and disagreements. As the movement expanded, many explanatory articles and essays appeared, increasing exponentially the bibliography in this field of inquiry. Whereas reader-oriented criticism did not dramatically alter literary canons or textbooks nor engender specialized dictionaries or handbooks, it did generate a large number of special sessions at conferences and special issues of journals. The proliferation of helpful published materials reached a high point in 1980 with the publication of two exemplary anthologies of reader-response criticism, complete with useful introductions and lengthy bibliographies: (1) *The Reader in the Text: Essays on Audience and Interpretation*, edited by Susan Suleiman and Inge Crosman, published by Princeton University Press, containing sixteen original articles; and (2) *Reader-Response Criticism: From Formalism to Post-Structuralism*, edited by Jane Tompkins, published by the Johns Hopkins University Press, reprinting eleven key texts of the movement. Sponsored by major university presses and frequently reprinted, these anthologies signaled a certain culmination of the shift from text-centered to reader-oriented criticism within the field of literary studies in American universities.

In her extensive introduction, 'Varieties of Audience-Oriented Criticism', Susan Suleiman surveyed six approaches to receptionist criticism, including rhetorical, structuralist–semiotic, phenomenological, psychoanalytical, sociological–historical, and hermeneutical modes. She argued that 'audience-oriented criticism is not one field but many, not a single widely trodden path but a multiplicity of crisscrossing, often divergent tracks that cover a vast area of the critical landscape . . . '.[1] Unlike Jane Tompkins in 'An Introduction to Reader-Response Criticism', Suleiman allotted considerable space to European critics who played a significant role in the 'revolution' set off by reader-oriented theory. Her canon of important American critics included Bleich, Booth, Fish, Holland, Prince, Riffaterre, and certain Yale deconstructors, namely

de Man, Hartman, and Miller. While Tompkins too presented
reader-response criticism as heterogeneous, observing it was 'not a
conceptually unified critical position',[2] she nevertheless argued that the
movement exhibited a 'coherent progression' over its two decades of
growth and displayed a 'main line of theoretical development' (ix, xxvi).
According to this account, two stages characterized the internal history
of the movement as it progressed from formalism through structuralism
and phenomenology to psychoanalysis and post-structuralism. First,
reader-response criticism envisaged the reader's activity as instrumental
to the understanding of the literary text without denying that the
ultimate object of critical attention was the text. Second, it conceived the
reader's activity as identical with the text so that this activity became the
source of concern and value. This 'revolutionary shift' from text to
reading, from product to process, opened new areas of inquiry,
resituated theories of meaning and interpretation, and reconnected
criticism with ethics and eventually with politics. The key American
critics in this development, in Tompkins' view, were Prince, Riffaterre,
Fish, Culler, Holland, and Bleich. Unlike Suleiman, Tompkins left out of
account the works of European sociological and historical
Reader-Response Critics and of Continental and native Hermeneutical
Critics. Both editors omitted consideration of feminist reader-oriented
critics. Perhaps this was so because feminist criticism did not reach its
peak until the mid-1980s, evidently some years after the reader-response
anthologies were first planned. As with other historians of
reader-response criticism, Suleiman and Tompkins disagreed about the
actual scope of the heterogeneity and disunity within the movement.
That it constituted a more or less fragmented site of inquiry was never in
question. Usually presented as a cultural paradigm shift, the new focus
on the reader seemed to preoccupy an era rather than one school or
another.

Reading: from phenomenology to post-structuralism

During the sixties the most well-known and popular work of
reader-response criticism was Stanley Fish's *Surprised by Sin: The Reader
in Paradise Lost* (1967). Here and in his *Self-Consuming Artifacts: The
Experience of Seventeenth-Century Literature* (1972), Fish focused
single-mindedly on the reader's experience of literature. In contrast to
the long-standing formalist idea that a literary text was an autonomous
object like a well-wrought urn, Fish insisted that a work of literature
entered reality for the critic through the act of reading – the process of
reception. Because reading occurred through time, the experience of

literature involved a continuous readjustment of perceptions, ideas, and evaluations. The meaning of a work, therefore, was to be encountered in the experience of it, not in the detritus left after the experience. Literature was process, not product. Criticism required the microprocessing of phrases and sentences in a slow sequence of decisions, revisions, anticipations, reversals, and recoveries. Here the phenomenology of reading replaced both the traditional formalist project of spatial unity and the old hermeneutical project of recollective interpretation.

Fish described the basis of his phenomenological theory in the 1971 Preface to the paperback edition of *Surprised by Sin:* 'Meaning is an *event*, something that happens, not on the page, where we are accustomed to look for it, but in the interaction between the flow of print (or sound) and the actively mediating consciousness of a reader-hearer. *Surprised by Sin*, although it nowhere contains any reference to such a theory of meaning, is nevertheless the product of it.'[3] True to this description, the focus throughout Fish's book was on Milton's reader in *Paradise Lost*, particularly on the reader's participation, humiliation, and education during the course of the poem. As Fish conceived it, Milton's procedure was to render in the reader's mind the action of the Fall of Man, thereby causing the reader himself to fall just as Adam did. The meaning (or content) of the poem was embodied in the experience of the reader, not in the poem. Such experience was intellectually and morally uplifting.

Fish's concept of meaning entailed an unorthodox conception of literary form. He was unabashed about this matter, arguing that 'if the meaning of the poem is to be located in the reader's experience of it, the form of the poem is the form of that experience; and the outer or physical form, so obtrusive, and, in one sense, so undeniably there, is, in another sense, incidental and even irrelevant' (p. 341). Fish dismissed the traditional dualistic notion of the artwork as constructed object composed of form and content, replacing it with a monism (reader's experience = meaning = form), which earlier the New Critics had labeled a fallacy – the so-called 'affective fallacy'. Fish staked out a clear position on this presumed liability:

> I am courting the 'affective fallacy'. Indeed I am embracing it and going beyond it. . . . That is, making the work disappear into the reader's experience of it is precisely what should happen in our criticism, because it is what happens when we read. The lines of plot and argument, the beginnings, middles, and ends, the clusters of imagery, all the formal features that are observable when we step back from the reading experience, are, during that experience, components of a response; and the . . . structure of response.
>
> (pp. ix–x)

Methodically, Fish asserted a temporal basis for literary form as well as meaning. Spatial forms – poetic patterns objectified retrospectively – were illusory. Meaning and form were coextensive with the reader's experience; they were not produced after the reading activity. The phenomenology of time determined both the meaning and the form of a work.

Like the phenomenological criticism practised earlier by J. Hillis Miller, Fish's reader-oriented criticism abolished the text as the sole object of attention and advocated a primary role for the reader's consciousness. The interaction of reader and text, the co-implication of subject and object, effected a strong antiformalist emphasis on the experiential features of the engaged critical mind rather than on the formal features of the text (imagery, plot, genre). Fish, like Miller, more or less bracketed extrinsic social realities and historical issues, substituting for such broad matters an all-consuming sense of engagement experienced by the reader–critic working with the text. Despite their shared antiformalism and their tendency to ahistoricism, these two critics had different views of the text, of the text–reader relationship, and of meaning. Whereas Miller regarded the oeuvre as the unit text, Fish considered the individual work as text. For Miller, the 'text' embodied the consciousness of the author which was shared mystically with the sensitive reader: the reader served as acolyte or cocelebrant of the holy 'text'. For Fish, however, the text functioned as a rigorous, authoritative controller of the reader's developing responses. According to Miller's formulation, the meaning of a 'text' emerged from the persistent themes, motifs, and tones that recurred throughout the works of an author, revealing an essential selfhood or center of consciousness. To re-create the quintessential spiritual adventure of the author was to render the meaning of his work. According to Fish, however, meaning was created in the reader by the author as the text developed in the reading process: meaning was the reader's sequential experience of the work unfolding. To constitute meaning required describing in detail the moment-by-moment experience of reading.

Several years after *Surprised by Sin*, Fish articulated at some length and for the first time the basis of his reader-response theory in 'Literature in the Reader: Affective Stylistics' (1970), which he later appended to *Self-Consuming Artifacts* as an essential theoretical credo. In addition to depicting his theories of meaning, of form, and of the text, he offered in this manifesto a profile of his 'informed reader'. In moving from the text to the reading process to the reader, Fish opened for consideration a new array of problems, which would dominate his criticism throughout the seventies and eighties. The informed reader, in Fish's account, was 'neither an abstraction nor an actual living reader, but a hybrid – a real reader (me) who does everything within his power to make himself informed'.[4] The informed reader possessed both linguistic and literary competence – language experience and knowledge of literary conventions. Such minimal competency formed the necessary precondition for all potential reader responses. Not until the late 1970s would Fish begin to work out the implications of his theories about competence and convention. In the meantime, he attracted much harsh criticism, serving as *the* point man for the reader-response movement in America.

During the early seventies, Paul de Man criticized Fish for his theory of meaning and his view of the author. According to de Man, Fish substituted 'a regressive notion of unmediated "experience" for meaning',[5] which had the effect of covering over the inherent duplicity of language. The materiality and complexity of language were dissolved by Fish. In addition, Fish posited an intentional auctorial consciousness that controlled the complications of meanings through manipulation of linguistic and poetic conventions. This dubious formulation cast the reader in an eternal catch-up role with the author and actually minimized the reader's labor and creativity. What especially bothered de Man was a retrograde concept of intention surviving in Fish's reader-response criticism. According to de Man's assessment, Fish unwittingly projected the author as the ideal reader of the text.

Jonathan Culler criticized Fish in the mid-seventies for his refusal to take seriously the concepts of linguistic competence and literary convention, which formed the foundation of his theory of the informed reader. Given the logic of his position, Fish ought to have carried out 'an investigation of reading as a rule-governed, productive process'.[6] Instead, he retreated to individualistic thematic interpretation in a phenomenological mode. By simply assuming that the informed reader had internalized essential knowledge and ability, Fish closed off a whole area for inquiry – 'to make explicit the procedures and conventions of reading, to offer a comprehensive theory of the ways in which we go about making sense of various kinds of texts' (p. 125). This project, the goal of structuralist literary theory carefully outlined in Culler's *Structuralist Poetics* (1975), required a shift of focus from the individual to the communal reader.

In 1976, Fish recast his early view of the informed reader with the productive concept of 'interpretive communities', first introduced in the important essay, 'Interpreting the *Variorum*'. This new turn initiated a shift from phenomenological to poststructuralist modes of thinking. Fish sought to account for the variety as well as the stability of reader responses to a text. He did so by theorizing that 'interpretive communities are made up of those who share interpretive strategies not for reading (in the conventional sense) but for writing texts, for constituting their properties and assigning their intentions. In other words, these strategies exist prior to the act of reading and therefore determine the shape of what is read rather than, as is usually assumed, the other way around'.[7] Each community of interpreters deciphered texts in the manner demanded by its interpretive strategies. Thus numerological and psychoanalytical strategies, for instance, each reproduced one text. Moreover, any one reader could respond in different ways at different times because he or she could change to or belong to other communities. In any event, a reader always employed a set of interpretive strategies in spite of the desire for or impression of objectivity. Traditionally, meanings were thought to be embedded in a work prior to, and independent of, any individual interpretation. According to Fish, all meanings were created through particular reading acts and interpretive strategies during the reader's moment-to-moment experience of the text. As such, Fish proposed not just an informed reader, but an informed reader as a member of one community of interpreters or another, that is, a communal reader predisposed to create particular meanings.

When he moved from the informed reader to the interpretive community, Fish altered the nature of his enterprise. He left behind former notions about authors, about texts, and about individually cultivated readers, adopting new concepts about institutional readers, about interpretive strategies and (re)writing protocols, and about the sociology and professional politics of interpretation. He concerned himself not with the events of reading but with the systems of constraints controlling interpretive activity and with the communally based rationality engendering predictable interpretations. He denied the possibility of disinterested inquiry and 'objective' facts. Communal interests, beliefs, and values shaped knowledge, formed facts, and directed inquiry and interpretation. The understanding of a text – its (re)writing – emerged out of the preexisting interests and beliefs of the particular reading community. 'One can only read what one has already read.'[8]

From the mid-1970s through the mid-1980s, Fish promoted a pragmatist view of linguistic competence, literary convention, and interpretive strategy, opposing the universalism of traditional Baconian science and rationalism, the abstract mathematical structuralism of Chomskian linguistics, and the general hermeneutics of Hirschian criticism. He preferred the special differential historicism of Foucault, the 'ordinary language' ideas of Wittgenstein and Grice, and the antifoundationalist philosophies of Rorty and Derrida. About language competence, for example, he insisted:

> Linguistic knowledge is contextual rather than abstract, local rather than general, dynamic rather than invariant; every rule is a rule of

thumb; every competence grammar is a performance grammar in disguise. This then is why [universalist or foundational] theory will never succeed: it cannot help but borrow its terms and its content from that which it claims to transcend, the mutable world of practice, belief, assumptions, point of view, and so forth.[9]

All interpreters were situated. No point of transcendence – free from situation, context, and values – existed. Literary criticism could not bracket communally established and historically determined interests and beliefs. As a result, Fish was led to initiate inquiries into the sociology of knowledge and the nature of literary professionalism.

While Fish changed his approach over the course of two decades from a phenomenological to a poststructuralist mode of inquiry, he was in the 1980s subject to mounting criticism from numerous theorists, particularly those of the leftist cultural studies movement. According to Edward Said, for instance, 'If, as we have recently been told by Stanley Fish, every act of interpretation is made possible and given force by an interpretive community, then we must go a great deal further in showing what situation, what historical and social configuration, what political interests are concretely entailed by the very existence of interpretive communities.'[10] In other words, Fish needed to move much further in the direction of sociology, history, and politics.

Frank Lentricchia concurred, complaining that 'Fish's reader is purely literary: his membership in a community of literary critics somehow cancels out the forces that shape his political, social, or ethnic status. . . . A literary community walled off from larger enclosures of social structure and historical process is a repetition of aestheticist isolationism.'[11] Similar criticisms appeared in William Cain's *The Crisis in Criticism* (1984), Terry Eagleton's *Literary Theory* (1983), and other works published in the opening years of the 1980s. Having moved from the text to the informed reader to the interpretive community, Fish jumped beyond formalism to phenomenology and poststructuralism, stopping short of the ideological analysis characteristic of cultural studies as practised in America during the seventies and eighties.

Psychoanalysis of readers

Over the course of two decades, Norman Holland developed a detailed account of literary transactions in a series of articles and books, particularly *The Dynamics of Literary Response* (1968), *Poems in Persons*

(1973), *5 Readers Reading* (1975), *Laughing: A Psychology of Humor* (1982), and *The I* (1985). These works emanated from an abiding interest in the psychoanalytic nature of response. While the traditional insights and methods of Psychoanalytical Critics in the past elucidated the activities of authors and of literary characters, Holland's studies focused primarily on the transactions between readers and texts, using the findings of 'ego psychology' as a means of understanding the nature of text reception. By analyzing transcripts of actual readings performed by experimental subjects, Holland was enabled to conceptualize the dynamics of response in a refined psychoanalytical formulation. Essentially, he propounded a model in which the identity (or personality) of the reader constructed from the text a unified interpretation of the text: he offered a psychological account of the way personality affected the perception and interpretation of literature. Holland argued that belief in uniformity of response was erroneous because individual personality determined response in all cases.

Whereas in *The Dynamics of Literary Response* Holland used his own personal responses to extrapolate a schematic view of the reader–text transaction, he later employed the responses of others to formulate an empirically derived transactive model, especially in *Poems in Persons* and *5 Readers Reading*. In a key essay written just after these three books, he distilled the essentials of his model and, in so doing, put his project in its most succinct form. At the outset of 'UNITY IDENTITY TEXT SELF' (1975), published in *PMLA* and reprinted in Tompkins' anthology, Holland briefly defined the four terms of his title (since they underpinned his basic formulation). By 'text' he meant the words on the page; by 'self' he designated the whole person of an individual – mind and body. Using standard notions, Holland conceived literary 'unity' in a traditional way as a union of parts or a structural whole resembling a living organism. And he conceptualized 'identity' as a unified configuration of subordinate themes and patterns in a life – an unchanging and invariant essence typically called 'character' or 'personality'. Correlating these four concepts, Holland outlined various sets of mathematical relationships among them: '*Unity* is to *text*', to cite only the most important ratio, 'as *identity* is to *self*'.[12] That is to say, the unity of a text is like the identity of a self.

The point of all this preliminary labor was quickly made clear: 'The ratio, unity to text, equals the ratio, identity to self, but the terms on the right side of the equation cannot be eliminated from the left side. The unity we find in literary texts is impregnated with the identity that finds that unity' (p. 816). To put it another way, the literary transaction between reader and text ended with a sense of the unity of the text because of the shaping and unifying presence of the identity of the reader. As Holland summed it up, '*interpretation is a function of identity*'

(p. 816). Elaborating on this basic model of the reader–text transaction, Holland explained:

> The overarching principle is: identity re-creates itself, or, to put it another way, style – in the sense of personal style – creates itself. That is, all of us, as we read, use the literary work to symbolize and finally to replicate ourselves. We work out through the text our own characteristic patterns of desire and adaptation. We interact with the work, making it part of our own psychic economy and making ourselves part of the literary work – as we interpret it.
>
> (p. 816)

To account for the sequence of specific operations in the reader–text transaction, Holland depicted three psychological phases of response discovered in his research. The first phase of the process brought into play the reader's desire for pleasure and fear of pain. That is, the operation of the pain–pleasure mechanism and its attendant defense system constituted the initial set of events in the response process. Essentially, the reader shaped the work or found in the material what he or she both wished and feared, defending in a habitual way against what was feared and adapting through characteristic strategies what was desired. If the process did not take place, the reader shut out the experience. (Holland presented an exemplary case study of blockage in *Poems in Persons*.) The second phase of the response process brought to bear the reader's pleasure in fantasy. The reader recreated from the text a personal fantasy and thereby realized deep gratification. The third phase of the process brought into action anxiety and guilt over raw fantasy and the fantasy's consequent transformation into a coherent and significant experience of moral, intellectual, social, or aesthetic unity and wholeness. In the end, therefore, a synthesis of the reader's responses typically occurred in which defenses, gratifications, and anxieties were balanced so as to maintain mental and emotional stability.

Holland succinctly summarized and generalized this operational process of response transaction in 'The New Paradigm: Subjective or Transactive?' (1976):

> Very briefly, the literent (or the perceiver of another person or any other reality) comes to that other reality [a text, for instance] with a set of characteristic expectations, typically a balance of related desires and fears. The perceiver adapts the 'other' to gratify those wishes and minimize those fears – that is, the perceiver re-creates his characteristic modes of adaptation and defense (aspects of his identity theme) from the materials literature or reality offers. He or she projects characteristic fantasies into them (and these fantasies

can also be understood as aspects of identity). Finally, the individual may transform these fantasies into themes – meanings – of characteristic concern. . . .[13]

Because the phases of response involved *de*fenses, *e*xpectations, *f*antasies, and *t*ransformations, Holland employed the acronym DEFT to designate his model of literary transaction.

DEFT, the process of identity re-creation, was derived from the reading practices of experimental subjects (undergraduate students) recorded in great detail in *5 Readers Reading*. However, as Holland's generalized description implied, this model accounted for the manner in which identity or style shaped all interpretations of experience and all human transactions, including the interactions of institutions, cultures, and nations – not just interpretations of literary experience.[14]

Significantly, Holland extended the application of identity re-creation theory by analyzing the thematic preoccupations and techniques of writers, specifically of Hilda Doolittle in *Poems in Persons* and of Robert Frost in 'UNITY IDENTITY TEXT SELF'. In addition, he subjected his own critical interests and methods to DEFT analysis in *Poems in Persons*. Thus, by the mid-seventies, the point at which Fish had turned from the informed reader to interpretive communities, Holland had applied the model of identity re-creation with its phasic components to texts, authors, readers, and himself, suggesting that it could be extended to institutions and societies.

The main features of Holland's mature reader-response criticism resembled traits characteristic of Miller's Geneva criticism and Fish's early phenomenology. To be sure, there were differences also. It exhibited little commitment to historical inquiry, formalist explication, or ideological analysis. It attended to the reader–text transaction, allotting a primary role to the reader in shaping and determining the text. Whereas Miller's and Fish's work examined the role of temporality and consciousness in the creation of meaning, Holland's project scrutinized the drive of the unconscious toward producing organic unity. The reader had little freedom in interpreting the text; identity determined response. The reliance of Holland's enterprise on science, mathematics, and ego psychology distinguished it from other kinds of reader-oriented criticism. Where Miller spoke of mystical insights and moments of transcendence and Fish wrote about readers' continuous readjustments and consequent cognitive improvements, Holland talked of psychosexual fixations, defense strategies, and fantasy wishes.

Holland's psychological criticism represented a break with the main line of psychological criticism in American literary studies. The important book by Holland published in the 1970s revealed no indebtedness to Van Wyck Brooks, Kenneth Burke, Leslie Fiedler,

Frederick Hoffman, J.W. Krutch, Ludwig Lewisohn, Lionel Trilling, or Edmund Wilson. Moreover, Holland downplayed contemporary existential, Jungian, Lacanian, Frankfurt School, and third-force psychology (which was made clear in 'Guide to Further Reading' in *Poems in Persons*, and in the Appendix on 'Other Psychoanalyses' in *The I*). He relied most heavily on ego psychology as developed in certain key works by Erik Erikson, Anna Freud, Ernst Kris, Heinz Lichtenstein, Roy Schafer, Robert Waelder, and D.W. Winnicott. In *Out of My System* (1975) Frederick Crews, a fellow Psychoanalytic Critic, roundly criticized Holland for relying on the theory of identity derived from ego psychology, which he characterized as impoverished and reductive. As far as Crews was concerned, Holland was 'forgetting the entire *raison d'être* of critical activity' and was 'conducting a highly unusual going-out-of-business sale'.[15]

Critics of Holland's psychoanalysis of readers registered numerous complaints. Among such criticisms were: he imprudently shifted the concept of unity from the text to the self; he renounced literary criticism for case studies; he rendered all reading self-interested; he undermined standards of interpretative validity, professional authority, and classroom procedure; he reductively modeled criticism on the Freudian theory of transference; he characterized reading as a neurotic process of filtering and subtracting; he unwisely presented all criteria of aesthetic value as matters of individual psychology; he portrayed readers as fixated and static egos; he fostered an apolitical pluralism denuded of communal and social values; his own readings were solipsistic and merely confessional; his type of criticism made the literary text a victim; his depictions of 'ego style' remained caught in an interpretive circle; and his 'transactive paradigm' retained vestiges of a commitment to the obsolescent goal of objectivity. Because Holland's work attracted a great deal of attention, often of a negative sort, it served as a site of intense focus within the American reader-response movement. Holland, like Fish, was a point man in the movement for over a decade.

The subject of pedagogy

When Stanley Fish collected in book form his many credos and essays of the seventies, he titled the work *Is There a Text in This Class?* When Norman Holland shifted in the early seventies from an objective to a transactive paradigm, he grounded his research in analyses of student responses as his magnum opus of the decade, *5 Readers Reading*, memorably demonstrated. When David Bleich wrote *Readings and*

Feelings (1975) and *Subjective Criticism* (1978), he committed both books unequivocally to effecting 'changes in existing pedagogical institutions' and to outlining new teaching methods based on 'actual classroom experiences'.[16] Characteristically, the leaders of the American reader-response movement closely linked literary criticism and theory with classroom pedagogy and academic practices. Such a linkage, however, seemed neither inevitable nor desirable to other groups of critics ranging from the early Marxists and New York Intellectuals to the later existentialists and deconstructors. Lionel Trilling put the issue pointedly in the opening pages of *Beyond Culture* when he observed that 'pedagogy is a depressing subject to all persons of sensibility'. No doubt, the characteristic preoccupation with pedagogy reflected the growing absorption of most criticism into the university and the widespread student demands for 'relevance' typical of the sixties. Starting in the mid-sixties and continuing to the mid-eighties, Geoffrey Hartman, like several other influential philosophically-minded critics, was prompted to warn against the increasing reduction of criticism to pedagogy.

No Reader-Response Critic was more insistent than David Bleich in promoting the gains for pedagogy of adopting an antiformalist and non-objectivist paradigm for literary studies. His project, as first detailed in *Readings and Feelings: An Introduction to Subjective Criticism* (published by the National Council of Teachers of English), advocated the virtues of tutorial modes of teaching based on small classes and personal interactions of teachers and students. Holland's enterprise similarly advised small seminar formats where student–teacher interactions engendered intimacy and trust, conditions essential to reader-response pedagogy. 'In large classes', insisted Bleich, 'this method is impossible.'[17] Located at mega-universities regularly offering large literature classes, reader-response teachers like Bleich, Holland, and others positioned themselves as critics of the widespread practice during the Space Age of presenting literature in huge lecture halls. The concern with pedagogy became the ground of criticism.

In Bleich's view, *interpretation* of literature entailed the belated recreation and presentation of primary emotional response, consisting of personal (1) perceptions, (2) affects, and (3) associations. The fourth phase of a complex psychological process, interpretation involved objectification and potential falsification of individual subjective experience. 'The true scope of feeling – or perhaps the true limitations of feeling – is essentially denied by intellectual reformulations' (p. 69). What Bleich stressed and sought to demonstrate was the subjective ground of all objective formulations. He distrusted 'objectivity'. Epistemologically, feeling and passion preceded and directed thinking and knowledge. 'Ultimately, the separation of conscious judgment from its subjective roots is false and artificial' (p. 49). As a classroom teacher,

Bleich was mainly interested in what a student felt rather than what she thought; he cared most about affect, not interpretation.

Because reading depended on personal psychology, it necessarily engendered 'distortions' – exaggerations, omissions, associations, insertions, errors. No response to a text could meet the unreal orthodox criteria of objectivity and completeness. As an inherent element of response, 'distortion' for Bleich was both revealing and valuable: it displayed features of perceptual style and testified to authentic engagement with a text. Valuing subjectivity required crediting personal peculiarities. Objectivity sought to eradicate just such essential and predetermining personal idiosyncrasies. Bleich deplored the critical taboo on private feelings and subjective values.

For Bleich, response was one thing and interpretation was another: one was private; the other was communal. To make an interpretation was to go public with a private experience: 'experience of peremptory feelings and images precedes the onset of deliberate thought' (p. 5). Thus, 'dealing with subjective experiences in a community should be preceded by the student's working things out on an individual basis . . .' (p. 79). Unlike Fish, Bleich pictured the community as a late arrival in the formulation of a response rather than as the determining factor in the formation of an interpretation. Like Holland, Bleich worked as a psychological rather than a sociological critic. Without question, the community helped shape interpretation, but it did so late in the process and it involved risks of falsification. In particular, the conventional social format for interpretation – the proposition-proof argument – directed primary reader response, especially personal affect and association, away from actual experience. Although he didn't say so in *Readings and Feelings*, Bleich evidently would have liked to scrap altogether the genre of the critical essay as inimical to reader-oriented pedagogy.

Like Fish, Bleich regarded literature as an experience, not as an autonomous object. Unlike Fish, he showed no interest in the temporality of reading. From his students he expected multiple readings of a text as a prerequisite of response as well as interpretation. A reader's 'initial' response to a whole text might hinge completely on a work's last word. Bleich was no phenomenologist. As with other Reader-Response Critics, Bleich joined a didactic to an affective poetics: the emotional experience of literature 'can produce new understanding of oneself – not just a moral here and a message there, but a genuinely new conception of one's values and tastes as well as one's prejudices and learning difficulties' (pp. 3–4). The strong emphasis on subjectivity in Bleich's work made him the least attached of all the leading Reader-Response Critics to a textual poetics. The power of the text to direct reading and survive distortion was inconsiderable. In literary study, ontological priority belonged to written response statements, not poetic texts.

Criticism was not an operation of textual decoding but an experience of developing important personal feelings and associations.

Readings and Feelings was based on six years of experience teaching in reader-response classrooms and analyzing the actual responses of numerous undergraduate students. Thirty such responses were examined in Bleich's book. Where other contemporary literary intellectuals like Myth Critics and hermeneuticists prized erudition, philological rigor, and scholarly mastery, Reader-Response Critics working in the empirical mode of Holland and Bleich valued depth of personal engagement, individual frankness and authenticity, and freedom from institutional authority. They made public their own private responses as well as the responses of their students. As Susan Suleiman noted, such 'criticism takes us as far as we can go in the investigation of reading as private experience – an experience in which the determining factor is the individual "life history", not the history of groups and nations' (pp. 31–2). Privileging the idiosyncratic over the norm and the singular over the collective, Bleich's subjective criticism left the text completely behind as a regulator of response. In this he differed from Holland, whose transactive criticism credited textual constraints.[18] Both critics, however, promoted efforts to renew literary pedagogy and to value individual student readers. Such a project prompted even sympathetic critics to doubts, as was clear in Steven Mailloux's *Interpretive Conventions* (1982) and William Ray's *Literary Meaning* (1984), both of which stressed the absence of adequate sociological and institutional analyses inherent in contemporary reader-response psychological criticism.

Reading as resistance: feminism and Marxism

During the heyday of the reader-response movement, none of the leaders explicitly addressed the matter of gender – an issue that Feminist Critics began to raise in the 1970s. Do women read differently from men? Does sexual identity influence understanding? What role does gender play in literature? In criticism? Here Fish, Holland, and Bleich had nothing to say. Neither Suleiman and Crosman nor Tompkins considered such questions in their antnologies. In fact, the issue of gender remained unexplored by leading Phenomenological, Existential, Hermeneutical, Structuralist, and Deconstructive Critics during the early Space Age. Yet important work was done in the field of feminine reader response.

Among the most influential of feminist works of the 1970s in the area of reader-response theory was Judith Fetterley's *The Resisting Reader* (1978), which argued that classic American fiction from Irving and

Hawthorne to Hemingway and Mailer was not 'universal' but masculine, and that women readers of this literature were constrained to identify against themselves. What Fetterley aimed to do was offer a 'survival manual for the woman reader lost in "the masculine wilderness of the American novel"'.[19] She took her inspiration from Kate Millett's *Sexual Politics* (1970) – a pioneering book that first examined texts in light of their male assumptions.

Fetterley argued that to be an American woman reading the nation's classic fiction was to find oneself excluded: one's experience was neither expressed nor legitimized in art. Reading such literature required identifying with it as a male. Under such conditions women were powerless. 'Not only does powerlessness characterize woman's experience of reading, it also describes the content of what is read' (p. xiii). Ultimately, Fetterley criticized both male-dominated literature and the sexist academic institutions of criticism grown up around it. 'As readers and teachers and scholars, women are taught to think as men, to identify with a male point of view, and to accept as normal and legitimate a male system of values . . .' (p. xx). Committing herself to feminist criticism, Fetterley aimed to remedy the anomalous situation of being sexually female and intellectually male. Accordingly, 'the first act of the feminist critic must be to become a resisting rather than an assenting reader and, by this refusal to assent, to begin the process of exorcizing the male mind that has been implanted in us' (p. xxii). This project entailed not only psychological and sociological analysis but political criticism. Feminist resistance had to do with one's identity, one's class, and one's power relations. Fetterley never doubted 'the power of men as a class over women as a class' (p. xvii), nor the present-day oppressive 'function of literary sexual politics' (p. xx).

Following in the wake of other Feminist Critics, especially Carolyn Heilbrun, Kate Millett, Adrienne Rich, and Lillian Robinson, Fetterley indicted the patriarchal exclusions and sexist practices endemic to American institutions of literature. What characterized such male-dominated culture was sex–class hostility and oppression. The task at hand was clear:

> To expose and question that complex of ideas and mythologies about women and men which exist in our society and are confirmed in our literature is to make the system of power embodied in the literature open not only to discussion but even to change. Such a questioning and exposure can, of course, be carried on only by a consciousness radically different from the one that informs the literature. . . . Feminist criticism provides that point of view and embodies that consciousness.
>
> (p. xx)

By foregrounding female consciousness, feminist reader-response criticism could uncover, expose, and question the ideas, myths, and power relations encoded in culture as a way to foster change. This program depended on a new and radically different *female* consciousness. The goal was clear. 'To create a new understanding of our literature is to make possible a new effect of that literature on us. And to make possible a new effect is in turn to provide the conditions for changing the culture that the literature reflects' (pp. xix–xx). The job of feminist criticism was to produce new interpretations as a means to alter consciousness and change society.

In Fetterley's feminist project, poetics encompassed affective, didactic and mimetic frameworks. To begin with, 'what we read affects us' (p. viii). We can be moved by literature. Moreover, we can be instructed and shaped by it. For example, we can construe ourselves as powerless, schizophrenic, or unworthy, as Fetterley personally testified. Finally, literature both embodies and reflects the reigning culture. American society and art, in Fetterley's account, were patriarchal and sexist. So too was academic criticism. What most obviously distinguished the literary theory and criticism of Fetterley from that of Fish, Holland, and Bleich was its recuperation of mimetic poetics and its dedication to a political program. These two were of a piece.

Since literature and its criticism moved, shaped, and mirrored our minds and worlds, both possessed the power to effect positive change. 'At its best, feminist criticism is a political act whose aim is not simply to interpret the world but to change it by changing the consciousness of those who read' (p. viii). Like other reader-response theorists, Fetterley linked reading with identity formation; however, she credited literary texts with much more power over readers. As a result, she envisaged feminist critical activity as an operation of resistance to power. For Fetterley, as for Fish, the reader was not isolated and idiosyncratic, which Holland and Bleich believed, but a member of an interpretive community. The readers represented in Fetterley's work belonged to a particular class with a specific experience of history, set of goals, and program of protocols. About the sociology and politics of the community, Fetterley was much more deeply concerned than Fish. In this regard, the enterprise of Fetterley had a great deal in common with the cultural studies movement initiated in the 1970s and less in common with contemporary phenomenology, hermeneutics, structuralism, deconstruction, or male reader-response criticism.

As is typical of most reader-response criticism, Fetterley's work had close connections with pedagogy. Her text's opening words were: 'This book began in the classroom.' She then related her eight years of experience teaching women's literature, revealing that her book started as a classroom journal kept during a course and shared with students. 'I have continued to develop, refine, and change my ideas through interaction and exchange with my students. It is my sincere wish that this book will extend that dialogue even further and that it will be itself a form of teaching' (p. vii). Here, as elsewhere in the reader-response movement, the beginning and the end of criticism was pedagogy, which was in keeping with its affective-didactic poetics and its student-oriented critical methods. What Fetterley added to this common nexus was a mimetic-political dimension, which lodged her work in an objective paradigm.

That some female practitioners and theoreticians of reader-response criticism were committed to both sociological and political analysis was evident not only in the book of Judith Fetterley, but in the later works, for instance, of Jane Tompkins and of Mary Louise Pratt. At the conclusion of her anthology Tompkins, for example, surprisingly offered a strong critique of the reader-response movement, singling out six weaknesses. First, it did not undermine New Criticism but 'merely transposed formalist principles into a new key' (p. 201). Second, it limited critical activity to specifying 'meaning'. Third, it continued to restrict analysis to individual texts. Fourth, it maintained the long-standing pernicious separation of literature from the forces of political and social life, exacerbating its puerile privatization and loss of moral effectiveness. Fifth, it accepted the removal of literature from history and the tendency to monumentalize or universalize art. And, sixth, it regarded literary language as special or as aesthetic rather than as a form or instrument of power.

In her important essay, 'Interpretive Strategies/Strategic Interpretations: On Anglo-American Reader-Response Criticism' (1982), Mary Louise Pratt employed the ideological analysis typical of the cultural studies movement to criticize American reader-oriented theory and criticism. Using insights from the Marxist intellectuals Louis Althusser, Raymond Williams, and Terry Eagleton, Pratt condemned reader-response criticism as a new formalist practice tied closely to 'bourgeois esthetics, notably to a kind of consumerist view of art which calls for dehistoricizing the art object, detaching it from its context of production and making it available for privatized leisure use'.[20] Like Fetterley and Tompkins, Pratt deplored the avoidance of history, sociology, and politics. What Pratt recommended for reader-response criticism was an expanded program that would undertake 'exploring the specifics of reception as a socially and ideologically determined process and coming to grips with the question of artistic *production*. . . . Obviously it is not in the slightest degree necessary for reader-response criticism to exclude questions of production from the domain of literary studies' (p. 205). Reader-response criticism needed to extend its notion that reception was psychologically and communally determined to the idea that artistic production itself was similarly determined. Actually, argued Pratt, the movement could profitably apply the model of production also to the act of reception: response to literature was itself a form or process of production.

Though Fish's work came closest to meeting Pratt's goals for reader-oriented criticism, it provoked her dismay on several grounds. While Fish's theory of interpretive communities propounded the useful axioms of the socially constituted subject and of the social constitution of literature, it did so at considerable cost: it overlooked or ignored the reality of disagreements, uncertainty, and change within interpretive groups (ideological circles). It thus denied the possibility of power struggles. In Pratt's assessment, Fish portrayed 'interpretive communities as spontaneously forming, egalitarian entities which couldn't be coercive' (p. 225). In this way 'the question of power relations is ruthlessly avoided' (p. 226). The harmony within such communities was established by Fish's utopian concept of consensus – a happy endpoint always insured because the self-selected members of each community perfectly shared beliefs and reading conventions. Instead of politicizing the labors of interpretive communities, Fish depicted the variability and relativity of their critical efforts as signs of the healthy equality and fraternity within groups and the vital freedoms and energies between groups. Where Bleich celebrated the individual liberty of readers, Fish championed the communal agreements of like-minded critics. In both cases, these critics suppressed the fundamental fact of power relations and struggles.

In her earlier work, *Toward a Speech Act Theory of Literary Discourse* (1977), Pratt had attacked formalist and structuralist poetics because they distanced literary language from ordinary language, divorcing literature and criticism from the broad realm of social existence. She looked with hope toward new developments in reader-response theory as well as speech-act theory since both promised to reintegrate literary studies into material social life. In her later essay, she continued to hope for a renewal of criticism by its adoption of an account of discursive production indebted now to Marxist and feminist critical ideas and theories. She singled out Fetterley's work as a model for her enterprise. In Pratt's vision, the intersection of reader-response criticism with the Marxist concept of production and the feminist practice of sociopolitical analysis stood to broaden and improve the movement. In the early 1980s mainline American reader-response criticism lacked adequate treatment of sociological and political realities, as feminists and Marxists in increasing numbers documented. While the shift from a text-centered to a reader-oriented criticism was widely heralded as a positive transformation of literary studies by both feminists and Marxists, matters needed to go further so as to make contact with the facts of gender, class, power, and resistance.

German reception theory in America

Independent of the American reader-response movement, a school of reception theory developed during the sixties and seventies in West Germany, primarily at the University of Constance. The leaders of this tight-knit group were Hans Robert Jauss and Wolfgang Iser, whose works frequently appeared in the biannual series *Poetik und Hermeneutik: Arbeitsergebnisse einer Forschungsgruppe* (*Poetics and Hermeneutics: Findings of a Research Group*), which presented material from important colloquia regularly held at Constance. From the mid-seventies and lasting for a decade, the phenomenological project of Iser drew a great deal of attention in America, whereas the historicist work of Jauss did not receive much consideration until the early eighties when his *Aesthetic Experience and Literary Hermeneutics* (1977) and his collected essays, *Toward an Aesthetic of Reception* (1982), obtained a sympathetic hearing. Iser's major books, *The Implied Reader* (1972) and the *Act of Reading* (1976), were translated by 1974 and 1978, respectively, and were widely and promptly reviewed in American journals. Throughout the seventies both Jauss and Iser lectured at American universities, which included several long sojourns at various major institutions. Significantly, however, the American anthologies of reader-oriented criticism, published by Suleiman and Crosman and by Tompkins in 1980, contained contributions only from Iser, not from Jauss. When a selection of the Constance material from *Poetik und Hermeneutik* was translated and published in 1979 as *New Perspectives in German Literary Criticism*, edited by Richard Amacher and Victor Lange, it offered two essays by Jauss and two by Iser – a more balanced presentation than other English-language collections of reader-oriented materials. Even though Jauss and Iser appeared in translation equally often during the seventies in the influential journal *New Literary History*, it was Iser who most often represented German reception theory for American intellectuals. There were two major reasons why Wolfgang Iser was hospitably received by American literary critics: first, he specialized in classic English fiction, unlike Jauss, whose main interest was in early romance-language literature; and, second, he practiced close reading in a phenomenological mode, whereas Jauss engaged in wide-ranging historicist speculations.

Just as American reader-response criticism provoked attacks for its apparent indifference to sociological and political issues, so West German reception theory incited parallel, though earlier, assaults from

East German Marxists. By the opening years of the 1970s the East Germans, particularly Manfred Naumann and Robert Weimann, had lodged a series of critiques, published mainly in the pages of *Weimarer Beiträge*, the leading journal of literary theory during the post-Stalinist era in the German Democratic Republic. The Marxists had three major complaints. First, they condemned Constance reception theory for focusing exclusively on the consumption of literature, leaving out all consideration of its production. Second, they complained about the tendency of West German reader-oriented critics to subjectivize human cultural history. And third, they deplored Western receptionists' proclivity to privatize the reading process – which was a bourgeois idealization that circumvented all analysis of the social origins and determinants of individual response. Neither Jauss nor Iser escaped these charges similar to ones later made against Fish, Holland, and Bleich.

Americans interested in Iser were most attentive to his accounts of the 'implied reader', the reading process, and the role of 'textual gaps'. Positing an implied reader prestructured by a text and actualized by a critic, Iser was able to focus reception theory on a transcendental or transhistorical reader, thereby bracketing actual, empirical readers and predetermined informed readers. In other words, Iser avoided entanglement with the history of reception in favor of involvement with potential response. This strategy comported well with long-standing formalist doctrines. As depicted by Iser, the reading process entailed a continuous readjustment of expectations and evaluations in a dynamic event dedicated to consistency-building. Unlike the holistic unity pictured as the endpoint in Holland's model of identity re-creation, the sequential consistency portrayed in Iser's account respected the unfolding temporality of the reading experience. The copartnership of reader and text emphasized the aesthetic and didactic dimensions of reading rather than the psychological, sociological, or historical aspects. Patterning the elements or schemata of the text, the reader actively engaged in a self-correcting operation that heightened self-awareness and reinforced humane openness. Because texts contained gaps, blanks, vacancies – indeterminacies – readers were constrained in the process of concretizing works and producing consistency to attend carefully and creatively to textual cues. Iser's reception theory thus respected the text, reminiscent of 'objective' modes of criticism; it refused to transform or dissolve the text into the reader's subjectivity or the interpretive community's codes and conventions. At the same time it depended on and promoted the creativity of the reader in the work of surmounting indeterminacies.

In 1981 a debate broke out between Stanley Fish and Wolfgang Iser in the pages of the poststructuralist journal *Diacritics*. The main issue turned out to be epistemological. Fish insisted that 'perception' was inherently interpretive, that 'facts' were predetermined by values, that 'knowledge' was always interested, that the 'given' was in fact supplied, and that the 'text' was constituted by the reader. Not only was perception thus mediated, but it was conventional. That is to say, perception was prestructured by public and communal rather than individual and unique categories. Consequently, the textual gaps or indeterminacies activating the labors of reading in Iser's model were not built into the text but resulted from the interpretive strategies or perceptual proclivities of the communal reader. Iser replied: 'Interpretation is always informed by a set of assumptions or conventions, but these are also acted upon by what they intend to tackle. Hence the 'something' which is to be mediated exists prior to interpretation, acts as a constraint on interpretation, has repercussions on the anticipations operative in interpretation, and thus contributes to a hermeneutical process. . . .'[21] By insisting that the text preexisted and constrained interpretation, Iser unabashedly made clear the 'objectivist' or textual poetics that distinguished his overall interactive or phenomenological model of interpretation from the various models proposed by Fish, Miller, Holland, Bleich, Fetterley, and others.

In his introductory book on German reader-oriented criticism titled *Reception Theory* (1984), Robert Holub separated American reader-response criticism from German reception theory. None of the American critics campaigned under the banner 'reader-response criticism'; instead this designation was applied after the fact to a number of theorists having little contact with or influence upon one another. 'If reader-response criticism has become a critical force', argued Holub, 'it is by virtue of the ingenuity of labeling rather than any commonality of effort.'[22] In contrast, German reception theory was a cohesive, self-conscious, collective enterprise responding to similar circumstances and predecessors. Forerunners included Slavic formalists and structuralists, European phenomenologists and hermeneuticists, and various sociologists and speech-act theorists. Significantly, psychoanalysis and feminism were conspicuously absent. As far as Holub was concerned, 'the similarities in general critical perspective between reader-response criticism and reception theory are ultimately too superficial and too abstract for a merging here' (pp. xiii–xiv). Yet Holub's subsequent account of the numerous internal disagreements and differences within the German enterprise illustrated a lack of cohesiveness easily a match for American diversity. This important similarity – diversity and struggle – highlighted the operation within all reader-oriented work of differing philosophical commitments (formalism, phenomenology, hermeneutics, Marxism) characteristic of German and of American reader-oriented criticism. Whether part of a tight-knit group or a loose movement, reader-centered critics in Germany and in America typically operated at the intense intersection of numerous contending philosophical forces. Iser was as different from Jauss as Miller was from Fish. What significantly separated the leading Americans from the main Germans were preoccupations with pedagogy and with psychology. Later the concern with feminism would further differentiate the American movement from the German School of Constance.

Of limits and changes

Except for feminist and leftist criticism, no critical group or school appeared as 'pluralistic' or heterogeneous during the 1970s in America as the reader-response movement. In Jane Tompkins' account, this movement encompassed various formalist, phenomenological, structuralist, post-structuralist, and psychoanalytical modes of approach. In the view of Susan Suleiman, it included a half dozen discreet methodologies, ranging from rhetorical, semiotic, and phenomenological to psychoanalytical, hermeneutical, and sociological–historical modes of analysis. (The latter category admittedly applied mainly to European reception theory.) The limits of the movement could have been expanded even further by including in such accounts the receptionist work undertaken by new hermeneuticists like Spanos and by feminists like Fetterley – both of whom promised to reinvigorate reader-oriented practice during its first period of stagnation in the late seventies. It was the force of the ideological analysis promoted by these latter two representative critics – and by certain of the emerging cultural studies theorists – that signaled change for the reader-centered enterprise.

Despite its broadness, the evident pluralism of American reader-response criticism could not accommodate the text-dominated methodology of certain formalists, structuralists, deconstructors, and hermeneuts. In addition, it could not comfortably accommodate the programmatic, theme-centered criticism common to most Myth Critics, existentialists, and Black Aestheticians.

In a certain sense, reader-response criticism was the least pluralistic of contemporary schools and movements. Generally, pluralists seek to avoid two main dangers: they resist any theory that insists there is (only) one correct interpretation of a work; and they deny any theory that promotes as many acceptable readings as there are readers. Pluralists encourage yet constrain hermeneutic liberty; they characteristically celebrate limited diversity and condemn outright arbitrariness. Because reader-response critics like Bleich, Holland, and Fish located meaning in individual readers, they exceeded, quite forcefully, the limits essential to pluralism. The reader-response movement assaulted traditional American pluralism not only by giving the critical franchise to individual readers, but paradoxically by insisting that for each reader there was really only one 'valid' interpretation. Just as the conventions of an interpretive community directed reading along certain preestablished paths, so the personal psychology or identities of readers predetermined the outcomes of their reading experiences. Reader-response criticism undermined the two main limits of traditional pluralism.

Various telling changes characterized American higher education during the formative years of the reader-response movement. Among these were widespread expansions in the sizes of universities and classrooms, successful cries for students' rights, effective demands for relevance in subject matter, fulfilled requests for individualized majors, utopian attempts at deschooling society, scattered triumphant efforts to dismantle traditional grading policies, and heeded calls for formal teacher evaluations. What occurred was a broad shift of emphasis in education from the teacher to the student, from erudition to experience, from disinterested scholarship to personal self-development. The new reference source appeared to be the diary, not the encyclopedia. The source of authority became the self rather than the scholar. Confession seemed a productive activity. The small seminar was preferable to the huge lecture hall. The response statement replaced the critical essay. In such an environment, it was not surprising that text-centered literary studies faced a challenge from reader-response criticism. Nor was it surprising that charges against reader-oriented analysis included accusations of narcissism, of anti-intellectualism, of capitulation to vulgar consumerism, and of making classroom pedagogy *the* measure of effective theory and practice. In this context, the receptionists' early strategy of attacking New Criticism became symbolic of much broader changes taking place in American education during the Space Age.

In its later stages reader-response criticism often broke through its earlier limiting personalism and narcissism, catching glimpses of the impersonal sociological and cultural forces that conditioned the self and its activities. The result was that the magnified self of early formulations soon became a minimal self in later theories. The work of Fish and Fetterley best illustrated this significant change. By the time Holland published *The I*, he had added a new dimension to his theory of identity re-creation so as to account for the essential role of culture: 'culture enables and limits the individual' or, put in terms of identity theory, 'identities are social and political as well as individual' (p. 149). Similarly, Bleich's *Subjective Criticism* marked an expansion of his earlier project precisely because it added a detailed account of how interpretations were negotiated collectively. According to Bleich, all knowledge 'finds itself, at least in part, under the authority of communal and societal motives' (p. 265). What distinguished such latter-day sociological theories formulated by leading receptionists was the degree to which they credited for the first time the determining powers of social practices and communal conventions.

While most of the leading critics associated with the reader-response movement sought to change traditional pedagogical practice and theory, they did not attempt to alter the canon of established great works. Consequently, they limited the scope of their enterprise. What was, in part, at issue here was the applicability of the techniques of personalized reading promoted by receptionists. Because reader-response methods applied to any literature from any period and genre, there was no drive to invent or privilege a special canon the way the New Critics did. However, Reader-Response Critics, particularly of the phenomenological and hermeneutical variety, slowed the pace of 'normal' reading (as did certain Deconstructive Critics). This change entailed an attack on theories of spatial form in favor of new concepts of serial, or sequential, or temporal 'form'. Unlike the New Critics, who preferred short, poetic kinds of literature, Reader-Response Critics were as comfortable with long as with short kinds and as content with prose as with poetry. Consequently, long-standing limits on the canon were loosened somewhat. Although a more generous and inclusive view of the canon evolved, a countervailing need to assess and judge works aesthetically did not emerge. Like historical criticism, judicial criticism remained out of favor. In the absence of these two discredited practices, reformation of the canon was unlikely to occur in reader-response criticism. Not surprisingly, feminists, Black Aestheticians, and other ethnic critics had reason to complain about the status of the canon in the hands of leading Reader-Response Critics. Even in later years, when they turned toward sociological theory, Reader-Response Critics focused primarily on small communities of students and professors, avoiding analysis of society and culture at large. Starting in the late seventies, feminist receptionists set out to change this narrow focus and to revise the limited canon – a project in line with the new turn to historical, political, and ideological analysis.

To arrive at a fuller understanding of the various branches of American reader-response criticism, we shall have to consider the contributions of certain Structuralist Critics to theories of reading and the reader.

The conventions and codes of reading

When they were published in 1980, the two leading anthologies of reader-oriented criticism, Jane Tompkins' *Reader-Response Criticism* and

Susan Suleiman's and Inge Crosman's *The Reader in the Text*, contained essays by three American literary structuralists – Culler, Prince, and Riffaterre. Others could have been added. Often American Structuralist Critics made detailed observations about and contributions to theories of the reader and of reading. In his *A Glossary of Literary Terms* (1981), M.H. Abrams noted: 'The focus of structuralist criticism is on the activity of reading which, by bringing into play the requisite conventions and codes, makes literary sense – that is, endows with form and significance the sequence of words, phrases, and sentences which constitute a piece of literary writing.'[23] To give a straightforward example, Chatman formulated a working distinction between 'reading' the surface level of a narrative and 'reading out' its deep structures, which entailed laborious interlevel deciphering of conventions and codes. In general, the structuralist project could not have proceeded without amplifications and renovations of the ordinary understanding of reading, as we shall see in the works of Riffaterre, Prince, Culler, and Scholes.

In his essay, 'Describing Poetic Structures', Riffaterre insisted that the segmentation and analysis of poetry depended on readers' perceptions of pertinent features of the text, which frequently were unpredictable obscurities unclear in content. To account for such relevant and crucial textual aspects, he posited the presence of a 'super-reader' – an imaginary composite reader who respected the unfolding temporality of the work and responded with hypersensitivity especially to its telling ungrammaticalities. This theoretical construct enabled Riffaterre to carry out formalistic micro-analysis focused on significant moments of perceptible peculiarity. In Riffaterre's view, the text determined response and response invariably required linguistic and literary knowledge. The super-reader possessed an encyclopedic store of information as well as aesthetic hypersensitivity.

When the French translation of 'Describing Poetic Structures' was published five years later in his *Essais de stylistique structurale*, Riffaterre added a new paragraph outlining three interlocking phases of reading. In the first phase, the reader faithfully followed the unfolding event of the text. In the second, he examined certain contradictory passages retroactively as a way to resolve dilemmas. In the third, he performed a global and memorial rereading. All three moments were essential to the dynamics of reading. When he turned from stylistics to semiotics, Riffaterre collapsed these three phases into two. First, 'heuristic reading' attended to the linear, mimetic aspects of a work, confronting surface linguistic ungrammaticalities. Second, 'hermeneutic reading' entailed a retroactive focus on the vertical, semiotic features of a text, particularly its deep structural hypograms and matrix. A set of oppositions characterized the two levels of reading: ideally, the process of reading progressed from *parole* to *langue*, sociolect to idiolect, meaning to significance, content to form, mimesis to semiosis, ungrammaticalities to grammaticalities, syntagm to paradigm, transformation to matrix, surface to depth. Such shifting of levels was labeled by Chatman 'reading out'. In Riffaterre's account, this process was highly stimulating, though disturbingly circular and unstable: 'the reader is reconverted to proper reading when the structural equivalences become apparent all at once in a blaze of revelation. This revelation is always chancy, must always begin anew . . . .'[24] Semiotic 'double reading' forced the reader into a productive and continuous shuttling between textual levels – a process construed by Riffaterre as a hallmark of literariness.

In his essay, 'Introduction à l'étude du narrataire' (1973; trans. 1980), Prince added to the growing typology of readers by distinguishing the 'narratee' from the real reader, the virtual reader, and the ideal reader. Like Riffaterre's super-reader, the ideal reader understood the text fully. The virtual reader was the one the author believed himself to be addressing, whereas the real reader was the one actually reading the work. The narratee was the one or the ones to whom the text was directed as, for example, the Caliph in the *Thousand and One Nights* or the four companions of Marlow in *Heart of Darkness*. 'All narration, whether it is oral or written, whether it recounts real or mythical events, whether it tells a story or relates a simple sequence of actions in time, presupposes not only (at least) one narrator but also (at least) one narratee, the narratee being someone whom the narrator addresses.'[25] The narratee occupied a position like a character in a novel; he was immanent to the text. In Prince's model of reading, the line of communication flowed from the author to the narrator to the narratee to the virtual reader to the real reader to the ideal reader. To be able to characterize the narratee, Prince posited a hypothetical 'zero-degree narratee' against whom he could measure the actual narratee. Unlike most overt or covert real narratees, the zero-degree narratee existed in a psychological, social, and ethical vacuum, possessing mainly minimal linguistic competence, a literal mind, and a good memory. With this fixed point of reference, Prince was able to sketch portraits of various textual narratees in a highly formalistic operation faithful to individual works. Among the functions served by narratees were establishing narrative frameworks, revealing the personalities of narrators, contributing to plot developments, relaying messages from narrators to readers, and pointing to the morals of stories. According to Prince, to read a narrative adequately depended on taking into account the functions served by narratees.

Concerning the extratextual 'real reader', Prince had something to say in *Narratology*. He distinguished between minimal and maximal reading. To understand and to paraphrase linguistic or denotational meaning was to read minimally. To grasp all the relevant and meaningful aspects of a text was to read maximally. Prince also distinguished between propounding a reading of a text and producing a response. In a reading, the critic selected, developed, and reordered materials gathered while reading. In a response, the reader allowed free associations and personal fantasies to condition his reception. Prince denigrated response on the grounds that it introduced irrelevancies and that it lost contact with the text by avoiding textual constraints. Just as Riffaterre insisted that 'the literary text is first of all a grid of constraints upon and directions for a very special type of reading behavior',[26] so Prince declared that 'the text I read acts as a constraint on my reading' (p. 112). Prince wanted a real reader to go beyond minimal reading in order to create a reading attentive to the constraints of the text in the process of extracting a maximum of meaning. For Prince, as for Riffaterre, meaning resided in the text and was extracted by the reader.

It was essential to Prince's real reader, as it was to Riffaterre's super-reader and hermeneutic reader, to be familiar with linguistic and literary conventions and codes. According to Prince, 'reading a narrative, understanding it, implies organizing it and interpreting it in terms of several codes' (p. 125). Among requisite codes and conventions, he included knowledge of language, mastery of elementary logic, familiarity with interpretive conventions, and appreciation of traditional symbols, genres, and characters. Such information constituted a set of norms, limitations, and rules that rendered texts decipherable and understandable. Given textual constraints, linguistic conventions, and literary codes, reading emerged in Prince's account as an impersonal and restricted activity.

Generally speaking, the structuralist theorists of reading, especially Riffaterre, Prince, and Culler, differed from other reader-response theorists, like Bleich, early Fish, and Holland, in their depictions of reading as a highly determined operation of decoding directed by textual and cultural constraints rather than by psychological and emotional proclivities. When Fish in the mid-seventies introduced the concept of interpretive communities into his theory of reading, he adopted a structuralist perspective, that is, he acknowledged the limitations on reading enforced by conventions and codes. What the structuralist concept of convention (or code) introduced was the sense of an underlying social and historical system (or deep structure) of rules determining literature and its interpretation, as Claudio Guillén following Harry Levin memorably demonstrated (*Literature as System*, pp. 59–68). No one did more to promote the study of conventions and codes in American literary circles than Jonathan Culler.

In *Structuralist Poetics* and elsewhere, Culler argued that readers of literature acquired mastery of codes and conventions, which allowed them to process sets of sentences as literary works endowed with shape and meaning. The task of structuralist criticism, therefore, was 'to render as explicit as possible the conventions responsible for the production of attested effects' (p. 31). Among interpretive conventions and codes shared by authors and readers, Culler singled out, for example, the following six. The 'rule of significance' dictated that a literary work expressed a significant attitude about man and/or his world. The 'convention of metaphorical coherence' affirmed that metaphorical tenors and vehicles were always coherent. The 'code of poetic tradition' provided a stock of symbols and types with agreed upon meanings. The 'convention of genre' offered stable sets of norms against which to measure texts. The 'rule of totality' required works to be coherent on as many levels as possible. And the 'convention of thematic unity' indicated that semantic and figurative oppositions fit into symmetrical binary patterns. In Culler's view, the whole system of such rules, codes, and conventions constituted literary competence and comprised the institution of literature.

Although reading conventions were often unconscious and sometimes changeable, they were social rather than subjective phenomena and thus capable of being analyzed the way grammar was examined in linguistics. What Culler advocated for literary studies, therefore, was a shift from scrutinizing separate works to investigating interpretive conventions. This turn from personal performance to social competence, from individual critics at work to the institution of literature, from surface phenomena to deep structure, recapitulated Saussure's move from *parole* to *langue*. Not surprisingly, Culler criticized the American preoccupation since the days of New Criticism with the close reading of individual texts. He discounted hermeneutics and championed semiotics for 'granting precedence to the task of formulating a theory of literary competence and relegating critical interpretation to a secondary role' (p. 128). Culler particularly deplored the tendency of contemporary critical interpretation toward premature foreclosure in the interests of unity and meaning, as was most clear in his *Flaubert: The Uses of Uncertainty* (1974) – a book that celebrated Flaubert's various strategies of undermining conventional modes of understanding. What the book on Flaubert illustrated was the crucial role not only of conventions but of convention-breaking for the institution of literary studies.

Throughout the seventies and early eighties, Culler incorporated more and more of deconstruction into his project of semiotics. While this effort was a minor affair in *Structuralist Poetics*, it became a major endeavor by the time of *The Pursuit of Signs* (1981) and *On Deconstruction* (1982). In the latter text, Culler almost seemed to have given up semiotics in favor of deconstruction while in the former he unequivocally aimed to appropriate deconstruction for semiotics. Such a change in his theoretical commitments altered his conception of the reading activity. In

On Deconstruction, for example, he presented reading as itself a type of narration. Readings of texts were cast as stories of reading texts. By nature such stories were dualistic; they depended on 'an interpreter and something to interpret, a subject and an object, an actor and something he acts upon or that acts on him'.[27] To account for the linkages in the reading process, literary theorists had to construct various monisms in which the borders between texts and readers or between textual contents and interpretative inferences were, in Culler's view, ultimately undecidable. This paradoxical logic, typical of deconstruction, seemed to undermine Culler's earlier structuralist goal of mapping the system of conventions underlying the institution of literature. However, Culler portrayed structuralism and deconstruction as complementary projects: the one categorized the grammar of texts and the other charted textual ungrammaticalities. Each dealt with systems and their breakdowns but from different vantage points. In a way, *On Deconstruction* sought to systematize the new conventions and codes brought into being by various deconstructionist protocols of reading.

What the structuralist theories of reading and readers worked out by Riffaterre, Prince, and Culler had in common was a foundation in deep structures linked to society. Communal conventions or codes took the place typically occupied in other theories by the individual reader. Systems replaced subjectivity. Reading emerged as a rule-governed process subject to textual and interpretive constraints. The various readers posited by structuralists had this in common: they were impersonal, collective, theoretical constructs, not empirical or real readers. For structuralists, the main interest in the reader concerned, in Culler's words, 'not what actual readers happen to do but what an ideal reader must know implicitly in order to read and interpret works' (*Structuralist Poetics*, pp. 123–4). The empathetic reading cherished by certain Phenomenological, Hermeneutical, Psychoanalytical, and Feminist Critics epitomized the approach most at odds with structuralist and semiotic criticism. To produce a maximal reading, the ideal reader had to decode the text in a manner consonant with superior competence in all matters of linguistic and literary convention. More or less ignored or downplayed in this process were the full resources of biographical, historical, and judicial modes of criticism.

Unlike other leading American literary semioticians, Robert Scholes became increasingly preoccupied with both classroom pedagogy and 'ideological analysis', as attested especially in his *Textual Power: Literary Theory and the Teaching of English* (1985), the third in a sequence of books dealing with structuralism and semiotics. These twin interests emerged out of a concern with the conventions and codes of culture and its various institutions. In constructing a three-phase semiotic model of 'reading', Scholes was heavily influenced by the 'structuralism' of

Michel Foucault, whose political and sociological works influenced significantly the cultural studies movement with which Scholes had increasingly more in common during the eighties.

The encounter with a text involved three interlocking and ascending stages labeled by Scholes as 'reading', 'interpretation', and 'criticism'. Reading entailed the submissive decipherment of a work dependent on largely unconscious knowledge of generic and cultural codes. Interpretation took place when difficulties occurred in reading, precipitating a conscious thematizing of oppositions and implications linked with shared cultural codes. Criticism entailed an antagonistic critique of the themes and/or codes in the name of certain specified group or class values. In Scholes' view, the encounter with a text ultimately required not passive consumption but active production, not reverential exegesis or close reading but judicious and skeptical questioning. Consequently, critics and teachers 'must open the way between the literary or verbal text and the social text in which we live'.[28] In his own readings and demonstrations, Scholes continually linked the literary text with the social text and engaged in ideological analysis indebted to psychoanalysis and feminism as well as structuralism and semiotics. He was committed to analysis and teaching of both interpretive codes and conventions and cultural codes and their values, rendering him the least formalistic of leading American literary semioticians. Scholes was not content with formulations like Prince's minimal/maximal reading or Riffaterre's heuristic/hermeneutic reading. He sought to add to such textual criticisms a judicial worldly criticism so as to empower the institution of criticism and render students as well as critics effective citizens. What Scholes did was to restore the referential and mimetic functions of discourse and dissolve the formalistic constraints erected by early structuralism. To Chatman's process of 'reading out' texts, he added 'reading against' texts, emerging in the eighties as one of a growing number of important and influential 'resisting readers'.

Notes

1. Susan R. Suleiman, 'Introduction: Varieties of Audience-Oriented Criticism', *The Reader in the Text: Essays on Audience and Interpretation*, ed. Susan R. Suleiman and Inge Crosman (Princeton: Princeton University Press, 1980), p. 6.

2. Jane P. Tompkins, 'An Introduction to Reader-Response Criticism', *Reader-Response Criticism: From Formalism to Post-Structuralism* (Baltimore: Johns Hopkins University Press, 1980), p. ix.

3. STANLEY EUGENE FISH, *Surprised by Sin: The Reader in Paradise Lost* (1967; Berkeley: University of California Press, 1971), p. x.

4. STANLEY E. FISH, 'Literature in the Reader: Affective Sylistics', *New Literary History*, 2 (Autumn 1970); reprinted with omissions in *Self-Consuming Artifacts: The Experience of Seventeenth-Century Literature* (Berkeley: University of California Press, 1972); reprinted with omissions in TOMPKINS, pp. 70–100; and reprinted in FISH, *Is There a Text in This Class? The Authority of Interpretive Communities* (Cambridge: Harvard University Press, 1980), p. 49. *Is There a Text* contains sixteen articles – twelve of which were previously published between 1970 and 1980.

5. PAUL DE MAN, 'Literature and Language: A Commentary', *New Literary History*, 4 (Autumn 1972): 192.

6. JONATHAN CULLER, 'Stanley Fish and the Righting of the Reader' (1975), in *The Pursuit of Signs: Semiotics, Literature, Deconstruction* (Ithaca: Cornell University Press, 1981), p. 131.

7. STANLEY E. FISH, 'Interpreting the *Variorum*', *Critical Inquiry*, 2 (Spring 1976); reprinted in *Is There a Text*, p. 171.

8. STANLEY FISH, *The Living Temple: George Herbert and Catechizing* (Berkeley: University of California Press, 1978), p. 172.

9. STANLEY FISH, 'Consequences', *Critical Inquiry*, 11 (March 1985): 438.

10. EDWARD W. SAID, *The World, the Text, and the Critic* (Cambridge: Harvard University Press, 1983), p. 26.

11. FRANK LENTRICCHIA, *After the New Criticism* (Chicago: University of Chicago Press, 1980), p. 147.

12. NORMAN HOLLAND, 'UNITY IDENTITY TEXT SELF', *PMLA*, **90** (October 1975): 815.

13. NORMAN HOLLAND, 'The New Paradigm: Subjective or Transactive?', *New Literary History*, 7 (Winter 1976): 338.

14. According to Holland, 'the same large principle seems to apply not only to interactions of people but to interactions by anything that can be said to have a style the way a person does: an institution, for example, or a culture or a nation' – 5 *Readers Reading* (New Haven: Yale University Press, 1975), p. xiii. See also HOLLAND, *The I* (New Haven: Yale University Press, 1985), pp. 145–55.

15. FREDERICK CREWS, *Out of My System: Psychoanalysis, Ideology, and Critical Method* (New York: Oxford University Press, 1975), pp. 179–80.

16. DAVID BLEICH, *Subjective Criticism* (Baltimore: Johns Hopkins University Press, 1978), pp. 297, 299.

17. DAVID BLEICH, *Readings and Feelings: An Introduction to Subjective Criticism* (Urbana: National Council of Teachers of English, 1975), p. 81.

18. Bleich and Holland debated this difference in articles published in *College English* and *New Literary History* during 1975 and 1976.

19. JUDITH FETTERLEY, *The Resisting Reader: A Feminist Approach to American Fiction* (Bloomington: Indiana University Press, 1978), p. viii.

20. MARY LOUISE PRATT, 'Interpretive Strategies/Strategic Interpretations: On Anglo-American Reader-Response Criticism', *Boundary* 2 11 (Fall/Winter 1982–83): 209.

21. WOLFGANG ISER, 'Talk like Whales: A Reply to Stanley Fish', *Diacritics*, 11 (Fall 1981): 84.

22. ROBERT C. HOLUB, *Reception Theory: A Critical Introduction* (London: Methuen, 1984), p. xiii.

23. M. H. ABRAMS, *A Glossary of Literary Terms*, 4th edn (New York: Holt, Rinehart and Winston, 1981), p. 189.

24. MICHAEL RIFFATERRE, *Semiotics of Poetry* (Bloomington: Indiana University Press, 1978), p. 166.

25. GERALD PRINCE, 'Introduction to the Study of the Narratee' (1973), trans. Francis Mariner in *Reader-Response Criticism: From Formalism to Post-Structuralism*, ed. Jane P. Tompkins (Baltimore: Johns Hopkins University Press, 1980), p. 7.

26. MICHAEL RIFFATERRE, 'Interview', *Diacritics*, 11 (Winter 1981): 13. See also *Semiotics of Poetry*, pp. 12, 150, 165.

27. JONATHAN CULLER, *On Deconstruction: Theory and Criticism after Structuralism* (Ithaca: Cornell University Press, 1982), p. 75.

28. ROBERT SCHOLES, *Textual Power: Literary Theory and the Teaching of English* (New Haven: Yale University Press, 1985), p. 24.

3 Reading Ourselves: Toward a Feminist Theory of Reading*

PATROCINIO P. SCHWEICKART

The single most important development in reading theory during the 1980s was produced in response to the recognition that reading is inescapably gendered. In her landmark essay, Patrocinio Schweickart explores the developments in feminist reading theory up to the mid-1980s. Schweickart critically adduces two separate strands in feminist reading theory: in the first place there is the resisting reader, the woman reader who resists the patriarchal assumptions and 'immasculating' forces of canonical texts. Secondly, there is a rewriting of the canon, necessitated by a specifically feminist reading of women's (hitherto largely non-canonical) texts: implicit even if not explicit in such a rereading is a critique of androcentric reading and a redescription of women reading. In both cases, Schweickart argues, reading theory 'needs feminist criticism' to escape from the eternal dualism of conventional reader-response criticism which seeks to locate authority in the text or in the reader. Finally, Schweickart is concerned throughout her essay to address the question of what it would mean to read 'as a woman', and approaches this question by way of Adrienne Rich's reading of Emily Dickinson.

For more on feminism and reading, see Flynn and Schweickart's important collection of essays, *Gender and Reading* (1986), and a more recent collection of essays, edited by Sara Mills, *Gendering the Reader* (1994); and see Jonathan Culler's influential Chapter 'Reading as a Woman', from *On Deconstruction* (1983). The subject-centred approach of Schweickart has been criticized recently by Pamela Caughie in 'Women Reading/Reading Women' (1988); for alternative feminist approaches, see Chapters 4 and 5 by Mary Jacobus and Wai-Chee Dimock.

* Reprinted from ELIZABETH A. FLYNN and PATROCINIO P. SCHWEICKART (eds), *Gender and Reading: Essays on Readers, Texts, and Contexts* (Baltimore: The Johns Hopkins University Press, 1986), pp. 35–62.

(In the introductory section of this essay, which is not included here, Schweickart contrasts three 'stories of reading' – by Wayne Booth, Malcolm X and Virginia Woolf. Wayne Booth's story of reading, Schweickart declares, is 'utopian' in its elision of the race and gender differences which are explored in the stories of Malcolm X and Woolf. But Booth's story is also utopian in a more positive sense, Schweickart asserts, in its prefiguration of a time when, having overcome the 'pervasive systemic injustice of our time', everyone will be able to read with 'critical understanding'.)

Reader-response theory and feminist criticism

Reader-response criticism, as currently constituted, is utopian in the same two senses [see above]. The different accounts of the reading experience that have been put forth overlook the issues of race, class, and sex, and give no hint of the conflicts, sufferings, and passions that attend these realities. The relative tranquility of the tone of these theories testifies to the privileged position of the theorists. Perhaps, someday, when privileges have withered away or at least become more equitably distributed, some of these theories will ring true. Surely we ought to be able to talk about reading without worrying about injustice. But for now, reader-response criticism must confront the disturbing implications of our historical reality. Paradoxically, utopian theories that elide these realities betray the utopian impulses that inform them.

To put the matter plainly, reader-response criticism needs feminist criticism. The two have yet to engage each other in a sustained and serious way, but if the promise of the former is to be fulfilled, such an encounter must soon occur. Interestingly, the obvious question of the significance of gender has already been explicitly raised, and – this testifies to the increasing impact of feminist criticism as well as to the direct ideological bearing of the issue of gender on reader-response criticism – not by a feminist critic, but by Jonathan Culler, a leading theorist of reading:

> If the experience of literature depends upon the qualities of a reading self, one can ask what difference it would make to the experience of literature and thus to the meaning of literature if this self were, for example, female rather than male. If the meaning of a work is the experience of a reader, what difference does it make if the reader is a woman?[1]

Until very recently this question has not occurred to reader-response critics. They have been preoccupied with other issues. Culler's survey of the field is instructive here, for it enables us to anticipate the direction reader-response theory might take when it is shaken from its slumber by feminist criticism. According to Culler, the different models (or 'stories') of reading that have been proposed are all organized around three problems. The first is the issue of control: Does the text control the reader, or vice versa? For David Bleich, Normal Holland, and Stanley Fish, the reader holds controlling interest. Readers read the poems they have made. Bleich asserts this point most strongly: the constraints imposed by the words on the page are 'trivial', since their meaning can always be altered by 'subjective action'. To claim that the text supports this or that reading is only to 'moralistically claim . . . that one's own objectification is more authoritative than someone else's'.2

At the other pole are Michael Riffaterre, Georges Poulet, and Wolfgang Iser, who acknowledge the creative role of the reader, but ultimately take the text to be the dominant force. To read, from this point of view, is to create the text according to *its* own promptings. As Poulet puts it, a text, when invested with a reader's subjectivity, becomes a 'subjectified object', a 'second self' that depends on the reader, but is not, strictly speaking, identical with him. Thus, reading 'is a way of giving way not only to a host of alien words, images and ideas, but also to the very alien principle which utters and shelters them. . . . I am on loan to another, and this other thinks, feels, suffers and acts within me'.3 Culler argues persuasively that, regardless of their ostensible theoretical commitments, the prevailing stories of reading generally vacillate between these reader-dominant and text-dominant poles. In fact, those who stress the subjectivity of the reader as against the objectivity of the text ultimately portray the text as determining the responses of the reader. 'The more active, projective, or creative the reader is, the more she is manipulated by the sentence or by the author' (p. 71).

The second question prominent in theories of reading is closely related to the first. Reading always involves a subject and an object, a reader and a text. But what constitutes the objectivity of the text? What is 'in' the text? What is supplied by the reader? Again, the answers have been equivocal. On the face of it, the situation seems to call for a dualistic theory that credits the contributions of both text and reader. However, Culler argues, a dualistic theory eventually gives way to a monistic theory, in which one or the other pole supplies everything. One might say, for instance, that Iser's theory ultimately implies the determinacy of the text and the authority of the author: 'The author guarantees the unity of the work, requires the reader's creative participation, and through his text, prestructures the shape of the aesthetic object to be produced by the reader.'[4] At the same time, one can also argue that the 'gaps' that structure the reader's response are not built into the text, but appear (or not) as a result of the particular interpretive strategy employed by the reader. Thus, 'there is no distinction between what the text gives and what the reader supplies; he supplies *everything*'.[5] Depending on which aspects of the theory one takes seriously, Iser's theory collapses either into a monism of the text or a monism of the reader.

The third problem identified by Culler concerns the ending of the story. Most of the time stories of reading end happily. 'Readers may be manipulated and misled, but when they finish the book their experience turns into knowledge . . . as though finishing the book took them outside the experience of reading and gave them mastery of it' (p. 79). However, some critics – Harold Bloom, Paul de Man, and Culler himself – find these optimistic endings questionable, and prefer instead stories that stress the impossibility of reading. If, as de Man says, rhetoric puts 'an insurmountable obstacle in the way of any reading or understanding', then the reader 'may be placed in impossible situations where there is no happy issue, but only the possibility of playing out the roles dramatized in the text' (Culler, p. 81).

Such have been the predominant preoccupations of reader-response criticism during the past decade and a half. Before indicating how feminist critics could affect the conversation, let me consider an objection. A recent and influential essay by Elaine Showalter suggests that we should not enter the conversation at all. She observes that during its early phases, the principal mode of feminist criticism was 'feminist critique', which was counter-ideological in intent and concerned with the feminist as reader. Happily, we have outgrown this necessary but theoretically unpromising approach. Today, the dominant mode of feminist criticism is 'gynocritics', the study of woman as writer, of the 'history, styles, themes, genres, and structures of writing by women; the psychodynamics of female creativity; the trajectory of the individual or collective female career; and the evolution and laws of a female literary tradition'. The shift from 'feminist critique' to 'gynocritics' – from emphasis on woman as reader to emphasis on woman as writer – has put us in the position of developing a feminist criticism that is 'genuinely woman-centered, independent, and intellectually coherent'.

> To see women's writing as our primary subject forces us to make the leap to a new conceptual vantage point and to redefine the nature of the theoretical problem before us. It is no longer the ideological dilemma of reconciling revisionary pluralisms but the essential question of difference. How can we constitute women as a distinct literary group? What is the *difference* of women's writing?[6]

But why should the activity of the woman writer be more conducive to theory than the activity of the woman reader is? If it is possible to formulate a basic conceptual framework for disclosing the 'difference' of women's writing, surely it is no less possible to do so for women's reading. The same difference, be it linguistic, biological, psychological, or cultural, should apply in either case. In addition, what Showalter calls 'gynocritics' is in fact constituted by feminist *criticism* – that is, *readings* – of female texts. Thus, the relevant distinction is not between woman as reader and woman as writer, but between feminist readings of male texts and feminist readings of female texts, and there is no reason why the former could not be as theoretically coherent (or irreducibly pluralistic) as the latter.

On the other hand, there are good reasons for feminist criticism to engage reader-response criticism. Both dispute the fetishized art object, the 'Verbal Icon', of New Criticism, and both seek to dispel the objectivist illusion that buttresses the authority of the dominant critical tradition. Feminist criticism can have considerable impact on reader-response criticism, since, as Culler has noticed, it is but a small step from the thesis that the reader is an active producer of meaning to the recognition that there are many different kinds of readers, and that women – because of their numbers if because of nothing else – constitute an essential class. Reader-response critics cannot take refuge in the objectivity of the text, or even in the idea that a gender-neutral criticism is possible. Today they can continue to ignore the implications of feminist criticism only at the cost of incoherence or intellectual dishonesty.

It is equally true that feminist critics need to question their allegiance to text- and author-centered paradigms of criticism. Feminist criticism, we should remember, is a mode of *praxis*. The point is not merely to interpret literature in various ways; the point is to *change the world*. We cannot afford to ignore the activity of reading, for it is here that literature is realized as *praxis*. Literature acts on the world by acting on its readers.

To return to our earlier question: What will happen to reader-response criticism if feminists enter the conversation? It is useful to recall the contrast between Booth's story and those of Malcolm X and Virginia Woolf. Like Booth's story, the 'stories of reading' that currently make up reader-response theory are mythically abstract, and appear, from a different vantage point, to be by and about readers who are fantastically privileged. Booth's story had a happy ending; Malcolm's and Mary's did not. For Mary, reading meant encountering a tissue of lies and silences; for Malcolm it meant the verification of Elijah Muhammad's shocking doctrines.

Two factors – gender and politics – which are suppressed in the dominant models of reading gain prominence with the advent of a feminist perspective. The feminist story will have *at least* two chapters: one concerned with feminist readings of male texts, and another with feminist readings of female texts. In addition, in this story, gender will have a prominent role as the locus of political struggle. The story will speak of the difference between men and women, of the way the experience and perspective of women have been systematically and fallaciously assimilated into the generic masculine, and of the need to correct this error. Finally, it will identify literature – the activities of reading and writing – as an important arena of political struggle, a crucial component of the project of interpreting the world in order to change it.

Feminist criticism does not approach reader-response criticism without preconceptions. Actually, feminist criticism has always included substantial reader-centered interests. In the next two sections of this paper, I will review these interests, first with respect to male texts, then with respect to female texts. In the process, I will uncover some of the issues that might be addressed and clarified by a feminist theory of reading.

The female reader and the literary canon

Although reader-response critics propose different and often conflicting models, by and large the emphasis is on features of the process of reading that do not vary with the nature of the reading material. The feminist entry into the conversation brings the nature of the text back into the foreground. For feminists, the question of *how* we read is inextricably linked with the question of *what* we read. More specifically, the feminist inquiry into the activity of reading begins with the realization that the literary canon is androcentric, and that this has a profoundly damaging effect on women readers. The documentation of this realization was one of the earliest tasks undertaken by feminist critics. Elaine Showalter's 1971 critique of the literary curriculum is exemplary of this work.

> [In her freshman year a female student] . . . might be assigned an anthology of essays, perhaps such as *The Responsible Man* . . . or *Conditions of Man*, or *Man in Crisis*, or again, *Representative Man: Cult Heroes of Our Time*, in which thirty-three men represent such categories of heroism as the writer, the poet, the dramatist, the artist, and the guru, and the only two women included are the actress Elizabeth Taylor, and the existential Heroine Jacqueline Onassis.

Perhaps the student would read a collection of stories like *The Young Man in American Literature: The Initiation Theme*, or sociological literature like *The Black Man and the Promise of America*. In a more orthodox literary program she might study eternally relevant classics, such as *Oedipus*; as a professor remarked in a recent issue of *College English*, all of us want to kill our fathers and marry our mothers. And whatever else she might read, she would inevitably arrive at the favorite book of all Freshman English courses, the classic of adolescent rebellion, *A Portrait of the Artist as a Young Man*.

By the end of her freshman year, a woman student would have learned something about intellectual neutrality; she would be learning, in fact, how to think like a man. And so she would go on, increasingly with male professors to guide her.[7]

The more personal accounts of other critics reinforce Showalter's critique.

The first result of my reading was a feeling that male characters were at the very least more interesting than women to the authors who invented them. Thus if, reading their books as it seemed their authors intended them, I naively identified with a character, I repeatedly chose men; I would rather have been Hamlet than Ophelia, Tom Jones instead of Sophia Western, and, perhaps, despite Dostoevsky's intention, Raskolnikov not Sonia.

More peculiar perhaps, but sadly unsurprising, were the assessments I accepted about fictional women. For example, I quickly learned that power was unfeminine and powerful women were, quite literally, monstrous. . . . Bitches all, they must be eliminated, reformed, or at the very least, condemned. . . . Those rare women who are shown in fiction as both powerful and, in some sense, admirable are such because their power is based, if not on beauty, then at least on sexuality.[8]

For a woman, then, books do not necessarily spell salvation. In fact, a literary education may very well cause her grave psychic damage: schizophrenia 'is the bizarre but logical conclusion of our education. Imagining myself male, I attempted to create myself male. Although I knew the case was otherwise, it seemed I could do nothing to make this other critically real.'[9]

To put the matter theoretically, androcentric literature structures the reading experience differently depending on the gender of the reader. For the male reader, the text serves as the meeting ground of the personal and the universal. Whether or not the text approximates the

particularities of his own experience, he is invited to validate the
equation of maleness with humanity. The male reader feels his affinity
with the universal, with the paradigmatic human being, precisely
because he is male. Consider the famous scene of Stephen's epiphany in
A Portrait of the Artist as a Young Man.

> A girl stood before him in midstream, alone and still, gazing out to
> sea. She seemed like one whom magic had changed into the likeness
> of a strange and beautiful seabird. Her long slender bare legs were
> delicate as a crane's and pure save where an emerald trail of
> seaweed had fashioned itself as a sign upon the flesh. Her thighs,
> fuller and softhued as ivory, were bared almost to the hips, where
> the white fringes of her drawers were like feathering of soft white
> down. Her slateblue skirts were kilted boldly about her waist and
> dovetailed behind her. Her bosom was a bird's, soft and slight,
> slight and soft, as the breast of some dark plumaged dove. But her
> long fair hair was girlish: and touched with the wonder of mortal
> beauty, her face.[10]

A man reading this passage is invited to identify with Stephen, to feel
'the riot in his blood', and, thus, to ratify the alleged universality of the
experience. Whether or not the sight of a girl on the beach has ever
provoked similar emotions in him, the male reader is invited to feel his
difference (concretely, *from the girl*) and to equate that with the universal.
Relevant here is Lévi-Strauss's theory that woman functions as currency
exchanged between men. The woman in the text converts the text into a
woman, and the circulation of this text/woman becomes the central
ritual that establishes the bond between the author and his male
readers.[11]

The same text affects a woman reader differently. Judith Fetterley
gives the most explicit theory to date about the dynamics of the woman
reader's encounter with androcentric literature. According to Fetterley,
notwithstanding the prevalence of the castrating bitch stereotype, 'the
cultural reality is not the emasculation of men by women, but the
immasculation of women by men. As readers and teachers and scholars,
women are taught to think as men, to identify with a male point of view,
and to accept as normal and legitimate a male system of values, one of
whose central principles is misogyny.'[12]

The process of immasculation does not impart virile power to the
woman reader. On the contrary, it doubles her oppression. She suffers

> not simply the powerlessness which derives from not seeing one's
> experience articulated, clarified, and legitimized in art, but more
> significantly, the powerlessness which results from the endless

division of self against self, the consequence of the invocation to identify as male while being reminded that to be male – to be universal – . . . is to be *not female*.[13]

A woman reading Joyce's novel of artistic awakening, and in particular the passage quoted above, will, like her male counterpart, be invited to identify with Stephen and therefore to ratify the equation of maleness with the universal. Androcentric literature is all the more efficient as an instrument of sexual politics because it does not allow the woman reader to seek refuge in her difference. Instead, it draws her into a process that uses her against herself. It solicits her complicity in the elevation of male difference into universality and, accordingly, the denigration of female difference into otherness without reciprocity. To be sure, misogyny is abundant in the literary canon.14 It is important, however, that Fetterley's argument can stand on a weaker premise. Androcentricity is a sufficient condition for the process of immasculation.

Feminist critics of male texts, from Kate Millett to Judith Fetterley, have worked under the sign of the 'Resisting Reader'. Their goal is to disrupt the process of immasculation by exposing it to consciousness, by disclosing the androcentricity of what has customarily passed for the universal. However, feminist criticism written under the aegis of the resisting reader leaves certain questions unanswered, questions that are becoming ripe for feminist analysis: Where does the text get its power to draw us into its designs? Why do some (not all) demonstrably sexist texts remain appealing even after they have been subjected to thorough feminist critique? The usual answer – that the power of male texts is the power of the false consciousness into which women as well as men have been socialized – oversimplifies the problem and prevents us from comprehending both the force of literature and the complexity of our responses to it.

Fredric Jameson advances a thesis that seems to me to be a good starting point for the feminist reconsideration of male texts: 'The effectively ideological is also at the same time necessarily utopian.'[15] This thesis implies that the male text draws its power over the female reader from authentic desires, which it rouses and then harnesses to the process of immasculation.

A concrete example is in order. Consider Lawrence's *Women in Love*, and for the sake of simplicity, concentrate on Birkin and Ursula. Simone de Beauvoir and Kate Millet have convinced me that this novel is sexist. Why does it remain appealing to me? Jameson's thesis prompts me to answer this question by examining how the text plays not only on my false consciousness but also on my authentic liberatory aspirations – that is to say, on the very impulses that drew me to the feminist movement.

The trick of role reversal comes in handy here. If we reverse the roles of Birkin and Ursula, the ideological components (or at least the most egregious of these, e.g., the analogy between women and horses) stand out as absurdities. Now, if we delete these absurd components while keeping the roles reversed, we have left the story of a woman struggling to combine her passionate desire for autonomous conscious being with an equally passionate desire for love and for other human bonds. This residual story is not far from one we would welcome as expressive of a feminist sensibility. Interestingly enough, it also intimates a novel Lawrence might have written, namely, the proper sequel to *The Rainbow*.

My affective response to the novel Lawrence did write is bifurcated. On the one hand, because I am a woman, I am implicated in the representation of Ursula and in the destiny Lawrence has prepared for her: man is the son of god, but woman is the daughter of man. Her vocation is to witness his transcendence in rapt silence. On the other hand, Fetterley is correct that I am also induced to identify with Birkin, and in so doing, I am drawn into complicity with the reduction of Ursula, and therefore of myself, to the role of the other.

However, the process of immasculation is more complicated than Fetterley allows. When I identify with Birkin, I unconsciously perform the two-stage rereading described above. I reverse the roles of Birkin and Ursula and I suppress the obviously ideological components that in the process show up as absurdities. The identification with Birkin is emotionally effective because, stripped of its patriarchal trappings, Birkin's struggle and his utopian vision conform to my own. To the extent that I perform this feminist rereading *unconsciously*, I am captivated by the text. The stronger my desire for autonomous selfhood and for love, the stronger my identification with Birkin, and the more intense the experience of bifurcation characteristic of the process of immasculation.

The full argument is beyond the scope of this essay. My point is that *certain* (not all) male texts merit a dual hermeneutic: a negative hermeneutic that discloses their complicity with patriarchal ideology, and a positive hermeneutic that recuperates the utopian moment – the authentic kernel – from which they draw a significant portion of their emotional power.[16]

Reading women's writing

Showalter is correct that feminist criticism has shifted emphasis in recent years from 'critique' (primarily) of male texts to 'gynocritics', or the study of women's writing. Of course, it is worth remembering that the latter has always been on the feminist agenda. *Sexual Politics*, for example, contains not only the critique of Lawrence, Miller, and Mailer that won Millett such notoriety, but also her memorable rereading of *Villette*.[17] It is equally true that interest in women's writing has not entirely supplanted the critical study of patriarchal texts. In a sense 'critique' has provided the bridge from the study of male texts to the study of female texts. As feminist criticism shifted from the first to the second, 'feminist critique' turned its attention from androcentric texts *per se* to the androcentric critical strategies that pushed women's writing to the margins of the literary canon. The earliest examples of this genre (for instance, Showalter's 'The Double Critical Standard', and Carol Ohmann's 'Emily Brontë in the Hands of Male Critics') were concerned primarily with describing and documenting the prejudice against women writers that clouded the judgment of well-placed readers, that is, reviewers and critics.[18] Today we have more sophisticated and more comprehensive analyses of the androcentric critical tradition.

One of the most cogent of these is Nina Baym's analysis of American literature.[19] Baym observes that, as late as 1977, the American canon of major writers did not include a single woman novelist. And yet, in terms of numbers and commercial success, women novelists have probably dominated American literature since the middle of the nineteenth century. How to explain this anomaly?

One explanation is simple bias of the sort documented by Showalter, Ohmann, and others. A second is that women writers lived and worked under social conditions that were not particularly conducive to the production of 'excellent' literature: 'There tended to be a sort of immediacy in the ambitions of literary women leading them to professionalism rather than artistry, by choice as well as by social pressure and opportunity.'[20] Baym adduces a third, more subtle, and perhaps more important reason. There are, she argues, 'gender-related restrictions that do not arise out of the cultural realities contemporary with the writing woman, but out of later critical theories . . . which impose their concerns anachronistically, after the fact, on an earlier period'.[21] If one reads the critics most instrumental in forming the current theories about American literature (Matthiessen, Chase, Feidelson, Trilling, etc.), one finds that the theoretical model for the canonical American novel is the 'melodrama of beset manhood'. To accept this model is also to accept as a consequence the exclusion from the canon of 'melodramas of beset womanhood', as well as virtually all fiction centering on the experience of women.[22]

The deep symbiotic relationship between the androcentric canon and androcentric modes of reading is well summarized by Kolodny.

Insofar as we are taught to read, what we engage are not texts, but paradigms. . . . Insofar as literature is itself a social institution, so too, reading is a highly socialized – or learned – activity. . . . We read well, and with pleasure, what we already know how to read; and what we know how to read is to a large extent dependent on what we have already read [works from which we have developed our expectations and learned our interpretive strategies]. What we then choose to read – and, by extension, teach and thereby 'canonize' – usually follows upon our previous reading.[23]

We are caught, in other words, in a rather vicious circle. An androcentric canon generates androcentric interpretive strategies, which in turn favor the canonization of androcentric texts and the marginalization of gynocentric ones. To break this circle, feminist critics must fight on two fronts: for the revision of the canon to include a significant body of works by women, and for the development of the reading strategies consonant with the concerns, experiences, and formal devices that constitute these texts. Of course, to succeed, we also need a community of women readers who are qualified by experience, commitment, and training, and who will enlist the personal and institutional resources at their disposal in the struggle.[24]

The critique of androcentric reading strategies is essential, for it opens up some ideological space for the recuperation of women's writing. Turning now to this project, we observe, first, that a large volume of work has been done, and, second, that this endeavor is coming to look even more complicated and more diverse than the criticism of male texts. Certainly, it is impossible in the space of a few pages to do justice to the wide range of concerns, strategies, and positions associated with feminist readings of female texts. Nevertheless, certain things can be said. For the remainder of this section, I focus on an exemplary essay: 'Vesuvius at Home: The Power of Emily Dickinson', by Adrienne Rich.[25] My commentary anticipates the articulation of a paradigm that illuminates certain features of feminist readings of women's writing.

I am principally interested in the rhetoric of Rich's essay, for it represents an implicit commentary on the process of reading women's writing. Feminist readings of male texts are, as we have seen, primarily resisting. The reader assumes an adversarial or at least a detached attitude toward the material at hand. In the opening pages of her essay, Rich introduces three metaphors that proclaim a very different attitude toward her subject.

The methods, the exclusions, of Emily Dickinson's existence could not have been my own; yet more and more, as a woman poet finding my own methods, I have come to understand her necessities, could have served as witness in her defense.

(p. 158)

I am traveling at the speed of time, along the Massachusetts Turnpike. . . . 'Home is not where the heart is', she wrote in a letter, 'but the house and adjacent buildings'. . . . I am traveling at the speed of time, in the direction of the house and buildings. . . . For years, I have been not so much envisioning Emily Dickinson as trying to visit, to enter her mind through her poems and letters, and through my own intimations of what it could have meant to be one of the two mid-nineteenth century American geniuses, and a woman, living in Amherst, Massachusetts.

(pp. 158–9)

For months, for most of my life, I have been hovering like an insect against the screens of an existence which inhabited Amherst, Massachusetts between 1830 and 1886. . . . Here [in Dickinson's bedroom] I become again, an insect, vibrating at the frames of windows, clinging to the panes of glass, trying to connect.

(pp. 158, 161)

A commentary on the process of reading is carried on silently and unobtrusively through the use of these metaphors. The first is a judicial metaphor: the feminist reader speaks as a witness in defense of the woman writer. Here we see clearly that gender is crucial. The feminist reader takes the part of the woman writer against patriarchal misreadings that trivialize or distort her work.[26] The second metaphor refers to a principal tenet of feminist criticism: a literary work cannot be understood apart from the social, historical, and cultural context within which it was written. As if to acquiesce to the condition Dickinson had imposed on her friends, Rich travels through space and time to visit the poet on her own *premises*. She goes to Amherst, to the house where Dickinson lived. She rings the bell, she goes in, then upstairs, then into the bedroom that had been 'freedom' for the poet. Her destination, ultimately, is Dickinson's mind. But it is not enough to read the poet's poems and letters. To reach her heart and mind, one must take a detour through 'the house and adjacent buildings'.

Why did Dickinson go into seclusion? Why did she write poems she would not publish? What mean these poems about queens, volcanoes, deserts, eternity, passion, suicide, wild beasts, rape, power, madness, the daemon, the grave? For Rich, these are related questions. The revisionary re-reading of Dickinson's work is of a piece with the revisionary re-reading of her life. 'I have a notion genius knows itself; that Dickinson chose her seclusion, knowing what she needed. . . . She carefully selected her society and controlled the disposal of her time. . . . Given her vocation, she was neither eccentric nor quaint; she was determined to survive, to use her powers, to practise necessary economies' (p. 160).

> To write [the poetry that she needed to write] she had to enter chambers of the self in which
>
> > Ourself, concealed –
> > Should startle most –
>
> and to relinquish control there, to take those risks, she had to create a relationship to the outer world where she could feel in control
>
> .(p. 175)

The metaphor of visiting points to another feature of feminist readings of women's writing, namely, the tendency to construe the text not as an object, but as the manifestation of the subjectivity of the absent author – the 'voice' of another woman. Rich is not content to revel in the textuality of Dickinson's poems and letters. For her, these are doorways to the 'mind' of a 'woman of genius'. Rich deploys her imagination and her considerable rhetorical skill to evoke 'the figure of powerful will' who lives at the heart of the text. To read Dickinson, then, is to try to visit with her, to hear her voice, to make her live *in* oneself, and to feel her impressive 'personal dimensions'.[27]

At the same time, Rich is keenly aware that visiting with Dickinson is only a metaphor for reading her poetry, and an inaccurate one at that. She signals this awareness with the third metaphor. It is no longer possible to visit with Dickinson; one can only enter her mind through her poems and letters as one can enter her house – through the backdoor out of which her coffin was carried. In reading, one encounters only a text, the trail of an absent author. Upstairs, at last, in the very room where Dickinson exercised her astonishing craft, Rich finds herself again 'an insect, vibrating at the frames of windows, clinging to panes of glass, trying to connect'. But though 'the scent is very powerful', Dickinson herself is absent.

Perhaps the most obvious rhetorical device employed by Rich in this essay, more obvious even than her striking metaphors, is her use of the personal voice. Her approach to Dickinson is self-consciously and unabashedly subjective. She clearly describes her point of view – what she saw as she drove across the Connecticut Valley toward Amherst (ARCO stations, MacDonald's, shopping plazas, as well as 'light-green spring softening the hills, dogwood and wild fruit trees blossoming in the hollows'), and what she thought about (the history of the valley, 'scene of Indian uprisings, religious revivals, spiritual confrontations, the blazing-up of the lunatic fringe of the Puritan coal', and her memories of college weekends in Amherst). Some elements of her perspective – ARCO and MacDonald's – would have been alien to Dickinson; others – the sight of dogwood and wild fruit trees in the spring, and most of all, the experience of being a woman poet in a patriarchal culture – would establish their affinity.

Rich's metaphors together with her use of the personal voice indicate some key issues underlying feminist readings of female texts. On the one hand, reading is necessarily subjective. On the other hand, it must not be wholly so. One must respect the autonomy of the text. The reader is a visitor and, as such, must observe the necessary courtesies. She must avoid unwarranted intrusions – she must be careful not to appropriate what belongs to her host, not to impose herself on the other woman. Furthermore, reading is at once an intersubjective encounter and something less than that. In reading Dickinson, Rich seeks to enter her mind, to feel her presence. But the text is a screen, an inanimate object. Its subjectivity is only a projection of the subjectivity of the reader.

Rich suggests the central motivation, the regulative ideal, that shapes the feminist reader's approach to these issues. If feminist readings of male texts are motivated by the need to disrupt the process of immasculation, feminist readings of female texts are motivated by the need 'to connect', to recuperate, or to formulate – they come to the same thing – the context, the tradition, that would link women writers to one another, to women readers and critics, and to the large community of women. Of course, the recuperation of such a context is a necessary basis for the nonrepressive integration of women's point of view and culture into the study of a Humanities that is worthy of its name.[28]

Feminist models of reading: a summary

As I noted in the second section, mainstream reader-response theory is preoccupied with two closely related questions: (1) Does the text manipulate the reader, or does the reader manipulate the text to produce the meaning that suits her own interests? and (2) What is 'in' the text? How can we distinguish what it supplies from what the reader supplies? Both of these questions refer to the subject–object relation that is established between reader and text during the process of reading. A feminist theory of reading also elaborates this relationship, but for feminists, gender – the gender inscribed in the text as well as the gender of the reader – is crucial. Hence, the feminist story has two chapters, one concerned with male texts and the other with female texts.

The focus of the first chapter is the experience of the woman reader. What do male texts *do* to her? The feminist story takes the subject–object relation of reading through three moments. The phrasing of the basic question signals the first moment. Control is conferred on the text: the woman reader is immasculated by the text. The feminist story fits well at this point in Iser's framework. Feminists insist that the androcentricity of the text and its damaging effects on women readers are not figments of their imagination. These are implicit in the 'schematized aspects' of the text. The second moment, which is similarly consonant with the plot of Iser's story, involves the recognition of the crucial role played by the subjectivity of the woman reader. Without her, the text is *no-thing*. The process of immasculation is latent in the text, but it finds its actualization only through the reader's activity. In effect, the woman reader is the agent of her own immasculation.[29]

Here we seem to have a corroboration of Culler's contention that dualistic models of reading inevitably disintegrate into one of two monisms. Either the text (and, by implication, the author) or the woman reader is responsible for the process of immasculation. The third moment of the subject–object relation – ushered in by the transfiguration of the heroine into a feminist – breaks through this dilemma. The woman reader, now a feminist, embarks on a critical analysis of the reading process, and she realizes that the text has power to structure her experience. Without androcentric texts she will not suffer immasculation. However, her recognition of the power of the text is matched by her awareness of her essential role in the process of reading. Without her, the text is nothing – it is inert and harmless. The advent of feminist consciousness and the accompanying commitment to emancipatory *praxis* reconstitutes the subject–object relationship within a dialectical rather than a dualistic framework, thus averting the impasse described by Culler between the 'dualism of narrative' and the 'monism of theory'. In the feminist story, the breakdown of Iser's dualism does not indicate a mistake or an irreducible impasse, but the necessity of *choosing* between two modes of reading. The reader can submit to the power of the text, or she can take control of the reading experience. The recognition of the existence of a choice suddenly makes visible the normative dimension of the feminist story: She *should* choose the second alternative.

But what does it mean for a reader to take control of the reading experience? First of all, she must do so without forgetting the androcentricity of the text or its power to structure her experience. In addition, the reader taking control of the text is not, as in Iser's model, simply a matter of selecting among the concretizations allowed by the text. Recall that a crucial feature of the process of immasculation is the woman reader's bifurcated response. She reads the text both as a man and as a woman. But in either case, the result is the same: she confirms her position as other. Taking control of the reading experience means reading the text as it was *not* meant to be read, in fact, reading it against itself. Specifically, one must identify the nature of the choices proffered by the text and, equally important, what the text precludes – namely, the possibility of reading as a woman *without* putting one's self in the position of the other, of reading so as to affirm womanhood as another, equally valid, paradigm of human existence.

All this is easier said than done. It is important to realize that reading a male text, no matter how virulently misogynous, could do little damage if it were an isolated event. The problem is that within patriarchal culture, the experience of immasculation is paradigmatic of women's encounters with the dominant literary and critical traditions. A feminist cannot simply refuse to read patriarchal texts, for they are everywhere, and they condition her participation in the literary and critical enterprise. In fact, by the time she becomes a feminist critic, a woman has already read numerous male texts – in particular, the most authoritative texts of the literary and critical canons. She has introjected not only androcentric texts, but also androcentric reading strategies and values. By the time she becomes a feminist, the bifurcated response characteristic of immasculation has become second nature to her. The feminist story stresses that patriarchal constructs have objective as well as subjective reality; they are inside and outside the text, inside and outside the reader.

The pervasiveness of androcentricity drives feminist theory beyond the individualistic models of Iser and of most reader-response critics. The feminist reader agrees with Stanley Fish that the production of the meaning of a text is mediated by the interpretive community in which the activity of reading is situated: the meaning of the text depends on the interpretive strategy one applies to it, and the choice of strategy is regulated (explicitly or implicitly) by the canons of acceptability that govern the interpretive community.[30] However, unlike Fish, the feminist reader is also aware that the ruling interpretive communities are androcentric, and that this androcentricity is deeply etched in the strategies and modes of thought that have been introjected by all readers, women as well as men.

Because patriarchal constructs have psychological correlates, taking control of the reading process means taking control of one's reactions and inclinations. Thus, a feminist reading – actually a re-reading – is a kind of therapeutic analysis. The reader recalls and examines how she would 'naturally' read a male text in order to understand and therefore undermine the subjective predispositions that had rendered her vulnerable to its designs. Beyond this, the pervasiveness of immasculation necessitates a collective remedy. The feminist reader hopes that other women will recognize themselves in her story, and join her in her struggle to transform the culture.[31]

'Feminism affirms women's point of view by revealing, criticizing and examining its impossibility.'[32] Had we nothing but male texts, this sentence from Catherine MacKinnon's brilliant essay on jurisprudence could serve as the definition of the project of the feminist reader. The significant body of literature written by women presents feminist critics with another, more heartwarming, task: that of recovering, articulating, and elaborating positive expressions of women's point of view, of celebrating the survival of this point of view in spite of the formidable forces that have been ranged against it.

The shift to women's writing brings with it a shift in emphasis from the negative hermeneutic of ideological unmasking to a positive hermeneutic whose aim is the recovery and cultivation of women's culture. As Showalter has noted, feminist criticism of women's writing proposes to articulate woman's difference: What does it mean for a woman to express herself in writing? How does a woman write as a woman? It is a central contention of this essay that feminist criticism should also inquire into the correlative process of *reading*: What does it mean for a woman to read without condemning herself to the position of other? What does it mean for a woman, reading as a woman, to read literature written by a woman writing as a woman?[33]

The Adrienne Rich essay discussed in the preceding section illustrates a contrast between feminist readings of male texts and feminist readings of female texts. In the former, the object of the critique, whether it is regarded as an enemy or as symptom of a malignant condition, is the text itself, *not* the reputation or the character of the author.[34] This impersonal approach contrasts sharply with the strong personal interest in Dickinson exhibited by Rich. Furthermore, it is not merely a question of friendliness toward the text. Rich's reading aims beyond 'the unfolding of the text as a living event', the goal of aesthetic reading set by Iser. Much of the rhetorical energy of Rich's essay is directed toward evoking the personality of Dickinson, toward making *her* live as the substantial, palpable presence animating her works.

Unlike the first chapter of the feminist story of reading, which is centered around a single heroine – the woman reader battling her way out of a maze of patriarchal constructs – the second chapter features two protagonists – the woman reader and the woman writer – in the context of two settings. The first setting is judicial: one woman is standing witness in defense of the other; the second is dialogic: the two women are engaged in initimate conversation. The judicial setting points to the larger political and cultural dimension of the project of the feminist reader. Feminist critics may well say with Harold Bloom that reading always involves the 'art of defensive warfare'.[35] What they mean by this, however, would not be Bloom's individualistic, agonistic encounter between 'strong poet' and 'strong reader', but something more akin to 'class struggle'. Whether concerned with male or female texts, feminist criticism is situated in the larger struggle against patriarchy.

The importance of this battle cannot be overestimated. However, feminist readings of women's writing open up space for another, equally important, critical project, namely, the articulation of a model of reading that is centered on a female paradigm. While it is still too early to present a full-blown theory, the dialogic aspect of the relationship between the feminist reader and the woman writer suggests the direction that such a theory might take. As in all stories of reading, the drama revolves around the subject–object relationship between text and reader. The feminist story – exemplified by the Adrienne Rich essay discussed earlier – features an intersubjective construction of this relationship. The reader encounters not simply a text, but a 'subjectified object': the 'heart and mind' of another woman. She comes into close contact with an interiority – a power, a creativity, a suffering, a vision – that is *not* identical with her own. The feminist interest in construing reading as an intersubjective encounter suggests an affinity with Poulet's (rather than Iser's) theory, and, as in Poulet's model, the subject of the literary work is its author, *not* the reader: 'A book is not only a book; it is a means by which an author actually preserves [her] ideas, [her] feelings, [her] modes of dreaming and living. It is a means of saving [her] identity from death. . . . To understand a literary work, then, is to let the individual who wrote it reveal [herself] to us *in* us.'[36]

For all this initial agreement, however, the dialogic relationship the feminist reader establishes with the female subjectivity brought to life in the process of reading is finally at odds with Poulet's model. For the interiorized author is 'alien' to Poulet's reader. When he reads, he delivers himself 'bound hand and foot, to the omnipotence of fiction'. He becomes the 'prey' of what he reads. 'There is no escaping this takeover.' His consciousness is 'invaded', 'annexed', 'usurped'. He is 'dispossessed' of his rightful place on the 'center stage' of his own mind. In the final analysis, the process of reading leaves room for only one subjectivity. The work becomes 'a sort of human being' at 'the expense of the reader whose life it suspends'.[37] It is significant that the metaphors of mastery and submission, of violation and control, so prominent in Poulet's essay, are entirely absent in Rich's essay on Dickinson. In the paradigm of reading implicit in her essay, the dialectic of control (which shapes feminist readings of male texts) gives way to the dialectic of communication. For Rich, reading is a matter of 'trying to connect' with the existence behind the text.

This dialectic also has three moments. The first involves the recognition that genuine intersubjective communication demands the duality of reader and author (the subject of the work). Because reading removes the barrier between subject and object, the division takes place *within* the reader. Reading induces a doubling of the reader's subjectivity, so that one can be placed at the disposal of the text while the other remains with the reader. Now, this doubling presents a problem, for in fact there is only one subject present – the reader. The text – the words on the page – has been written by the writer, but meaning is always a matter of interpretation. The subjectivity roused to life by reading, while it may be attributed to the author, is nevertheless not a separate subjectivity but a projection of the subjectivity of the reader. How can the duality of subjects be maintained in the absence of the author? In an actual conversation, the presence of another person preserves the duality. Because each party must assimilate and interpret the utterances of the other, we still have the introjection of the subject–object division, as well as the possibility of hearing only what one wants to hear. But in a real conversation, the other person can interrupt, object to an erroneous interpretation, provide further explanations, change her mind, change the topic, or cut off conversation altogether. In reading, there are no comparable safeguards against the appropriation of the text by the reader. This is the second moment of the dialectic – the recognition that reading is necessarily subjective. The need to keep it from being *totally* subjective ushers in the third moment of the dialectic.

In the feminist story, the key to the problem is the awareness of the double context of reading and writing. Rich's essay is wonderfully illustrative. To avoid imposing an alien perspective on Dickinson's poetry, Rich informs her reading with the knowledge of the circumstances in which Dickinson lived and worked. She repeatedly reminds herself and her readers that Dickinson must be read in light of her *own* premises, that the 'exclusions' and 'necessities' she endured, and, therefore, her choices, were conditioned by her own world. At the same time, Rich's sensitivity to the context of writing is matched by her sensitivity to the context of reading. She makes it clear throughout the essay that her reading of Dickinson is necessarily shaped by her experience and interests as a feminist poet living in the twentieth-century United States. The reader also has her own premises. To forget these is to run the risk of imposing them surreptitiously on the author.

To recapitulate, the first moment of the dialectic of reading is marked by the recognition of the necessary duality of subjects; the second, by the realization that this duality is threatened by the author's absence. In the third moment, the duality of subjects is referred to the duality of contexts. Reading becomes a mediation between author and reader, between the context of writings and the context of reading.

Although feminists have always believed that objectivity is an illusion, Rich's essay is the only one, as far as I know, to exhibit through its rhetoric the necessary subjectivity of reading coupled with the equally necessary commitment to reading the text as it was meant to be read.[38] The third moment of the dialectic is apparent in Rich's weaving – not blending – of the context of writing and the context of reading, the perspective of the author and that of the reader. The central rhetorical device effecting this mediation is her use of the personal voice. As in most critical essays, Rich alternates quotes from the texts in question with her own commentary, but her use of the personal voice makes a difference. In her hands, this rhetorical strategy serves two purposes. First, it serves as a reminder that her interpretation is informed by her own perspective. Second, it signifies her tactful approach to Dickinson; the personal voice serves as a gesture warding off any inclination to appropriate the authority of the text as a warrant for the validity of the interpretation. Because the interpretation is presented as an *interpretation*, its claim to validity rests on the cogency of the supporting arguments, *not* on the authorization of the text.

Rich accomplishes even more than this. She reaches out to Dickinson not by identifying with her, but by establishing their affinity. Both are American, both are women poets in a patriarchal culture. By playing this affinity against the differences, she produces a context that incorporates both reader and writer. In turn, this common ground becomes the basis for drawing the connections that, in her view, constitute the proper goal of reading.

One might ask: Is there something distinctively female (rather than 'merely feminist') in this dialogic model? While it is difficult to specify what 'distinctively female' might mean, there are currently very interesting speculations about differences in the way males and females conceive of themselves and of their relations with others. The works of Jean Baker Miller, Nancy Chodorow, and Carol Gilligan suggest that men define themselves through individuation and separation from others, while women have more flexible ego boundaries and define and experience themselves in terms of their affiliations and relationships with others.[39] Men value autonomy, and they think of their interactions with others principally in terms of procedures for arbitrating conflicts between individual rights. Women, on the other hand, value relationships, and they are most concerned in their dealings with others to negotiate between opposing needs so that the relationship can be maintained. This difference is consistent with the difference between mainstream models of reading and the dialogic model I am proposing for feminist readings of women's writing. Mainstream reader-response theories are preoccupied with issues of control and partition – how to distinguish the contribution of the author/text from the contribution of the reader. In the dialectic of communication informing the relationship between the feminist reader and the female author/text, the central issue is not of control or partition, but of managing the contradictory implications of the desire for relationship (one must maintain a minimal distance from the other) and the desire for intimacy, up to and including a symbiotic merger with the other. The problematic is defined by the drive 'to connect', rather than that which is implicit in the mainstream preoccupation with partition and control – namely, the drive to get it right. It could also be argued that Poulet's model represents reading as an intimate, intersubjective encounter. However, it is significant that in his model, the prospect of close rapport with another provokes both excitement and anxiety. Intimacy, while desired, is also viewed as a threat to one's integrity. For Rich, on the other hand, the prospect of merging with another is problematical, but not threatening.

Let me end with a word about endings. Dialectical stories look forward to optimistic endings. Mine is no exception. In the first chapter the woman reader becomes a feminist, and in the end she succeeds in extricating herself from the androcentric logic of the literary and critical canons. In the second chapter the feminist reader succeeds in effecting a mediation between her perspective and that of the writer. These 'victories' are part of the project of producing women's culture and literary tradition, which in turn is part of the project of overcoming patriarchy. It is in the nature of people working for revolutionary change to be optimistic about the prospect of redirecting the future.

Culler observes that optimistic endings have been challenged (successfully, he thinks) by deconstruction, a method radically at odds with the dialectic. It is worth nothing that there is a deconstructive moment in Rich's reading of Dickinson. Recall her third metaphor: the reader is an insect 'vibrating the frames of windows, clinging to the panes of glass, trying to connect'. The suggestion of futility is unmistakable. At best, Rich's interpretation of Dickinson might be considered as a 'strong misreading' whose value is in its capacity to provoke other misreadings.

We might say this – but must we? To answer this question, we must ask another: What is at stake in the proposition that reading is impossible? For one thing, if reading is impossible, then there is no way of deciding the validity of an interpretation – the very notion of validity becomes problematical. Certainly it is useful to be reminded that the validity of an interpretation cannot be decided by appealing to what the author 'intended', to what is 'in' the text, or to what is 'in' the experience of the reader. However, there is another approach to the problem of validation, one that is consonant with the dialogic model of reading described above. We can think of validity not as a property inherent in an interpretation, but rather as a *claim* implicit in the *act* of propounding an interpretation. An interpretation, then, is not valid or invalid in itself. Its validity is contingent on the agreement of others. In this view, Rich's interpretation of Dickinson, which is frankly acknowledged as conditioned by her own experience as a twentieth-century feminist poet, is not necessarily a misreading. In advancing her interpretation, Rich implicitly claims its validity. That is to say, to read a text and then to write about it is to seek to connect not only with the author of the original text, but also with a community of readers. To the extent that she succeeds and to the extent that the community is potentially all-embracing, her interpretation has that degree of validity.[40]

Feminist reading and writing alike are grounded in the interest of producing a community of feminist readers and writers, and in the hope that ultimately this community will expand to include everyone. Of course, this project may fail. The feminist story may yet end with the recognition of the impossibility of reading. But this remains to be seen. At this stage I think it behoves us to *choose* the dialectical over the deconstructive plot. It is dangerous for feminists to be overly enamored with the theme of impossibility. Instead, we should strive to redeem the claim that it is possible for a woman, reading as a woman, to read literature written by women, for this is essential if we are to make the literary enterprise into a means for building and maintaining connections among women.

Notes

I would like to acknowledge my debt to David Schweickart for the substantial editorial work he did on this chapter.

1. JONATHAN D. CULLER, *On Deconstruction: Theory and Criticism after Structuralism* (Ithaca: Cornell University Press, 1982), p. 42. (Subsequent references are cited parenthetically in the text.) Wayne Booth's essay 'Freedom of Interpretation: Bakhtin and the Challenge of Feminist Criticism', *Critical Inquiry* 9 (1982): 45–76, is another good omen of the impact of feminist thought on literary criticism.

2. DAVID BLEICH, *Subjective Criticism* (Baltimore: Johns Hopkins University Press, 1978), p. 112.

3. GEORGES POULET, 'Criticism and the Experience of Interiority', trans. Catherine and Richard Macksey, in *Reader-Response Criticism: From Formalism to Structuralism*, ed. Jane Tompkins (Baltimore: Johns Hopkins University Press, 1980), p. 43. Poulet's theory is not among those discussed by Culler. However, since he will be useful to us later, I mention him here.

4. This argument was advanced by SAMUEL WEBER in 'The Struggle for Control: Wolfgang Iser's Third Dimension', cited by Culler in *On Deconstruction*, p. 75.

5. STANLEY E. FISH, 'Why No One's Afraid of Wolfgang Iser', *Diacritics*, 11 (1981): 7. Quoted by Culler in *On Deconstruction*, p. 75.

6. ELAINE SHOWALTER, 'Feminist Criticism in the Wilderness', *Critical Inquiry* 8 (1981): 182–5. Showalter argues that if we see feminist critique (focused on the

reader) as our primary critical project, we must be content with the 'playful pluralism' proposed by Annette Kolodny: first because no single conceptual model can comprehend so eclectic and wide-ranging an enterprise, and second because 'in the free play of the interpretive field, feminist critique can only compete with alternative readings, all of which have the built-in obsolescence of Buicks, cast away as newer readings take their place' (p. 182). Although Showalter does not support Wimsatt and Beardsley's proscription of the 'affective fallacy', she nevertheless subscribes to the logic of their argument. Kolodny's 'playful pluralism' is more benign than Wimsatt and Beardsley's dreaded 'relativism', but no less fatal, in Showalter's view, to theoretical coherence.

7. ELAINE SHOWALTER, 'Women and the Literary Curriculum', *College English* 32 (1971): 855. For an excellent example of recent work following in the spirit of Showalter's critique, see PAUL LAUTER, *Reconstructing American Literature* (Old Westbury, N.Y.: Feminist Press, 1983).

8. LEE EDWARDS, 'Women, Energy, and *Middlemarch*', *Massachusetts Review*, 13 (1972): 226.

9. Ibid.

10. JAMES JOYCE, *A Portrait of the Artist as a Young Man* (London: Jonathan Cape, 1916), p. 195.

11. See also FLORENCE HOWE's analysis of the same passage, 'Feminism and Literature', in *Images of Women in Fiction: Feminist Perspectives*, ed. Susan Koppelman Cornillon (Bowling Green, Ohio: Bowling Green State University Press, 1972), pp. 262–3.

12. JUDITH FETTERLEY, *The Resisting Reader: A Feminist Approach to American Fiction* (Bloomington: Indiana University Press, 1978), p. xx. Although Fetterley's remarks refer specifically to American Literature, they apply generally to the entire traditional canon.

13. Ibid., p. xiii.

14. See KATHARINE M. ROGERS, *The Troublesome Helpmate: A History of Misogyny in Literature* (Seattle: University of Washington Press, 1966).

15. FREDRIC JAMESON, *The Political Unconscious: Narrative as a Socially Symbolic Act* (Ithaca: Cornell University Press, 1981), p. 286.

16. In *Woman and the Demon: The Life of a Victorian Myth* (Cambridge, Mass.: Harvard University Press, 1982), NINA AUERBACH employs a similar – though not identical – positive hermeneutic. She reviews the myths and images of women (as angels, demons, victims, whores, etc.) that feminist critics have 'gleefully' unmasked as reflections and instruments of sexist ideology, and discovers in them an 'unexpectedly empowering' mythos. Auerbach argues that the 'most powerful, if least acknowledged creation [of the Victorian cultural imagination] is an explosively mobile, magic woman, who breaks the boundaries of family within which her society restricts her. The triumph of this overweening creature is a celebration of the corporate imagination that believed in her' (p. 1). See also idem, 'Magi and Maidens: The Romance of the Victorian Freud', *Critical Inquiry*, 8 (1981): 281–300. The tension between the positive and negative feminist hermeneutics is perhaps most apparent when one is dealing with the 'classics'. See, for example, CAROL THOMAS NEELY, 'Feminist Modes of Shakespeare Criticism: Compensatory, Justificatory, Transformational', *Women's Studies*, 9 (1981): 3–15.

17. KATE MILLETT, *Sexual Politics* (New York: Avon Books, 1970).

18. ELAINE SHOWALTER, 'The Double Critical Standard and the Feminine Novel', Chapter 3 in *A Literature of Their Own: British Women Novelists from Brontë to Lessing* (Princeton: Princeton University Press, 1977), pp. 73–99; CAROL OHMANN, 'Emily Brontë in the Hands of Male Critics', *College English*, 32 (1971): 906–13.

19. NINA BAYM, 'Melodramas of Beset Manhood: How Theories of American Fiction Exclude Women Authors', *American Quarterly*, 33 (1981): 123–39.

20. Ibid., p. 125.

21. Ibid., p. 130. One of the founding works of American Literature is 'The Legend of Sleepy Hollow', about which Leslie Fiedler writes: 'It is fitting that our first successful homegrown legend would memorialize, however playfully, the flight of the dreamer from the shrew' (*Love and Death in the American Novel*, New York: Criterion, 1960, p. xx).

22. NINA BAYM's *Women's Fiction: A Guide to Novels by and about Women in America, 1820–1870* (Ithaca: Cornell University Press, 1978) provides a good survey of what has been excluded from the canon.

23. ANNETTE KOLODNY, 'Dancing through the Minefield: Some Observations on the Theory, Practice, and Politics of a Feminist Literary Criticism', *Feminist Studies*, 6 (1980): 10–12. Kolodny elaborates the same theme in 'A Map for Rereading: or, Gender and the Interpretation of Literary Texts', *New Literary History*, 11 (1980): 451–67.

24. For an excellent account of the way in which the feminist 'interpretive community' has changed literary and critical conventions, see JEAN E. KENNARD, 'Convention Coverage, or How to Read Your Own Life', *New Literary History*, 8 (1981): 69–88. The programs of the MLA Convention during the last twenty-five years offer more concrete evidence of the changes in the literary and critical canons, and of the ideological and political struggles effecting these changes.

25. In ADRIENNE RICH, *On Lies, Secrets, and Silence: Selected Prose, 1966–1978* (New York: W.W. Norton, 1979). Subsequent references are cited parenthetically in the text.

26. SUSAN GLASPELL's story 'A Jury of Her Peers' revolves around a variation of this judicial metaphor. The parable of reading implicit in this story has not been lost on feminist critics. Annette Kolodny, for example, discusses how it 'explores the necessary gender marking which *must* constitute any definition of "peers" in the complex process of unraveling truth or meaning'. Although the story does not exclude male readers, it alerts us to the fact that 'symbolic representations depend on a fund of shared recognitions and potential references', and in general, 'female meaning' is inaccessible to 'male interpretation'. 'However inadvertently, [the male reader] is a *different kind* of reader and . . . where women are concerned, he is often an inadequate reader' ('Map for Rereading', pp. 460–3).

27. There is a strong counter-tendency, inspired by French post-structuralism, which privileges the appreciation of textuality over the imaginative recovery of the woman writer as subject of the work. See, for example, MARY JACOBUS, 'Is There a Woman in This Text?' *New Literary History*, 14 (1982): 117–41, especially the concluding paragraph. The last sentence of the essay underscores the controversy: 'Perhaps the question that feminist critics

should be asking is not "Is there a woman in this text?" but rather: "Is there a text in this woman?" '

28. I must stress that although Rich's essay presents a significant paradigm of feminist readings of women's writing, it is not the only such paradigm. An alternative is proposed by CAREN GREENBERG, 'Reading Reading: Echo's Abduction of Language', in *Women and Language in Literature and Society*, ed. Sally McConnell-Ginet, Ruth Borker, and Nelly Furman (New York: Praeger, 1980), pp. 304–9.

Furthermore, there are many important issues that have been left out of my discussion.

For example:

(a) The relationship of her career as reader to the artistic development of the woman writer. In *Madwoman in the Attic* (New Haven: Yale University Press, 1980) SANDRA GILBERT and SUSAN GUBAR show that women writers had to struggle to overcome the 'anxiety of authorship' which they contracted from the 'sentences' of their predecessors, male as well as female. They also argue that the relationship women writers form with their female predecessors does not fit the model of oedipal combat proposed by Bloom. Rich's attitude toward Dickinson (as someone who 'has been there', as a 'foremother' to be recovered) corroborates Gilbert and Gubar's claim.

(b) The relationship between women writers and their readers. We need actual reception studies as well as studies of the way women writers conceived of their readers and the way they inscribed them in their texts.

(c) The relationship between the positive and the negative hermeneutic in feminist readings of women's writing. Rich's reading of Dickinson emphasizes the positive hermeneutic. One might ask, however, if this approach is applicable to *all* women's writing. Specifically, is this appropriate to the popular fiction written by women, e.g., Harlequin Romances? To what extent is women's writing itself a bearer of patriarchal ideology? JANICE RADWAY addresses these issues in 'Utopian Impulse in Popular Literature: Gothic Romances and "Feminist Protest"', *American Quarterly*, 33 (1981): 140–62, and 'Women Read the Romance: The Interaction of Text and Context', *Feminist Studies*, 9 (1983): 53–78. See also TANIA MODLESKI, *Loving with a Vengeance: Mass-Produced Fantasies for Women* (New York: Methuen, 1982).

29. Iser writes:

Text and reader no longer confront each other as object and subject, but instead the 'division' takes place within the reader [herself]. . . . As we read, there occurs an artificial division of our personality, because we take as a theme for ourselves something we are not. Thus, in reading there are two levels – the alien 'me' and the real, virtual 'me' – which are never completely cut off from each other. Indeed, we can only make someone else's thoughts into an absorbing theme for ourselves provided the virtual background of our personality can adapt to it.

('The Reading Process: A Phenomenological Approach', in TOMPKINS, *Reader-Response Criticism*, p. 67)

Add the stipulation that the alien 'me' is a male who has appropriated the universal into his maleness, and we have the process of immasculation described in the third section.

30. STANLEY E. FISH, *Is There a Text in This Class? The Authority of Interpretive Communities* (Cambridge: Harvard University Press, 1980), especially Part 2.

31. Although the woman reader is the 'star' of the feminist story of reading, this does not mean that men are excluded from the audience. On the contrary, it is hoped that on hearing the feminist story they will be encouraged to revise their own stories to reflect the fact that they, too, are gendered beings, and that, ultimately, they will take control of their inclination to appropriate the universal at the expense of women.

32. CATHERINE A. MACKINNON, 'Feminism, Marxism, Method, and the State: Toward Feminist Jurisprudence', *Signs*, 8 (1981): 637.

33. There is lively debate among feminists about whether it is better to emphasize the essential similarity of women and men, or their difference. There is much to be said intellectually and politically for both sides. However, in one sense, the argument centers on a false issue. It assumes that concern about women's 'difference' is incompatible with concern about the essential humanity shared by the sexes. Surely, 'difference' may be interpreted to refer to what is distinctive in women's lives and works, *including* what makes them essentially human; unless, of course, we remain captivated by the notion that the standard model for humanity is male.

34. Although opponents of feminist criticism often find it convenient to characterize such works as a personal attack on authors, for feminist critics themselves, the primary consideration is the function of the text as a carrier of patriarchal ideology, and its effect as such especially (but not exclusively) on women readers. The personal culpability of the author is a relatively minor issue.

35. HAROLD BLOOM, *Kabbalah and Criticism* (New York: Seabury, 1975), p. 126.

36. POULET, 'Criticism and the Experience of Interiority', p. 46.

37. Ibid., p. 47. As Culler has pointed out, the theme of control is prominent in mainstream reader-response criticism. Poulet's story is no exception. The issue of control is important in another way. Behind the question of whether the text controls the reader or vice versa is the question of how to regulate literary criticism. If the text is controlling, then there is no problem. The text itself will regulate the process of reading. But if the text is not necessarily controlling, then, how do we constrain the activities of readers and critics? How can we rule out 'off-the-wall' interpretations? Fish's answer is of interest to feminist critics. The constraints, he says, are exercised not by the text, but by the institutions within which literary criticism is situated. It is but a small step from this idea to the realization of the necessarily political character of literature and criticism.

38. The use of the personal conversational tone has been regarded as a hallmark of feminist criticism. However, as JEAN E. KENNARD has pointed out ('Personally Speaking: Feminist Critics and the Community of Readers', *College English*, 43 (1981): 140–5), this theoretical commitment is not apparent in the overwhelming majority of feminist critical essays. Kennard found only five articles in which the critic 'overtly locates herself on the page'. (To the five she found, I would add three works cited in this essay: 'Women, Energy, and *Middlemarch*', by LEE EDWARDS; 'Feminism and Literature', by Florence Howe; and 'Vesuvius at Home,' by ADRIENNE RICH.) Kennard observes further that, even in the handful of essays she found, the personal tone is confined to a few introductory paragraphs. She asks: 'If feminist criticism has on the

whole remained faithful to familiar methods and tone, why have the few articles with an overt personal voice loomed so large in our minds?' Kennard suggests that these personal introductions are invitations 'to share a critical response which depends upon unstated, shared beliefs and, to a large extent, experience; that of being a female educated in a male tradition in which she is no longer comfortable'. Thus, these introductory paragraphs do not indicate a 'transformed critical methodology; they are devices for transforming the reader. I read the later portions of these essays – and by extension other feminist criticism – in a different way because I have been invited to participate in the underground. . . . I am part of a community of feminist readers' (pp. 143–4).

I would offer another explanation, one that is not necessarily inconsistent with Kennard's. I think the use of a personal and conversational tone represents an overt gesture indicating the dialogic mode of discourse as the 'regulative ideal' for all feminist discourse. The few essays – indeed, the few introductory paragraphs – that assert this regulative ideal are memorable because they strike a chord in a significant segment of the community of feminist critics. To the extent that we have been touched or transformed by this idea, it will be implicit in the way we read the works of others, in particular, the works of other women. Although the ideal must be overtly affirmed periodically, it is not necessary to do so in all of our essays. It remains potent as long as it is assumed by a significant portion of the community. I would argue with Kennard's distinction between indicators of a transformed critical methodology and devices for transforming the reader. To the extent that critical methodology is a function of the conventions implicitly or explicitly operating in an interpretive community – that is, of the way members of the community conceive of their work and of the way they read each other – devices for transforming readers are also devices for transforming critical methodology.

39. JEAN BAKER MILLER, *Toward a New Psychology of Women* (Boston: Beacon Press, 1976); and NANCY CHODOROW, *The Reproduction of Mothering: Psycho analysis and the Sociology of Gender* (Berkeley and Los Angeles: University of California Press, 1978); and CAROL GILLIGAN, *In a Different Voice: Psychological Theory and Women's Development* (Cambridge: Harvard University Press, 1982).

40. I am using here JURGEN HABERMAS's definition of truth or validity as a claim (implicit in the act of making assertions) that is redeemable through discourse – specifically, through the domination-free discourse of an 'ideal speech situation'. For Habermas, consensus attained through domination-free discourse is the warrant for truth. See 'Wahrheitstheorien', in *Wirklichkeit und Reflexion: Walter Schulz zum 60. Geburtstag* (Pfullingen: Nesge, 1973), pp. 211–65. I am indebted to Alan Soble's unpublished translation of this essay.

4   An Unnecessary Maze of Sign-Reading*

MARY JACOBUS

During the 1980s, Charlotte Perkins Gilman's extraordinary story 'The Yellow Wallpaper' (1892), became something of a test case for feminist criticism and feminist accounts of reading. Mary Jacobus's essay positions itself in opposition to 'rationalist' feminist readings of the story and, as such, acts as a contrast to Schweickart's account of feminist reading in the previous chapter. Always alert to the figurative force of the language of both Gilman's story and her own text, Jacobus explores the unconscious of 'The Yellow Wallpaper' in a psychoanalytic reading which plots the text's uncanny figures. In particular, Jacobus suggests ways in which a reading of 'The Yellow Wallpaper' produces a disturbing repetition of the narrator's reading of the yellow wallpaper in her room – and the inescapable sense that, like the narrator's reading, ours must *literalize* the figure of the text. 'Learning to read', suggests Jacobus, 'might be called a hysterical process, since it involves substituting a bodily figure for the self-reproducing repetitions of textuality.' By contrast with Schweickart, then, who understands feminist reading in terms of an affirmation of female identity, in this chapter and in her book *Reading Woman: Essays in Feminist Criticism* (1986) more generally, Jacobus suggests that any such identity is itself constituted in and through acts of reading.

For another feminist reading of 'The Yellow Wallpaper', see the essay by Dimock reprinted below; for other accounts of the relationship between (Lacanian) psychoanalysis and reading, see Felman's essay (Chapter 9), together with her 'Turning the Screw of Interpretation' (1977).

I may here be giving an impression of laying too much emphasis on the details of the symptoms and of becoming lost in an unnecessary maze of sign-reading. But I have come to learn that the

* Reprinted from *Reading Woman: Essays in Feminist Criticism* (London: Methuen, 1986), pp. 229–48.

determination of hysterical symptoms does in fact extend to their subtlest manifestations and that it is difficult to attribute too much sense to them.

(*SE* 2: 93*n*.)

Freud's footnote to *Studies on Hysteria* amounts to saying that where hysteria is concerned it is impossible to over-read. The maze of signs, his metaphor for the hysterical text, invokes not only labyrinthine intricacy but the risk of self-loss. What would it be like to become lost in the subtleties of sign reading? Charlotte Perkins Gilman's short story, 'The Yellow Wallpaper', provides an answer of sorts. It would be like finding one's own figure replicated everywhere in the text; like going mad. This tale of hysterical confinement – a fictionalized account of Gilman's own breakdown in 1887 and the treatment she underwent at the hands of Freud's and Breuer's American contemporary, Weir Mitchell – could almost be read as Anna O.'s own version of 'Fräulein Anna O.'. The flower of fiction reproduces herself, hysterically doubled, in the form of a short story whose treatment by feminist readers raises questions not only about psychoanalysis, but about feminist reading.

Freud had favorably reviewed a German translation of Weir Mitchell's *The Treatment of Certain Forms of Neurasthenia and Hysteria* in 1887, the year of Gilman's breakdown, and himself continued to make use of the Weir Mitchell rest-cure alongside Breuer's 'cathartic treatment'. Gilman later wrote that after a month of the Weir Mitchell regimen ('I was put to bed and kept there. I was fed, bathed, rubbed, and responded with the vigorous body of twenty-six') she was sent home to her husband and child with the following prescription: 'Live as domestic a life as possible. Have your child with you all the time. . . . Lie down an hour after each meal. Have but two hours' intellectual life a day. And never touch pen, brush or pencil as long as you live.' Not surprisingly, she 'came perilously near to losing [her] mind' as a result.[1] Mitchell, who apparently believed that intellectual, literary, and artistic pursuits were destructive both to women's mental health and to family life, had prescribed what might be called the Philadelphian treatment (a good dose of domestication) rather than the Viennese treatment famously invoked by Chrobak in Freud's hearing ('*Penis normalis dosim repetatur*').[2]

Gilman, by contrast, believed that she only regained her sanity when she quit family life – specifically, married life – altogether and resumed her literary career. 'The real purpose of the story', according to Gilman herself, 'was to reach Dr S. Weir Mitchell, and convince him of the error of his ways.' Hearsay has it that he was duly converted: 'I sent him a copy as soon as it came out, but got no response. However, many years later, I met someone who knew close friends of Dr Mitchell's who said he had told them that he had changed his treatment of nervous prostration since reading "The Yellow Wallpaper". If that is a fact, I have not lived in vain.'[3] Weir Mitchell figures in this autobiographical account from *The Living of Charlotte Perkins Gilman* (1935) as a surrogate for the absent father whom Gilman also tried to 'convert' through her writing.[4] As Juliet Mitchell puts it, 'Hysterics tell tales and fabricate stories – particularly for doctors who will listen.'[5] But to read 'The Yellow Wallpaper' as a literary manifestation of transference reduces the figure in the text to Gilman herself; recuperating text as life, the diagnostic reading represses its literariness. Gilman's is a story that has forgotten its 'real purpose' (conversion), becoming instead a conversion narrative of a different kind – one whose major hysterical symptom is an unnecessary (or should one say 'hysterical'?) reading of the maze of signs.

John, the rationalist physician-husband in 'The Yellow Wallpaper', diagnoses his wife as suffering from 'temporary nervous depression – a slight hysterical tendency' and threatens to send her to Weir Mitchell.[6] This hysterical tendency is shared not only by a story whose informing metaphor is the maze of sign reading figured in the wallpaper, but by the readings which the story generates. If Gilman creates a literary double for herself in the domestic confinement of her hysterical narrator, her narrator too engages in a fantastic form of re-presentation, a doubling like that of Anna O.'s 'private theatre'. Just as we read the text, so she reads the patterns on the wallpaper; and like Freud she finds that 'it is difficult to attribute too much sense to them'. Hers is a case of hysterical (over-)reading. Lost in the text, she finds her own madness written there. But how does her reading of the wallpaper differ from readings of the story itself by contemporary feminist critics?

Two pioneering accounts of the assumptions involved in feminist reading have used as their example 'The Yellow Wallpaper' – by now as much part of the feminist literary canon as Freud's *Dora*. Both Annette Kolodny's 'A Map for Rereading: Or, Gender and the Interpretation of Literary Texts' and Jean E. Kennard's 'Convention Coverage or How to Read Your Own Life' focus on the feminist deciphering of texts which are seen as having deeper, perhaps unacceptable meanings hidden beneath their palimpsestic surfaces.[7] Kolodny's argument – that interpretative strategies are not only learned, but gender inflected – emphasizes the unreadability of texts by women embedded in a textual system which is controlled by men. Her own reading of 'The Yellow Wallpaper' repeats the gesture of Gilman's narrator, finding in Gilman's story an emblem of women's dilemma within an interpretive community from which they are excluded as both readers and writers. For Kolodny, the doctor-husband's diagnosis anticipates the story's contemporary reception; male readers thought it merely chilling, while female readers were as yet apparently unable to see its relevance to their own situation. The 'slight hysterical tendency' turns out to be, not that of Gilman's narrator or even of her story, but the hysterical blindness of Gilman's contemporary readers.

As Kolodny points out, John (the husband) 'not only appropriates the interpretive processes of reading', determining the meaning of his wife's symptoms ('reading to her, rather than allowing her to read for herself'); he also forbids her to write. Kolodny's retelling of the story involves the selective emphasis and repression which she views as normative in any attempt to make meaning out of a complex literary text:

> From that point on, the narrator progressively gives up the attempt to *record* her reality and instead begins to *read* it – as symbolically adumbrated in her compulsion to discover a consistent and coherent pattern [in the wallpaper]. Selectively emphasizing one section of the pattern while repressing others, reorganizing and regrouping past impressions into newer, more fully realized configurations – as one might with any complex formal text – the speaking voice becomes obsessed with her quest for meaning . . . .[8]

'What [the narrator] is watching . . . is her own psyche writ large', Kolodny concludes. But whose obsessive quest for meaning is this? Surely that of the feminist critic as she watches her interpretive processes writ small, finding a figure for feminist reading within the text. The result is a strange (that is, hysterical) literalization; the narrator, we are told, 'comes more and more to experience herself as a text', and ends by being 'totally surrendered to what is quite *literally* her own text'.[9] The literalization of figure (a symptom of the protagonist's hysteria) infects the interpretive process itself. Read as the case which exemplifies feminist reading, just as 'Fraulein Anna O.' exemplifies hysterical processes for Breuer and Freud, 'The Yellow Wallpaper' becomes, not the basis for theory, but the model on which it is constructed. Ostensibly, Kolodny emphasizes the need to re-learn interpretive strategies. But her reading ends by suggesting that re-vision is really pre-vision – that we can only see what we have already read into the text. Meaning is pre-determined by the story we know; there is no room for the one we have forgotten.

As Kennard points out, surveying approaches such as Kolodny's, or Gilbert and Gubar's in *The Madwoman in the Attic*, readings that stress the social message of 'The Yellow Wallpaper' (assuming both that the narrator's madness is socially induced and that her situation is common to all women) have become possible only as a result of 'a series of conventions available to readers of the 1970s which were not available to those of 1892'.[10] Kennard summarizes the concepts associated with these conventions as: *patriarchy, madness, space,* and *quest*. Feminist interpretations of 'The Yellow Wallpaper' have tended, inevitably, to see the story as an updated fictional treatment of Mary Wollstonecraft's theme in her novel, *The Wrongs of Woman: or, Maria* ('Was not the world a vast prison, and women born slaves?');[11] mental illness replaces imprisonment as the sign of women's social and sexual oppression. But how justifiable is it to read into Gilman's story a specifically feminist tendency of this kind? And what is the tendency of such thematic readings anyway? We have learned not only to symbolize (reading the narrator's confinement in a former nursery as symbolic of her infantilization) but to read confinement itself as symbolic of women's situation under patriarchy, and to see in madness not only the result of patriarchal attitudes but a kind of sanity – indeed, a perverse triumph; the commonsensical physician-husband is literally floored by his wife at the end of the story. As he loses consciousness, she finds herself in the madness whose existence he has denied.

The 'feminist' reading contradicts the tendency to see women as basically unstable or hysterical, simultaneously (and contradictorily) claiming that women are not mad and that their madness is not their fault. But a thematic reading cannot account for the Gothic and uncanny elements present in the text. The assumption of what Jacqueline Rose calls 'an unproblematic and one-to-one causality between psychic life and social reality' not only does away with the unconscious; it also does away with language.[12] In the same way, the assumption of a one-to-one causality between the text and social reality does away with the unconscious of the text – specifically, with its literariness, the way in which it knows more than it knows (and more than the author intended). Formal features have no place in interpretations that simply substitute latent content for manifest content, bringing the hidden story uppermost. A kind of re-telling, feminist reading as Kennard defines it ends by translating the text into a cryptograph (or pictograph) representing either women in patriarchal society or the woman as writer and reader. If we come to 'The Yellow Wallpaper' with this story already in mind, we are likely to read it with what Freud calls 'that blindness of the seeing eye' which relegates what doesn't fit in with our expectations to the realm of the un-known or unknowable.

The 'feminist' reading turns out to be the rationalist reading after all ('the narrator is driven mad by confinement'). By contrast, signs that might point to an irrationalist, Gothic reading ('the narrator is driven mad by the wallpaper') are ignored or repressed. Kennard admits that although the 'feminist' reading is the one she teaches her students, 'Much is made in the novella of the color yellow; feminist readings do little with this.'[13] The color of sickness ('old foul, bad yellow things', p. 28), yellow is also the color of decay and, in a literary context, of Decadence (although the *Yellow Book* was not to appear until 1894). In America, it gives its name to 'the yellow press' and to the sensationalism ushered in during the mid-1890s by color printing. Gilman's wallpaper is at once lurid, angry, dirty, sickly, and old: 'The color is repellent, almost revolting; a smouldering unclean yellow, strangely faded by the slow-turning sunlight . . . a dull yet lurid orange . . . a sickly sulphur tint' (p. 13). The sensational ugliness of yellow is an unexplained given in Gilman's story. Yet the adjectival excess seems to signal not just the narrator's state of mind, but an inexplicable, perhaps repressed element in the text itself.

If feminist readings do little with the color of Gilman's title, they do even less with the creepiness of her story. Both Kolodny and Kennard ignore the uncanny altogether. Like the yellowness of the wallpaper, it is unaccountable, exceeding meaning; or rather, suggesting a meaning which resides only in the letter. The uncanny resists thematization, making itself felt as a 'how' not a 'what' – not as an entity, but rather as a phenomenon, like repetition.[14] A symptom of this uncanny repetition in the letter of the text is the word 'creepy', which recurs with a spectrum of meanings spanning both metaphorical and literal senses (seeming to remind us, along with Freud, that figurative expressions have their origin in bodily sensations). Gilman's contemporary readers (to a man) found the story strange, if not ghostly. Her own husband thought it 'the most ghastly tale he ever read'.[15] The editor of *The Atlantic Monthly*, rejecting it, wrote that 'I could not forgive myself if I made others as miserable as I have made myself!' and when he reprinted it in 1920, William Dean Howells called it a story to 'freeze . . . our blood'.[16] The *OED* reveals that the word 'creepy' starts as 'characterized by creeping or moving slowly', only later taking on the sense of chill associated with the uncanny ('creeping of the flesh, or chill shuddering feeling, caused by horror or repugnance'). Toward the end of the nineteenth century, the term came to be used especially in a literary context (*OED*: 'A really effective romance of the creepy order'; 1892 – the year in which 'The Yellow Wallpaper' was finally published in the *New England Magazine*). If Gilman wrote a minor classic of female Gothic, hers is not only a tale of female hysteria but a version of Gothic that successfully tapped male hysteria about women. What but femininity is so calculated to induce 'horror or repugnance' in its male readers?

The story's stealthy uncanniness – its sidelong approach both to the condition of women and to the unspeakably repugnant female body – emerges most clearly in the oscillation of the word 'creepy' from figurative to literal. The link between female oppression, hysteria, and the uncanny occurs in the letter of the text; in a word whose meaning sketches the repressed connection between women's social situation, their sickness, and their bodies. A reading of the 'slight hysterical tendency' displayed by 'The Yellow Wallpaper' involves tracing the repression whereby the female body itself becomes a figure for the uncanny and the subjection of women can surface only in the form of linguistic repetition. A necessary first move would be to recover its lost literary and political 'unconscious'. The setting for Gilman's story is 'a colonial mansion, a hereditary estate, I would say a haunted house, and reach the height of romantic felicity – but that would be asking too much of fate!' (p. 9). The trouble with the narrator is that her husband doesn't believe she's sick: the trouble with the text is its refusal of 'romantic felicity'. The narrator is no Jane Eyre (though the sister-in-law who is her 'keeper', or 'housekeeper', is named Jane) and her husband no Rochester ('John is practical in the extreme', p. 9); yet she must play the role of both Jane Eyre, who at once scents and represses a mystery, and Bertha Mason, who explodes it while refusing all attempts at sublimation – 'I thought seriously of burning the house' (p. 29), the narrator confesses at one point.

In this prosaic present, romance can only take the form of hallucination (like Anna O.'s daydreaming); or perhaps, the form of a woman deranged by confinement. Female oppression has been de-eroticized, making the woman's story at best merely creepy and at worst sensational, just as the colonial mansion has been emptied of its romantic past. The empty house evokes romantic reading ('It makes me think of English places that you read about', p. 11), with its hedges and walls and gates that lock, its shady garden, paths, and arbors, and its derelict greenhouses. The rationalist explanation ('some legal trouble . . . something about the heirs and co-heirs', p. 11) 'spoils my ghostliness', writes the narrator; 'but I don't care – there is something strange about the house – I can feel it. I even said so to John one moonlight evening, but he said what I felt was a *draught*, and shut the window' (p. 11). Like the coolly rational Dr John in *Villette*, who diagnoses Lucy's hysteria as 'a case of spectral illusion . . . resulting from long-continued mental conflict' (p. 330), John comes to stand not only for unbelief ('He has no patience with faith', p. 9), but for the repression of romantic reading. His *'draught'* is a literary breeze from *Wuthering Heights* ('the *height* of romantic felicity'?), and his gesture a repetition of Lockwood's in the nightmare that opens Emily Brontë's book. Indeed, like Lockwood confronted with the ghost of Cathy in his dream, John has 'an intense horror of superstition' (p. 9) and scoffs at intangible presences ('things not to be felt and seen') as a way of shutting them out of house and mind. Hence his horrified loss of consciousness at the end of the story, when the narrator confronts him in all her feminine otherness.

Madness – the irrational – is what Doctor John's philosophy cannot dream of, and his repressive refusal of the unconscious makes itself felt in the narrator's inconsequential style and her stealthy confidences to the written page. But the same rationalist censorship also makes itself felt in Gilman's authorial relation to the uncanny. An age of doctors had

made the tale of supernatural haunting a story about hysteria; no one
dreamed of taking Anna O.'s death-head hallucinations seriously or
believed that her *'absences'* or 'split-off mind' were a form of demonic
possession.[17] As Freud points out, literature provides a much more fertile
province for the uncanny than real life. A deranged narrator is licensed
to think irrational thoughts and confide the unsayable to her journal ('I
would not say it to a living soul, of course, but this is dead paper and a
great relief to my mind', pp. 9–10). Gilman herself only differs from the
insane, in the words used by Alice James to describe the recollected
torments of her own hysteria, in having imposed on her 'not only all the
horrors and sufferings of insanity but the duties of doctor, nurse, and
straight-jacket'.[18] Medical knowledge, in other words, straight-jackets
Gilman's text as well as her narrator: 'I am a doctor, dear, and I know',
John tells his wife (p. 23). It is as if Gilman's story has had to repress its
own ancestry in nineteenth-century female Gothic, along with the entire
history of feminist protest. The house in 'The Yellow Wallpaper' is
strange because empty. An image of dispossession, it points to what
Gilman can't say about the subjection of women, not only in literary
terms, but politically – imaging the disinherited state of women in
general, and also, perhaps, the symptomatic dispossession which had
made Gilman herself feel that she had to take her stand against marriage
alone, without the benefit of feminist forebears.[19] Lacking a past,
privatized by the family, all she had to go on was her personal feeling.
'Personally', the narrator opines near the start of the story ('Personally, I
disagree with their ideas. Personally, I believe that congenial
work . . . would do me good', p. 10) – the subjection of women is also the
enforced 'subjectivity' of women, their constitution as subjects within an
economy which defines knowledge as power and gives to women the
disenfranchizing privilege of personal feeling uninformed by knowledge
('I am a doctor, dear, and I know'). In other words, an economy which
defines female subjectivity as madness and debases the literature of the
uncanny to the level of the merely creepy.

Mary Wollstonecraft's invective against the infantilization of women
through sensibility and ignorance in *The Rights of Woman* becomes
Gilman's depiction of marriage in terms of a disused attic room that has
formerly been a nursery ('It was nursery first and then play-room and
gymnasium, I should judge; for the windows are barred for little
children, and there are rings and things in the walls', p. 12). But where
Wollstonecraft had taken an enlightenment stance in her polemic (if not
in her novel), Gilman is compelled to assume an irrationalist stance
which she has no means of articulating directly; in her story, the
irrational inhabits or haunts the rational as its ghostly other, hidden
within it like the figure of a mad woman hidden in the nursery
wallpaper. The site of repression, above all the family, is also the place

that contains both strangeness and enslavement (as Engels reminds us in *The Origin of the Family, Private Property and the State*, the word 'family', derives from *'famulus'*, or household slave). For Freud, *'Heimlich'* and *'Unheimlich'* are never far apart; what is familiar returns as strange because it has been repressed. John may shut out the 'draught', but the strangeness he fears is already within the home and creeps into the most intimate place of all, the marital bedroom – creeps in as both woman's estate and woman's body; at once timorous, stealthy, and abject; and then, because split off from consciousness, as alien.

The figure whom the narrator first glimpses in the wallpaper 'is like a woman stooping down and *creeping* about behind that pattern', and by the light of the moon which *'creeps* so slowly' she watches 'that undulating wall-paper till I felt *creepy'* (pp. 22–3; my italics). The meaning of the word 'creep', according to the *OED*, like that of 'creepy', starts from the body; and it too ends by encompassing a figurative sense: '1. To move with the body prone and close to the ground . . . a human being on hands and feet, or in a crouching posture'; '2. To move slowly, cautiously, timorously, or slowly; to move quietly or stealthily so as to elude observation'; and '3. *fig.* (of persons and things) a. To advance or come on slowly, stealthily, or by imperceptible degrees. . . . b. To move timidly or diffidently; to proceed humbly, abjectly, or servilely, to cringe.' As 'creepy' becomes 'creep' we are reminded of Freud's formulation about the language of hysteria: 'In taking a verbal expression literally . . . the hysteric is not taking liberties with words, but is simply reviving once more the sensations to which the verbal expression owes its justification' (*SE* 2: 181). 'Creepy' and 'creep' – the female uncanny, the subjection of women, and the body – are linked by a semantic thread in the textual patterning of Gilman's story; only by letting ourselves become 'lost in an unnecessary maze of sign-reading' like the narrator herself (and like Freud) can we trace the connection between female subjection and the repression of femininity; between the literature and the politics of women's oppression.

The narrator of 'The Yellow Wallpaper' enacts her abject state first by timorousness and stealth (her acquiescence in her own 'treatment', and her secret writing), then by creeping, and finally by going on all fours over the supine body of her husband. If she was Anna O., her creeping would be read as hysterical conversion, like a limp or facial neuralgia. At this point one can begin to articulate the relationship between the 'feminist' reading, the hysterical reading, and the uncanny. The story is susceptible to what Kennard calls the 'feminist' reading partly because the narrator herself glimpses not one but many women creeping both in and out of the wallpaper. But like the inconsequential, maddening pattern in the wallpaper – like a hysterical symptom – the repressed 'creeping' figure begins to proliferate all over Gilman's text:

It is the same woman, I know, for she is always
creeping, and most women do not creep by daylight.

I see her on that long road under the trees, creeping along, and when a carriage comes she hides under the
blackberry vines.

I don't blame her a bit. It must be very humiliating
to be caught creeping by daylight!

. . .

I often wonder if I could see her out of all the
windows at once.

But, turn as fast as I can, I can only see out of one
at one time.

And though I always see her, she *may* be able to
creep faster than I can turn!

I have watched her sometimes away off in the
open country, creeping as fast as a cloud shadow in a high
wind.

(pp. 30–1)

And finally: 'I don't like to *look* out of the windows even – there are so
many of those creeping women, and they creep so fast' (p. 35).

As the creeping women imprisoned both in and out of the wallpaper
become the creeping woman liberated from domestic secrecy ('I always lock
the door when I creep by daylight', p. 31) into overt madness ('It is so
pleasant to be out in this great room and creep around as I please', p. 35) –
as the 'creeping' figure is embodied in the narrator's hysterical acting out –
there emerges also a creeping sense that the text knows more than she;
perhaps more than Gilman herself. At the culmination of the story, the
rationalist husband tries to break in on his wife's madness, threatening to
take an axe to her self-enclosure in the repetitions of delusion and language.
The story's punchline has all the violence of his attempted break-in:

'What is the matter?' he cried. 'For God's sake, what are you doing!'

I kept on creeping just the same, but I looked at him over my
shoulder.

'I've got out at last,' said I, 'in spite of you and Jane. And I've
pulled off most of the paper, so you can't put me back!'

Now why should that man have fainted? But he did, and right
across my path by the wall, so that I had to creep over him every
time!

(p. 36)

The docile wife and compliant patient returns as a defiant apparition, her rebellious strength revealed as the other of domesticated invalidism. This time it is the doctor who faints on the floor. But the story leaves us asking a creepy question. Did she tear and score the wallpaper round her bed herself, or has her madness been pre-enacted in the 'haunted' house? Who bit and gnawed at the heavy wooden bed, gouged at the plaster, splintered the floor? What former inmate of the attic nursery was confined by those sinister rings in the wall? As readers versed in female gothic we know that Bertha Mason haunts this text; as readers of the feminist tradition from Wollstonecraft on, we know that the rights of women have long been denied by treating them as children. The uncanny makes itself felt as the return of a repressed past, a history at once literary and political – here, the history of women's reading.

'Now why should that man have fainted?' The narrator's question returns us to male hysteria. The body of woman is hystericized as the uncanny – defined by Freud as the sight of something that should remain hidden; typically, the sight of the female genitals. The woman on all fours is like Bertha Mason, an embodiment of the animality of woman unredeemed by (masculine) reason. Her creeping can only be physical – it is the story that assumes her displaced psychic uncanniness to become 'creepy' – since by the end she is all body, an incarnation not only of hysteria but of male fears about women. The female hysteric displaces her thoughts onto her body: the male hysteric displaces his fear of castration, his anxiety, on to her genitals. Seemingly absent from 'The Yellow Wallpaper', both the female body (female sexuality) and male hysteria leave their traces on the paper in a stain or a whiff – in a yellow 'smooch' and a yellow smell that first appear in metonymic proximity to one another in Gilman's text:

> But there is something else about that paper – the
> smell! I noticed it the moment we came into the room. . . .
> It creeps all over the house.
> I find it hovering in the dining-room, skulking in the parlor, hiding in the hall, lying in wait for me on the stairs.
> It gets into my hair.
> Even when I go to ride, if I turn my head suddenly and surprise it – there is that smell!
> Such a peculiar odor, too! I have spent hours in trying to analyze it, to find what it smelled like.
> It is not bad – at first, and very gentle, but quite the subtlest, most enduring odor I ever met.
> In this damp weather it is awful, I wake up in the night and find it hanging over me.
> It used to disturb me at first. I thought seriously of burning the house – to reach the smell.

But now I am used to it. The only thing I can think
of is that it is like the *color* of the paper! A yellow smell.

There is a very funny mark on this wall, low down, near the
mopboard. A streak that runs round the room. It goes behind every
piece of furniture, except the bed, a long, straight, even *smooch*, as
if it had been rubbed over and over.

(pp. 28–9)

At the end of the story, the narrator's own shoulder 'just fits in that long
smooch around the wall' (p. 35). The mark of repetition, the uncanny
trace made by the present stuck in the groove of the past, the 'smooch' is
also a smudge or smear, a reciprocal dirtying, perhaps (the wallpaper
leaves 'yellow smooches on all my clothes and John's', p. 27). In the
1890s, 'smooch' had not taken on its slangy mid-twentieth-century
meaning (as in 'I'd rather have hooch / And a bit of a smooch', 1945).[20]
The 'smooch' on the yellow wallpaper cannot yet be a sexual caress,
although dirty rubbing might be both Doctor John's medical verdict on
sexuality and the story's hysterical literalization of it. As such, the dirty
stain of smooching would constitute not just the unmentionable aspect
of the narrator's genteel marital incapacity, but the unsayable in
Gilman's story – the sexual etiology of hysteria, certainly (repressed in
Gilman's as in Breuer's text); but also the repression imposed by the
1890s on the representation of female sexuality and, in particular, the
repression imposed on women's writing.

And what of the 'yellow smell'? – a smell that creeps, like the figure in
the text; presumably the smell of decay, of 'old foul, bad yellow things'.
Studies on Hysteria provides a comparable instance of a woman
'tormented by subjective sensations of smell' (*SE*, 2: 106), the case of
'Miss Lucy R.', an English governess secretly in love with the widowed
father of her charges. Since, in Freud's words, 'the subjective olfactory
sensations . . . were recurrent hallucinations', he interprets them as
hysterical symptoms. Miss Lucy R. is troubled first by 'a smell of burnt
pudding', and then, when the hallucination has been traced back to its
originating episode, by the smell of cigar smoke. The episode of the
burnt pudding turns out to be associated not only with her tender
feelings for her employer's children but with tenderness for her
employer ('I believe', Freud informs her, 'that really you are in love with
your employer . . . and that you have a secret hope of taking their
mother's place', *SE* 2: 117). The smell of cigar smoke proves to be a
mnemonic symbol for a still earlier scene associated with the
disappointing realization that her employer doesn't share her feelings.
Here, hysterical smells function as a trace of something that has been
intentionally forgotten – marking the place where unconscious
knowledge has forced itself into consciousness, then been forcibly

repressed once more. Freud does not pursue the question of smell any further in this context, although he does so elsewhere.

Jane Gallop's *The Daughter's Seduction* intriguingly suggests not only that smell is repressed by Freud's organization of sexual difference around a specular image ('sight of a phallic presence in the boy, sight of a phallic absence in the girl') but that smell in the Freudian text may have a privileged relation to female sexuality.[21] The female stench, after all, is the unmentionable of misogynist scatology. Two disturbing or 'smelly' footnotes in *Civilization and Its Discontents* seem to argue, according to Gallop, that prior to the privileging of sight over smell, 'the menstrual process produced an effect on the male psyche by means of olfactory stimuli' (*SE* 21: 99*n*.) and that 'with the depreciation of his sense of smell . . . the whole of [man's] sexuality' fell victim to repression, since when 'the sexual function has been accompanied by a repugnance which cannot further be accounted for' (*SE* 21: 106*n*.). In other words (Gallop's own), 'The penis may be more visible, but female genitalia have a stronger smell'; and that smell becomes identified with the smell of sexuality itself.

Gallop connects Freud's footnotes with an essay by Michèle Montrelay associating the immediacy of feminine speech and what she terms, italianately, the *'odor di femina'* emanating from it. Montrelay is reviewing *Recherches Psychoanalytiques nouvelles sur la sexualité féminine* – a book which, combining theory with case histories like *Studies on Hysteria* 'take[s] us to the analyst's: there where the one who speaks is no longer the mouth-piece of a school, but the patient on the couch. . . . Here we have the freedom to follow the discourse of female patients in analysis in its rhythm, its style and its meanderings.' 'This book', Montrelay concludes, 'not only talks of femininity according to Freud, but it also makes it speak in an immediate way. . . . An *odor di femina* arises from it.'[22] For Montrelay, feminine immediacy – predicated on the notion of an incompletely mediated relation between the female body, language, and the unconscious – produces anxiety which must be managed by representation; that is, by the privileging of visual representations in psychic organization. Or, as Gallop explicates Montrelay, 'The *"odor di femina"* becomes odious, nauseous, because it threatens to undo the achievements of repression and sublimation, threatens to return the subject to the powerlessness, intensity, and anxiety of an immediate, unmediated connection with the body of the mother'.[23] The bad smell that haunts the narrator in 'The Yellow Wallpaper' is both the one she makes and the smell of male hysteria emanating from her husband – that is, fear of femininity as the body of the mother ('old, foul, bad yellow things') which simultaneously threatens the boy with a return to the powerlessness of infancy and with anxiety about the castration she embodies.

'The Yellow Wallpaper', like the Freudian case history or the speech whose immediacy Montrelay scents, offers only the illusion of feminine discourse. What confronts us in the text is not the female body, but a figure for it. The figure in the text of 'The Yellow Wallpaper' is 'a strange, provoking, formless sort of figure, that seems to skulk about behind that silly and conspicuous front design' (p. 18). A formless figure? '*Absences*' could scarcely be more provoking. Produced by a specular system as nothing, as lack or absence, woman's form is by definition formless. Yet both for the hysteric and for Freud, figuration originates in the body – in 'sensations and innervations . . . now for the most part . . . so much weakened that the expression of them in words seems to us only to be a figurative picture of them . . . hysteria is right in restoring the original meaning of the words and depicting its unusually strong innervations' (*SE* 2: 181). The hysterical symptom (a smell, a paralysis, a cough) serves as just such a trace of 'original' bodily meaning. Figuration itself comes to be seen as a linguistic trace, a 'smooch' that marks the body's unsuccessful attempt to evade the repressiveness of representation.

What is infuriating (literally, maddening – 'a lack of sequence, a defiance of law, that is a constant irritant to a normal mind', p. 25) about the yellow wallpaper is its resistance to being read: 'It is dull enough to confuse the eye in following, pronounced enough to constantly irritate and provoke study, and when you follow the lame uncertain curves for a little distance they suddenly commit suicide – plunge off at outrageous angles, destroy themselves in unheard-of contradictions' (p. 13). A hideous enigma, the pattern has all the violence of nightmares ('It slaps you in the face, knocks you down, and tramples upon you. It is like a bad dream', p. 25). But perhaps the violence is really that of interpretation. The 'figure' in the text is at once a repressed figure (that of a woman behind bars) and repressive figuration. Shoshana Felman asks, 'what, indeed, is the unconscious if not – in every sense of the word – a *reader*?'[24] Like the examinations undergone by Lucy Snowe and Anna O., interpretive reading involves the specular appropriation or silencing of the text. Only the insistence of the letter resists forcible translation.

In Gilman's story, the narrator-as-unconscious embarks on a reading process remarkably like Freud's painstaking attempts, not simply to unravel, but, more aggressively, to wrest meaning from the hysterical text in *Studies on Hysteria*: 'by detecting lacunas in the patient's first description . . . we get hold of a piece of the logical thread at the periphery. . . . In doing this, we very seldom succeed in making our way right into the interior along one and the same thread. As a rule it breaks off half-way . . .'; and finally, 'We drop it and take up another thread, which we may perhaps follow equally far. When we have . . . discovered the entanglements on account of which the separate threads could not be followed any further in isolation, we can think of attacking the resistance before us afresh' (*SE* 2: 294). The language of attack entangles Freud himself in a Thesean fantasy about penetrating the maze to its center ('I *will* follow that pointless pattern to some sort of a conclusion', writes Gilman's narrator, with similarly obsessional persistence; p. 19).

The meaningless pattern in the yellow wallpaper not only refuses interpretation; it refuses to be read as a text – as anything but sheer, meaningless reptition ('this thing was not arranged on any laws of radiation, or alternation, or repetition, or symmetry, or anything else that I ever heard of' p. 20). Attempts to read it therefore involve the (repressive) substitution of something – a figure – for nothing. At first the pattern serves simply to mirror the narrator's own specular reading, endlessly repeated in the figure of eyes ('the pattern lolls like a broken neck and two bulbous eyes stare at you upside down. . . . Up and down and sideways they crawl, and those absurd, unblinking eyes are everywhere', p. 16). But as the process of figuration begins to sprout its own autonomous repertoire of metaphors ('bloated curves and flourishes – a kind of "debased Romanesque" with *delirium tremens*'; 'great slanting waves of optic horror, like a lot of wallowing seaweeds in full chase', p. 20), it becomes clear that figures feed parasitically on resistance to meaning; the pattern 'remind[s] one of a fungus. If you can imagine a toadstool in joints, an interminable string of toadstools, budding and sprouting in endless convolutions – why, that is something like it' (p. 25). The function of figuration is to manage anxiety; any figuration is better than none – even a fungoid growth is more consoling than sheer absence.

Learning to read might be called a hysterical process, since it involves substituting a bodily figure for the self-reproducing repetitions of textuality. Significantly, the narrator's sighting of a figure in the text – her own – inscribes her madness most graphically. As the 'dim shape' becomes clearer, the pattern 'becomes bars! The outside pattern, I mean, and the woman behind as plain as can be. I didn't realize for a long time what the thing was that showed behind, that dim sub-pattern, but now I am quite sure it is a woman' (p. 26). The figure of bars functions in Gilman's text to make the narrator's final embodiment as mad woman look like a successful prison break from the tyranny of a meaningless pattern: 'The woman behind shakes it! . . . she crawls around fast, and her crawling shakes it all over . . . she just takes hold of the bars and shakes them hard. And she is all the time trying to climb through' (p. 30). The climax of Gilman's story has her narrator setting to work to strip off the paper and liberate the figure which by now, both she and we – hysterically identified with her reading – recognize as her specular double: 'As soon as it was moonlight and that poor thing began to crawl and shake the pattern, I got up and ran to help her. I pulled and she shook, I shook and she pulled, and before morning we had peeled off yards of that paper' (p. 32). And finally, 'I've got out at last . . . so you can't put me back!' (p. 36).

The figure here is the grammatical figure of chiasmus, or crossing (*OED*: 'The order of words in one of two parallel clauses is inverted in the other'). 'I pulled and she shook, I shook and she pulled' prepares us for the exchange of roles at the end, where the woman reading (and writing) the text becomes the figure of madness within it. Gilman's story hysterically embodies the formal or grammatical figure; but the same process of figuration dimly underlies (like the 'dim shape' or 'dim sub-pattern') our own reading. By the very fact of reading it as narrative, hysterical or otherwise, we posit the speaking or writing subject called 'the narrator'. '*Figure*' also means face, and face implies a speaking voice. In this sense, figure becomes the trace of the bodily presence without which it would be impossible to read 'The Yellow Wallpaper' as a first-person narrative, or even as a displaced form of autobiography.

The chiastic figure provides a metaphor for the hysterical reading which we engage in whenever the disembodied text takes on the aspect of a textual body. Since chiasmus is at once a specular figure and a figure of symmetrical inversion, it could be regarded as the structure of phallogocentrism itself, where word and woman mirror only the presence of the (masculine) body, reinforcing the hierarchy man/woman, presence/absence. Is there a way out of the prison? The bars shaken and mistaken by the madwoman might, in a different linguistic narrative, be taken for the constitutive bar between signifier and signified. The gap between sign and meaning is the absence that the hysteric attempts to abolish or conceal by textualizing the body itself. Montrelay writes of the analyst's discourse as 'not reflexive, but different. As such it is a *metaphor*, not a mirror, of the patient's discourse.'[25] For Montrelay, metaphor engenders a pleasure which is that of '*putting the dimension of repression into play on the level of the text itself*' – of articulating or designating what is not spoken, what is unspeakable, yet incompletely repressed, about the feminine body. The ultimate form of this unmentionable pleasure would be feminine jouissance, or meaning that exceeds the repressive effects of interpretation and figuration. Montrelay's formulation risks its own literalness, that of (hysterically) assuming an unmediated relation between feminine body and word. But her story follows the same trajectory as Gilman's. The end of 'The Yellow Wallpaper' is climactic because Doctor John, previously the censor of women's writing (as Felman demands, 'how can one write *for* the very figure who signifies the suppression of what one has to say *to* him?'),[26] catches the text, as it were, *in flagrante delicto*. The return of the repressed, in Freud's scenario, always figures the sight of the castrated of the letter in all its uncanny literalness to overwhelm us with the absence which both male and female hysteria attempt to repress in the name of woman.

Notes

1. *The Living of Charlotte Perkins Gilman: An Autobiography* (New York: Harper & Row, 1975), p. 96.

2. See *The History of the Psychoanalytic Movement, in Standard Edition of the Complete Psychological Works of Sigmund Freud*, ed. James Strachey et al., 24 vols. (London: Hogarth Press, 1957), hereafter *SE*, **14**: 13–15.

3. *The Living of Charlotte Perkins Gilman*, p. 121.

4. See MARY A. HILL, *Charlotte Perkins Gilman: The Making of a Radical Feminist 1860–1896* (Philadelphia: Temple University Press, 1980), pp. 27–43.

5. JULIET MITCHELL, 'The Question of Femininity', *Women: The Longest Revolution*, p. 299.

6. CHARLOTTE PERKINS GILMAN, *The Yellow Wallpaper*, ed. Elaine R. Hedges (Old Westbury, N.Y.: The Feminist Press, 1973), p. 10. Subsequent page references in the text are to this edition.

7. ANNETTE KOLODNY, 'A Map for Rereading: Or, Gender and the Interpretation of Literary Texts', *New Literary History* (Spring 1980): **11** (3): 451–67; JEAN E. KENNARD, 'Convention Coverage or How to Read Your Own Life', *New Literary History* (Autumn 1981), **13** (1): 69–88.

8. KOLODNY, 'A Map for Rereading', pp. 457–8.

9. Ibid., pp. 457, 459; my italics.

10. KENNARD, 'Convention Coverage', p. 74.

11. MARY WOLLSTONECRAFT, *Mary, A Fiction and the Wrongs of Woman*, ed. Gary Kelly (London and New York: Oxford University Press, 1976), p. 79.

12. See JACQUELINE ROSE, 'Femininity and its Discontents', *Feminist Review*, (June 1983), **14**: 17.

13. KENNARD, 'Convention Coverage', pp. 77–8.

14. See NEIL HERTZ's discussion of repetition and the uncanny in 'Freud and the Sandman', *The End of the Line: Essays on Psychoanalysis and the Sublime* (New York: Columbia University Press, 1985) pp. 97–121.

15. See HILL, *Charlotte Perkins Gilman*, p. 186.

16. See GILMAN, *The Yellow Wallpaper*, pp. 40, 37.

17. 'The split-off mind is the devil with which the unsophisticated observation of early superstitious times believed that these patients were possessed' (*SE* 2: 250).

18. *The Diary of Alice James*, ed. Leon Edel (Harmondsworth: Penguin, 1982), p. 149.

19. See HILL, *Charlotte Perkins Gilman*, pp. 98–9; but see also pp. 144–5 for the course of feminist reading which Gilman undertook in 1887, the year of her breakdown.

19. See HILL, *Charlotte Perkins Gilman*, pp. 98–9; but see also pp. 144–5 for the course of feminist reading which Gilman undertook in 1887, the year of her breakdown.

20. 'Once upon a time you "spooned", then you "petted", after that you "necked" . . . but now you may "smooch"' (1937); HAROLD WENTWORTH and STUART BERG FLEXNER, *Dictionary of American Slang* (New York: Thomas Y. Crowell Co., 1975).

21. See GALLOP, *Feminism and Psychoanalysis: The Daughter's Seduction* (London: Macmillan, 1982), pp. 27–28.

22. MICHÈLE MONTRELAY, 'Inquiry into Femininity', *m/f* (1978), 1: 84; see also the discussion and critique of Montrelay by PARVEEN ADAMS, 'Representation and Sexuality', ibid., 1: 65–82.

23. GALLOP, *The Daughter's Seduction*, p. 27.

24. See SHOSHANA FELMAN, 'Turning the Screw of Interpretation', *Yale French Studies* (1977): 55/56: 125.

25. MONTRELAY, 'Inquiry into Femininity', p. 96.

26. FELMAN, 'Turning the Screw of Interpretation', p. 146.

5 Feminism, New Historicism and the Reader*

WAI-CHEE DIMOCK

Wai-Chee Dimock begins by pointing to the apparently antagonistic relationship between new historicism and feminist criticism in recent theory, and proceeds to explore this relation through the figure of the reader. Dimock suggests that while feminists have privileged the reader as a site of conflict, subversion and empowerment, until very recently New Historicists have tended to ignore questions of readers and reading, concentrating instead on literary production. In order to sketch a historical reading theory, Dimock asks whether reading conventions governing literary texts produce 'structures of authority' and whether such structures might themselves be historically specific. As in Jacobus's essay (Chapter 4), Dimock chooses Charlotte Perkins Gilman's story 'The Yellow Wallpaper' (1892) to illustrate her point. Gilman's narrative is exemplary, for Dimock, in its dramatization of a professional conflict over the authority of reading: concerning the narrator's 'symptoms', her husband, who is a doctor, repeatedly insists on his interpretive authority over that of his wife. And Dimock argues that the question of professionalization – the professionalization of reading – puts into play conflicting readings from a new historicist perspective on the one hand, and from a feminist perspective on the other. Rather than opposing these two approaches, however, Dimock suggests that we should accept that feminism needs new historicism and that new historicism needs feminism in order that both might avoid essentializing and totalizing descriptions of readers and reading.

For more on reading and history, see two collections of essays: Machor (ed.), *Readers in History* (1993) and Cathy N. Davidson (ed.), *Reading in America* (1989). For alternative accounts of feminism and reading, see Chapters 3 and 4 by Schweickart and Jacobus, respectively.

The relation between feminist criticism and New Historicism is a peculiar one, exciting considerable interest and curiosity (not to say

---

* Reprinted from *American Literature* 63: 4 (1991): 601–22.

unease) and, especially in English Renaissance studies, occasioning some unusually acrimonious polemics. The acrimony has to do, at least in part, with the marginal status accorded by one to the other: figuring in each other's discourse at best as a point of departure and at worst as an *overlooked* point of departure, New Historicists and feminists seem to talk at cross purposes, keeping their mutual distance, relegating each other to a kind of non-presence.[1] If the feminist chronicling of women's oppression and celebration of women's difference have appeared misguided to many New Historicists, the New Historicist universalization of power and blurring of genders have struck many feminists as nothing short of reactionary.[2]

In this essay I want to rethink the relation between feminist criticism and New Historicism, using that *relation*, in turn, as a leverage point, an artificially concocted but no less serviceable juncture from which and against which both critical enterprises might be evaluated, held up for mutual reflection, and perhaps for mutual realignment. Eventually I want to challenge not only their supposed disagreement but also their presumed distinction, to show that the discrete identity imputed to each in fact impoverishes both. Still, it is useful, at the outset, to rehearse those presumed distinctions and supposed disagreements, if only to bring into focus some of the tacit premises that have given rise to so much hostility and mistrust. I begin, then, with an imaginary confrontation between New Historicism and feminist criticism, dressed up momentarily as parties at war, and, for dramatic effect, I stage the battle over the body of that most familiar and cherished of figures: the figure of the reader.

Or perhaps I should say, familiar and cherished by one side. For feminist critics as different as Nina Baym and Annette Kolodny, Margaret Homans and Louise Rosenblatt, Janice Radway and Cathy N. Davidson, the figure of the reader has served as a crucial organizing center: a site of contestation, a site of celebration, and a site from which to construct an alternative canon.[3] This is not true of New Historicists, who, preoccupied as they are with the sociocultural field at the text's moment of production (rather than its moment of reception), have been much less concerned with the reader either as a figure of the past or as a figure of the present moment.[4] Partly to redress the imbalance, and partly to manufacture an occasion for war, I begin with a more or less caricatured appearance of the reader in a more or less caricatured New Historicist exercise, one designed to be uncongenial to feminists.

My starting point, however, is neither a feminist text nor a New Historicist one, but an important (and eminently non-partisan) essay by Steven Marcus called 'Reading the Illegible'. Marcus uses the paradigm of reading to describe a cultural phenomenon generated by the complexity of modern life, which, 'not perceived as a coherent system of signs', demands to be read – to be organized and interpreted – into some semblance of clarity and order.[5] In the specific example Marcus analyzes, the subject for reading happens to be the urban landscape, but, beyond that, he seems also to be giving us a definition of reading in the broadest sense of the word, taking it beyond the generic boundaries of the literary text, and using it to include a wide range of activities, activities that have to do with the interpretation of signs, the adjudication of meanings, and the construction of reality. Understood in this non-generic sense, reading might be said to be a phenomenon peculiar to modernity. Unlike the medieval preoccupation with exegesis and the Puritan preoccupation with typology, reading in its modern guise is not centered on or authorized by one particular text, least of all the Bible. Modern society is a society of interpretation, interpretation at once deregulated and *de rigueur*,[6] for in this world, a world increasingly acted upon by forces unknown and unseen, and increasingly removed from our immediate comprehension, all of us, whether or not we accept the label, have to become readers of sorts. Indeed, from the mid-nineteenth century onward, reading might be said to be one of the most commonplace cultural activities, an activity dictated by the mysteries of modern life, by the gap, at once titillating and worrisome, between immediate experience and apprehended meaning, between what we see and what we think it signifies.[7]

Still, if all of us are readers, and if reading is what we do every minute of our lives, the phenomenon cannot be very interesting. What makes it interesting, a subject worthy of historical analysis, is its emergence, in its modern, non-generic form, as a field that sustains and indeed requires special knowledge, a field where the recession of meaning goes hand in hand with the concentration of expertise, and where standards of competence are erected over and against an illiteracy that is, paradoxically, the rule rather than the exception. The rise of the medical profession is a dramatic case in point. As we learn from Paul Starr's magisterial study, *The Social Transformation of American Medicine*, the spectacular ascent of physicians both in social status and in economic power had everything to do with their ability to institute a new set of reading conventions, conventions that established not only their own expertise, but also the lack of it in those they served. From being a more or less marginal, more or less disreputable group up to the mid-nineteenth century, medical practitioners effectively solidified their identity – by regulating certification and licensing and by building an elaborate system of specialized knowledge, technical procedures, and rules of behavior – so that, by the second half of the nineteenth century, the profession had come to occupy a central place in American society, and their success was reflected, according to Starr, not only in their authority over the 'construction of reality', the 'interpretation of experience', and the 'meaning of things', but also in the medical illiteracy of those they served, ordinary people who were incapable of reading their own symptoms and who had to defer to the judgment of these more qualified, or at least more certified, experts.[8]

The American Medical Association was not alone in its triumph. The same half-century also saw the rise of other professional groups, most notably the American Bar Association, as well as other organizations less powerful and less prosperous, such as the American Historical Association, the American Economic Association, and, of course, the MLA.[9] As the names of these august institutions suggest, the rise of professional communities has everything to do with the redistribution of social authority. And, whether we call such authority 'professional sovereignty' (as Paul Starr does) or 'professional jurisdiction' (as Andrew Abbott does),[10] it would seem to be predicated on a set of reading conventions, on the authority of expert readers, and conversely, on the dependency of the illiterate. Indeed, the rise of professionalism – a phenomenon that has fascinated sociologists from Emile Durkheim to Talcott Parsons to Daniel Bell[11] – might also be described as the rise of a new way of reading, with a new way of organizing knowledge and a new way of structuring authority.

Given the centrality of reading in a culture of professionalism, one obvious way to historicize the literary reader is to ask whether this figure inhabits a structure of authority comparable to that inhabited by its nonfictive counterparts, by the professionals who also happen to be expert readers. Along those lines, a New Historicist might be tempted to pursue a set of interrelated questions: In a culture more generally governed by the ideal of interpretive competence, what sort of *literary* reading conventions might we expect to find? If interpretation is itself a valuable social asset, an asset whose usefulness extends far beyond the domain of the literary, how might it in turn shape the literary domain? Do reading conventions in texts generate structures of authority in the same way that reading conventions in the social realm do? And are we prepared to argue that such structures are historically specific, that there might be a textual structure that would answer to the structure of authority underwritten by professionalism?

Charlotte Perkins Gilman's 'The Yellow Wallpaper', a story that has inspired numerous feminist readings,[12] turns out, from this perspective, also to be an ideal text for an imaginary New Historicist exercise, ideal not only because this is a story told by a mad narrator and therefore one that foregrounds the question of interpretive authority, and not only because there is actually a doctor in the story, but also because, by a happy coincidence, Gilman herself happened to be a paragon of professionalism in the late nineteenth century. For about thirteen years of her life, from 1887 to 1900, between the time she left her first husband and the time she married her second, Gilman supported herself in California, making a living as an editor of magazines (the *Impress* and the *Forerunner*), a veteran on the lecture circuit, and a respected authority on the economics of housework.[13] Between 1898 and 1904 she published four books on the subject, including *Women and Economics* (1898), *Concerning Children* (1900), *The Home: Its Work and Influence* (1903), and *Human Work* (1904). In the tradition of the scientific home-making movement (a movement begun by Catherine Beecher in the 1840s and reaching its zenith in the early twentieth century), Gilman believes that housework should be professionalized, arguing that this would secure not only gender equality for women, but, just as important, managerial efficiency for the home.[14] Her lifelong interest in architectural design reflects the same faith in professionalism.[15] For her, ideal apartment houses should provide 'trained professional service' for 'professional women with families'; they should have no kitchens, so that cooking would be done not by women but by professional cooks; and they should provide supervised cleaning by 'efficient workers' hired by 'the manager of the establishment', as well as day-care administered by 'well-trained professional nurses'.[16] Indeed, for her, the goals of feminism can be achieved only through the agency of professionalism, only by bringing specialized knowledge, rational authority, and administrative expertise to the home.

In itself, Gilman's commitment to professionalism is hardly remarkable. What is remarkable, however, is the apparent discrepancy between *Women and Economics* (1898) and 'The Yellow Wallpaper' (1892), written just six years before. In this story about mental collapse, a story that ends with the narrator crawling on all fours, where is the redeeming hand of professionalism? And, when we witness the terrible mistakes of the husband (who, of course, is a doctor), and when we see what befalls him at the end, are we not supposed to lose faith in the very ground of professional authority?

These questions, perplexing as they might seem, are actually not impossible to answer, especially if we are willing to entertain the possibility that the husband might not be the only model of professional authority, and that another, more commendable, figure might be lurking behind the scene. In any case, it is surely significant that the husband is not just a doctor but an emphatically bad one. This means, of course, that he is a bad reader, who, when confronted with a set of symptoms, repeatedly fails to come up with the right interpretation. As his wife becomes crazier and crazier, he becomes more and more optimistic in his diagnosis. Indeed he tells her: 'But you really are better, dear, whether you can see it or not. I am a doctor, dear, and I know.' And he adds, 'Can you not trust me as a physician when I tell you so?'[17]

Over and over again, the husband urges his wife to trust the soundness of his judgment by reminding her that as a doctor he has an interpretive authority over her life. But the point, of course, is that he really has no such authority, because, being a bad reader, he should never have been a doctor in the first place.[18] What makes him a villain of sorts, then, is not so much that he is a cruel husband as that he is an incompetent doctor. But if he is giving professionalism a bad name here, there is no reason why that bad name should be the last word on the subject. Indeed, the very fact that he is such a noticeably unworthy specimen should alert us to the possibility that there might be a worthier example somewhere else, a professional who not only occupies a position of authority, but actually has a legitimate claim to it.

Where might such an alternative position be found, what would be its structure of authority, and who would be the privileged figure within that structure? If we look for it merely within the actualized fictional world of 'The Yellow Wallpaper', only within that immanent structure where every available position is occupied by a particular character, we are bound to be disappointed, I think, because neither the mad narrator, nor her husband the doctor, nor the sister-in-law can claim to be a figure of authority. However, if we were to think of 'The Yellow Wallpaper' as a compositional structure – as a structure generated by a mode of rhetorical address – we might indeed argue for an alternative position, a position that is invisible, unembodied, and yet existing as an object of inference or perhaps even as a structural predicate. Such a position, we might further argue, can indeed function as a virtual repository where the absent attributes of professionalism – rational authority, expert knowledge, and interpretive competence – can be securely lodged.

As must be obvious by now, such a virtual position can be occupied only by one figure. In the absence of any competent reader inside the story, it is the outside reader – or, I should say, the implied reader – who is called upon to occupy the position of interpretive authority, functioning both as the text's ideal recipient and its necessary coordinate. As my vocabulary suggests, what is being invoked here is the model of reading associated with Wolfgang Iser, invoked in order to provide a supplement to the more familiar model of positionality, and to suggest an opening, a point of exit from the closed system of the text. Such a procedure, of course, runs the risk of conjuring up an idealized reader. Even more dangerously, at least to my mind, it also runs the opposite risk, that is, of turning the reader into a strictly textual phenomenon, strictly immanent within the text and ontologically dependent upon its functions, and so returning once again to a textual system of absolute closure.[19]

To reduce such risks, it is helpful to supplement Iser, in turn, with Tony Bennett's concept of the 'reading formation'. By this Bennett means a set of determinations which 'mediate the relation between text and context, connecting the two and providing the mechanisms . . . , [the] intertextual and discursive relations which produce readers for texts and texts for readers'.[20] Bennett's concept is especially important here, because, in speaking of reading as a 'formation', a reciprocal process by which readers and texts are mutually produced and mutually productive, he also restores a dialectical agency to the reading process, claiming for it a larger operating field as well as a larger instrumental effect.

This emphasis – on the dialectical agency of reading, on the interplay between production and reception – seems to me crucial in any attempt to historicize the reader. It is also crucial, I think, to any historical criticism (including New Historicism, though not confined to it) that, for various political or philosophical reasons, might wish not to reduce subject-positions merely to structural effects, merely to something that is given or entailed. Unlike Iser's model, which remains hostage to a system of textual immanence, Bennett's model is structurally contingent but not necessarily structurally determinate. It constitutes the reader not only as a figure of structural dictate but also as a figure of structural potential.

Of course, in 'The Yellow Wallpaper' the subject-position we are trying to imagine happens not at all to be a critical position but rather an authoritative one, which, as we have seen, none of the characters can occupy. But, as we have also seen, there is nonetheless a virtual position, commanded by a virtual figure. After all, quite aside from the meager cast of three characters, isn't someone else there as well, invisible to the others, but necessary to the unfolding of the text, someone who can do what the others seem incapable of doing for themselves, that is, interpret their story for them? When we come to the end of the story, when the husband is lying on the floor and the wife is crawling around, isn't someone else still sitting, still sane and still rational, whose sanity and rationality are the very credentials by which she can diagnose the ailments of these characters? Against the pathetic benightedness of all the characters in the story – who can hardly tell what is delusion or hallucination from what is 'real' – isn't someone else always there with open eyes, always granted a clear knowledge, both of the 'reality' of the wife's madness and of the 'reality' of the marital situation? And against the husband's less than professional expertise, isn't someone else always making a competent judgment or, should we say, a competent reading?

The position of authority in 'The Yellow Wallpaper' is occupied by the reader, and, we might add, not just any reader but a reader with a specific and historically recognizable profile, created in the image of professionalism at its most idealized, endowed with the sacred attributes of specialized knowledge and interpretive competence. To return, then, to my initial question about whether or not there might be a textual structure that would answer to the structure of authority underwritten by professionalism, the answer would seem to be yes. Indeed, one is almost obligated here to argue that, in the literary domain, what is professionalized is not just the careers of authors, but, less tangibly though no less significantly, the literary form itself, which, in the case of 'The Yellow Wallpaper', comprises a network of knowledge between author and reader, a network maintained largely at the expense of the characters in the story. Along those lines, one would have to argue that the literary domain is not really distinct from the social domain, that by a homologous process professionalism would seem also to have inscribed a differential structure here, a structure of authority and dependency. Within the text, the characters are 'professionalized', in the sense that they are organized into fields of subjectivities, which is also to say, fields of knowledge. They become subjects for us to know. And, presiding over the text, administering to its interpretation, is the reader, professionalized in the more familiar sense of the word, in the sense that she is assigned a privileged position, a position of readerly expertise and readerly knowledge.

Here, then, is the New Historicist reading, much simplified, to be sure, but still recognizable as such in its Foucauldian grid of power, knowledge, and subjectivity, and in its view of subjectivity as the determinate effect of discursive formations whose structural totality generates, saturates, and circumscribes all individual practices.[21] Such a reading would have argued that 'The Yellow Wallpaper' is a text embedded in and structured by the culture of professionalism, a text in which the unequal distribution of knowledge and the unequal distribution of authority are reproduced in its very literary form. Along those lines, such an argument would also have theorized about the homologous genesis of social and literary forms, about the power relations inscribed in such forms, and about the permeable boundary, or perhaps even the lack of boundary, between the literary and the social.

This is an argument I did make when I taught the book, but it is also an argument I now want to resist making.[22] Or rather, it is an argument I want both to make and to unmake, both to set forth and to destabilize. And one way to destabilize that argument, I think, is to consider the gender of the reader. I have been referring to the reader as a 'she'; this is not so much a polemical posture on my part as a deferential gesture to Gilman, because this is the pronoun she herself would have used.

In a little essay called 'Why I Wrote "The Yellow Wallpaper" ', Gilman explained why she had to write the book. She herself, she said, had been subjected to the 'rest cure' administered by Dr S. Weir Mitchell, the same treatment the narrator was subjected to, and it had left her 'so near the

borderline of utter mental ruin that I could see over'. What saved her,
and what restored to her 'some measure of power', was her decision to
defy the doctor and to go back to work – 'work, the normal life of every
human being; work, in which is joy and growth and service, without
which one is a pauper and a parasite'. And it was in the spirit of work
that she wrote 'The Yellow Wallpaper'. She wrote it, she said, 'to save
people from being driven crazy, and it worked'.[23] In a later essay, she
also explained for whose benefit all this work was being done: 'One girl
reads this, and takes fire! Her life is changed. She becomes a power – a
mover of others – I write for her.'[24]

What difference does it make to specify a 'she' here, or, to put the
question more generally, what difference does it make to introduce the
category of gender into the paradigm of reading? A big difference, I
think. Because if we are going to acknowledge that the implied reader in
'The Yellow Wallpaper' is not just a professional but also a woman, we
will also have to ask whether such a conjunction was actually in place
when the story was being written, whether gender and occupational
identity did indeed coincide and coalesce at that particular historical
moment. Once we put the question that way, it becomes clear that there
is in fact an interesting mismatch between the two defining attributes of
the implied reader. At the turn of the century, the professional who was
also a woman was a rare breed indeed. Professionalism was something
denied to women and something they were trying to attain. No women
practised law before the 1870s, and as late as 1873 the Supreme Court
still upheld a decision by the Illinois Supreme Court to refuse
Myra Bradwell admission to the Illinois bar solely on the grounds that
she was a woman.[25] Meanwhile, women made up no more than
2.8 per cent of the medical profession in 1880, and even by 1900 the
figure was a mere 5.6 per cent.[26] The reader in 'The Yellow Wallpaper'
who is both a woman and a professional is very much an ideal reader,
not only in the sense that she is the right reader, but also in the sense that
she is not quite real yet, not quite there in the flesh.

It is in this gap – in the non-identity between the ideal reader invoked
by the story and the actual women reading it – that we can speak of the
dialectical agency of the text, or, to use a more familiar phrase, of its
cultural work. For, given such a gap, a gap between the putative and the
actual, doesn't the story have its work cut out? Isn't that gap both the
space within which the story labors, and the space that it labors to
narrow and eventually to eliminate? As Gilman's own repeated
celebration of 'work' suggests, the idea is hardly foreign to her. 'The
Yellow Wallpaper', then, is not just the product of a culture of
professionalism, not just an inert index; it is also a transformative
agency, with the power to produce effects of its own. It has that power
because, within a gendered paradigm, the structure of professional

authority it ostensibly relies upon is actually something it is in the process of bringing into being. Its supposed ground turns out to be its desired consequence. A feminist reading of the story would focus on the reader, not as a site of homologous formation, not as the locus from which we can see a line of continuity between the text and the culture of professionalism, but as a figure constituted by a deliberate and enabling gap, a gap that, even as it shadows forth the temporal distance between what the female reader is and what she might become, also restores to the text the possibility of agency in the world.

I have dramatized the disagreement between a New Historicist and a feminist reading not to show that one is victorious over the other but to make a different – and somewhat paradoxical – point, namely, that the two readings are in fact not at odds, that, in some sense, they are not even adjacent, since the two phenomena that they describe turn out to be non-adjacent in the first place. This non-adjacency comes about because, even granting the primacy of a culture of professionalism, we must still point to a temporal discrepancy – a non-coincidence between what Raymond Williams calls the dominant, the residual, and the emergent – within that historical formation.[27] To the extent that 'The Yellow Wallpaper' is conditioned by history, this 'history' must itself be seen not as a field of synchronized unity but as a field of uneven development. The professionalism that prevails in one instance as a dominant standard can figure in another instance only as an emerging potential.[28] Given this structure of delays and relays – this non-adjacency between the established and the deferred – professionalism and feminism might be said to be in contact only through the mediated space of a temporal lag.

Even if we are to focus on a figure that seems common to both – the figure of the reader – we are still bound to encounter not a unified entity but a sedimented construct, a figure traversed by time and dispersed in time, making its staggered appearances in a variety of stages, in its residual, established, and emergent forms, and through its inflections by class, gender, and race.[29] There are readers and readers, it would seem, and, when we meditate on their points of divergence as well as their points of coincidence, when we think about their uneven genesis, conflicting identities, and different modes of reception, 'history' itself will have to be reconceived as something less than homogeneous, something less than synchronized.

This, at least to my mind, is one way to understand that well-known phrase 'the textuality of history'.[30] By this phrase we usually refer to the idea that the past is transmitted by texts, that it can never be recovered or apprehended as a lived totality. Here I want to use the phrase in a somewhat different sense, focusing not on the process of textual transmission but on the dynamics of historical development, on its sedimented, non-uniform, and therefore untotalizable *texture*. History itself has a texture, I argue, because at any given moment there is a precarious conjunction of the 'has been' and the 'not yet', the 'already' and the 'probably', a conjunction brought into play by the very passage of time, by the uneven velocities and shifting densities of social change. To historicize a text, then, is also to recover those uneven velocities and shifting densities, to deconstruct its spatial unity into a virtual (and uncharted) sequence, a momentary conjunction of temporal traces, with no particular center of gravity and no particular teleology. Any reading that tries to lock the text into a single posture – to impute to it a center and a teleology – can do so only through an act of historical repression, only by turning a temporal relation of multiple sedimentation into a spatial relation of either opposition or containment.[31]

But – and this is a 'but' that needs to be rendered in large print – if we are indeed committed to the idea of multiple sedimentation, as a practical program rather than a polemical statement, what we must then proceed to challenge, it would seem, is not just the model of containment associated with New Historicism but also the model of opposition associated with feminism. After all, it is not just New Historicism that threatens to lock the text into a single posture. Feminism (or, I should say, a certain brand of feminism, what its critics call essentialist feminism) threatens to do much the same thing, though obviously from the other direction. In celebrating gender as the ground of difference and in identifying the female as the positive term within this topography of difference, feminism also comes dangerously close to reifying gender into a binary opposition, and reifying opposition itself into a unitary term.

The shortcomings of essentialist feminism have been pointed out, most emphatically by Toril Moi, and they are indeed such as to deserve emphasis.[32] Still, the phrase 'essentialist feminism' might be guilty of doing some essentializing of its own, since the so-called essentialist feminists are by no means as rigid or ossified as their critics would like to make out.[33] What concerns me, then, is not the merit or shortcoming of individual practitioners so much as the general term 'feminism' itself, and it is this that I want to interrogate and unsettle. I want to bring a kind of heuristic weight to bear on the meaning of this word, to test its contents and its contours, and to ask to what extent a 'feminist' project can be understood as a self-sufficient and autonomous enterprise.

Indeed, playing the devil's advocate now, I want to deconstruct the neat opposition I have so far relied upon – the opposition between New Historicism and feminist criticism – and, with that in mind, I return to the second reading with the question, What is so 'feminist' about it? Such a question, I hope, is not without its shock effect. Most people, it is safe to say, will immediately label the second reading 'feminist', not only because it has vindicated both Gilman and 'The Yellow Wallpaper' but also because, in singling out the female reader as the text's privileged reader and in locating the text's agency in the trajectory of that figure, it has claimed for gender a centrally determinative (and indeed centrally redemptive) status. In all these respects it is identifiably feminist, tracing its genealogy most directly to Annette Kolodny's essay, 'A Map for Rereading: Gender and the Interpretation of Literary Texts', an essay instrumental in forging a new critical paradigm, the paradigm of gender and reading. Within this paradigm, the relation between two terms once considered separate – gender and reading – is now understood to be neither fortuitous nor incidental but primary and constitutive. Gender, that is to say, enters into the reading process not as an external or even secondary consideration, but as an organizing principle, as the perceptual coordinates by which details are selected and meaning imposed, in short, as the cognitive ground shaping an entire field of vision.

Kolodny's essay has inspired and informed an entire generation of feminist critics. And yet, to those of us sensitized to the dangers of essentialism, the essay also comes very close to embodying just those dangers. In introducing the category of gender into the reading process, Kolodny not only dismantles an older model, one that universalizes reading, but also puts a new one in its place, one that foregrounds gender differential and proceeds, on that basis, to separate reading into two distinct and distinctive modes, using gender, of course, as the line of division. What she emphasizes, accordingly, is the mutual illegibility between genders, and, more particularly, the illegibility of a female text to male readers. Summing up 'The Yellow Wallpaper' and 'A Jury of Her Peers' (a story by Susan Keating Glaspell), Kolodny suggests that while neither story 'necessarily excludes the male as reader – indeed, both in a way are directed specifically at educating him to become a better reader – they do nonetheless insist that, however inadvertently, he is a *different kind* of reader and that, where women are concerned, he is often an inadequate reader'.[34]

'A different kind of reader': the phrase is resounding but also problematic, because, in positing gender simply as a category of *difference* – simply as the ground of distinction between two discrete terms – Kolodny has put herself on the edge (and, some would say, over the edge) of a binary opposition, opposing male to female, and, in so doing, constituting each of them into a stable and unified identity. Gender, in short, operates as a principle of reification here, and it is within this reified landscape that Kolodny can speak of 'male texts' and 'female meaning' as if they were discrete and substantive terms.

All the same, it is a mistake simply to find fault with Kolodny or to critique her on absolute grounds. Rather, her critical practice must itself be contextualized, must be seen, that is, against the background of its inception, in 1980, when feminist theory was just beginning to emerge as a newly articulated and not fully legitimized form of discourse, one that had to struggle not just for visibility but also for a kind of internal coherence. If Kolodny's differential map of gender came close to being a binary opposition, and if her appeal to female unity came close to reifying female identity, those dangers were nonetheless necessary, and perhaps even beneficial, in an emerging discourse that was still struggling to be heard, still struggling to claim for itself a recognizable voice and a recognizable profile. Within this context, the traditional feminist appeal to 'female experience' or to 'the women's tradition' bespeaks not a theoretical naivete but a tactical wisdom.[35] By the same token, however, it is also understandable why a new generation of feminists writing today should feel the urgent need *not* to think about the female simply as a category of identity (which is also to say, not to think about gender simply as a category of difference): why Eve Sedgwick, for instance, would want to invoke the notion of the 'continuum' in order to describe the mobile distribution of sexual identities and the asymmetrical structuring of gender relations; why Alice Jardine would choose to analyze 'woman' as signifying effect rather than as originary subject; why Judith Butler would argue for a feminism that deconstructs the very concept of 'identity' itself ; and why Mary Poovey would seize upon the idea of 'uneven development' to emphasize the unstable ideological work of gender, its non-uniform institutional articulations, and hence its inability, at any given moment, to achieve anything like a totalization of the social field.[36]

I hope that by now I have contextualized my own reading of 'The Yellow Wallpaper' as well. Indebted to the paradigm of gender and reading but mindful of its potentially reifying hazards, I have tried not to posit a binary opposition between male and female reader, not to homogenize difference within the field of gender.[37] Instead I have tried to mobilize and multiply the grounds of difference, to analyze it as a relational and sequential rather than substantive phenomenon, and hence not a phenomenon that can be imputed to any single generative site or fixated along any single line of demarcation. What I have come up with, then, is a figure of internal difference,[38] who in this case happens to be the female reader, a figure not quite professionalized yet, not quite what she is supposed to be, and mobilized, therefore, by the very force of incipience, by the discrepancy which both constitutes and destablilizes her temporal being. Suspended between the dominant and the dormant, lagging behind the male reader but not willing to remain there for good, such an emerging figure also collapses the binary opposition between genders into a complexly imbricated and complexly sequential play of identity and difference.

And yet, to what extent is this female reader a *feminist* construct? It is a figure that pleases feminists, to be sure, one that is heartwarming and edifying to conjure up. Still, if this figure embodies an internal gap, as I have tried to argue, a gap that redeems both the text and the author, this redeeming feature is nonetheless not the effect of gender organization but the effect of temporal discrepancy. In other words, what makes the female reader the locus of 'not yet' – what suspends her between the 'not' and the 'yet' and preserves her as an indeterminate and therefore untotalized quantum – is not the agency of gender but the agency of history. Or, to be more precise, we might say that the agency of gender is itself historical, because it is history – understood as the medium of sequence, succession, and sedimentation – that produces the space between the 'not' and the 'yet', within which gender can operate as a principle of difference.

To put it this way is also to see how symbiotic 'gender' and 'history' are and how unfruitful it is to oppose a feminist reading to a historicist reading. Indeed, in order not to reify gender into an unvarying category of difference and in order not to limit difference to an unvarying site of production, a feminist reading must also be a historical reading. It must try, that is, not just to describe or taxonomize difference but also to trace its shifting contexts, modalities, and operative axes. It must study the changing pattern, throughout history, of what functions as difference and what counts as difference. In short, what I am emphasizing here is the grounding of gender in time, a grounding that is simultaneously its unsettling. Gender is most useful as an analytic category when it is seen as a temporal (and temporary) construct, when it is understood to be constituted in time and constrained by time, propelled by temporal necessity and subject to temporal reconfiguration.

Does that mean, then, that gender is completely subsumed by history and that a feminist reading is really no more than a historicist reading? This is a formulation I want to resist as well. If the relation between feminism and historicism is not one of categoric opposition, neither is it one of categoric subordination. For just as a vigorous historicizing of gender reorients the entire concept, so a vigorous engendering of history transforms the very meaning of what it is to be historical. Gender, that is, is to be understood not as an incidental addition to a stable historical field but as a principle productive of uneven textures, productive of the discrepancy between the dominant and the emergent, inflecting and disturbing the very shape of historical time, challenging not only normative temporality but also its spatial disposition of margins and limits. Since I have labored thus far to show that history is crucial as a category of gender studies, I want to turn my attention now to the other side of the argument – which also happens to echo the title of an important essay by Joan Wallach Scott – namely, that gender is equally crucial as a category of historical analysis.[39]

It is helpful here, in fact, to return to the New Historicist reading offered earlier in the essay, the reading that was inspected, found wanting, and set aside. What is it that makes that reading so unsatisfactory? The problem, I submit, is not that it is too historical but that it is not historical enough. Indeed, the charge of essentialism, so often leveled at feminism, can be directed against this reading as well, against its tendency to reify power relations within the literary *form* itself, as if power could inhere in a form and be ontological to that form, independent of the shifting contexts in which it figures, the varying uses to which it is put, and the changing audiences it speaks to and for. This essentializing tendency in New Historicism reinstates the very timelessness which it sets out to critique. The text, that is, is imaged here as an atemporal circulatory medium, ceaselessly negotiating with its synchronic social forms but otherwise untempered by diachronic inflections, untempered by the destabilizing effects of the passage of time.

The absence of the diachronic in New Historicism is regrettable but also forgivable, since a truly historical understanding – one based not on the knowledge of particular events but on the ability to generalize about continuity and change, to discern the shape of temporal movement and the facilitating conditions for that shape – is a gift rare not only among critics but (if I might say so) among historians as well. But it is precisely here, against this incapacity or impasse, that gender can intervene as a category of historical analysis, as a conceptual vehicle that urges upon us a version of the diachronic, more local and more modest, perhaps, but no less vital. For if gender is indeed to be understood as a principle of unevenness, as a fault line along which normative temporality is broken up, decentered, and dispersed into various stages of the residual, the dominant, and the emergent, any historical inquiry that takes gender as its analytic coordinate will also come to grips with that fractured temporality, which is to say it will be diachronic, the diachronicity here being generated not so much by the subject itself as by the analytic frame, which breaks up the seeming unity of time into its multiple sediments and infinite relays. In the case of 'The Yellow Wallpaper', it is the gendered reader, understood both as a historical figure and as a historied figure, that provides the point of entry for this radically destabilized sense of time. But, speaking more generally, we might also say that gender, as a principle of unevenness, will be important for any attempt to conceptualize history, not as a homologous or synchronized formation but as a field of endless mutations and permutations, a field where the temporal nonidentity between cause and effect and the structural nonidentity between system and subject quite literally open up a space for alternatives, however visionary and unsustained. History, thus engendered and thus decentered, is anything but a totalizing category. In fact, it is not even over and done with, but a realm of unexhausted and inexhaustible possibility.

Notes

1. This is a crude generalization, needless to say, but, at least to my mind, it describes the work of leading New Historicists such as Stephen Greenblatt and Walter Benn Michaels and the work of leading feminists such as Sandra Gilbert and Susan Gubar. Also needless to say, there are important exceptions here. For New Historicist work in American Studies that addresses gender, see RICHARD BRODHEAD, 'Sparing the Rod: Discipline and Fiction in Antebellum America', *Representations*, 21 (1988): 67–96; GILLIAN BROWN, 'The Empire of Agoraphobia', *Representations*, 20 (1987): 134–57; T. WALTER HERBERT, 'Nathaniel Hawthorne, Una Hawthorne, and *The Scarlet Letter*: Interactive Selfhoods and the Cultural Construction of Gender', *PMLA*, 103 (1988): 285–97; MYRA JEHLEN, 'The Ties that Bind: Race and Sex in *Pudd'nhead Wilson*', *American Literary History*, 2 (1990): 39–55; DAVID LEVERENZ, *Manhood and the American Renaissance* (Ithaca: Cornell University Press, 1989).

2. For an implicit New Historicist critique of feminists, see WALTER BENN MICHAELS, *The Gold Standard and the Logic of Naturalism* (Berkeley: University of California Press, 1987), pp. 3–28, 217–44. For a more explicit critique, see JONATHAN GOLDBERG, 'Shakespearean Inscriptions: The Voicing of Power', in *Shakespeare and the Question of Theory*, ed. Patricia Parker and Geoffrey Hartman (New York: Methuen, 1985), pp. 116–37. For feminist critiques of New Historicists, see LYNDA E. BOOSE, 'The Family in Shakespeare Studies; or – Studies in the Family of Shakespeareans; or – The Politics of Politics', *Renaissance Quarterly*, 40 (1987): 707–42, especially 727–42; MARGUERITE WALLER, 'Academic Tootsie: The Denial of Difference and the Difference it Makes', *Diacritics*, 17 (1987): 2–20; JUDITH LOWDER NEWTON, 'History as Usual? Feminism and the "New Historicism"', in *The New Historicism*, ed. H. Aram Veeser (New York: Routledge, 1989), pp. 152–67.

3. NINA BAYM, 'Melodramas of Beset Manhood: How Theories of American Fiction Exclude Women Authors', *American Quarterly*, 33 (1981): 123–39; ANNETTE KOLODNY, 'A Map for Rereading: Or, Gender and the Interpretation of Literary Texts', *New Literary History*, 11 (1980): 451–67, reprinted in *The New Feminist Criticism*, ed. Elaine Showalter (New York: Pantheon, 1985), pp. 46–62, and KOLODNY, 'Dancing Through the Minefield: Some Observations on the Theory, Practice, and Politics of a Feminist Literary Criticism', *Feminist Studies*, 6 (1980): 1–25; MARGARET HOMANS, 'Eliot, Wordsworth, and the Scenes of the Sister's Instruction', *Critical Inquiry*, 8 (1981): 223–41; LOUISE ROSENBLATT, *The Reader, The Text, The Poem: The Transactional Theory of the Literary Work* (Carbondale: Southern Illinois University Press, 1978); JANICE RADWAY, *Reading the Romance: Women, Patriarchy, and Popular Literature* (Chapel Hill: University of North Carolina Press, 1984); CATHY N. DAVIDSON, *Revolution and the Word* (New York: Oxford University Press, 1986). See also a useful collection, *Gender and Reading*, ed. Elizabeth Flynn and Patrocinio P. Schweickart (Baltimore: Johns Hopkins University Press, 1986).

4. On this point, see BROOK THOMAS, *The New Historicism and Other Old-Fashioned Topics* (Princeton: Princeton University Press, 1991). Significantly, this is *not* true of feminist New Historicists, who have been very attentive indeed to the figure of the reader. See, for example, NANCY ARMSTRONG, *Desire and Domestic Fiction* (New York: Oxford University Press, 1987); CATHY N. DAVIDSON, *Revolution and the Word*; JANE TOMPKINS, *Sensational Designs: The Cultural Work of American Fiction* (New York: Oxford University Press, 1985).

5. STEVEN MARCUS, 'Reading the Illegible', in *The Victorian City: Images and Realities*, 2 vols, ed. H.J. Dyos and Michael Wolff (London: Routledge & Kegan Paul, 1973), I, 257–76.

6. See SACVAN BERCOVITCH, *The Office of 'The Scarlet Letter'* (Baltimore: Johns Hopkins University Press, 1991).

7. Most American historians have pointed to the second half of the nineteenth century as a cultural divide, when modern habits of perception and interpretation came into being. See, for instance, THOMAS HASKELL, *The Emergence of Professional Social Science* (Urbana: University of Illinois Press, 1977); JOHN HIGHAM, 'The Reorientation of American Culture in the 1890s', in his *Writing American History: Essays on Modern Scholarship* (Bloomington: Indiana University Press, 1970), pp. 73–102; SAMUEL P. HAYS, *The Response to Industrialism: 1885–1914* (Chicago: University of Chicago Press, 1957); ROBERT WIEBE, *The Search for Order, 1877–1920* (New York: Hill and Wang, 1967).

8. PAUL STARR, *The Social Transformation of American Medicine* (New York: Basic Books, 1982). See especially pp. 3–29, on 'the social origins of professional sovereignty'. Quotations from pp. 13, 19, 13. For related arguments, see ELIOT FREIDSON, *Profession of Medicine: A Study of the Sociology of Applied Knowledge* (New York: Dodd, Mead, 1970), and FREIDSON, *Professional Dominance: The Social Structure of Medical Care* (New York: Atherton, 1970).

9. The American Bar Association was founded in 1878, the MLA in 1883, the AHA in 1884, and the AEA in 1885. For the rise of professionalism, see BURTON J. BLEDSTEIN, *The Culture of Professionalism: The Middle Class and the Formation of Higher Education in America* (New York: Norton, 1976); ANTON-HERMANN CHROUST, *The Rise of the Legal Profession in America* (Norman: University of Oklahoma Press, 1965); MARY FURNER, *Advocacy and Objectivity: A Crisis in the Professionalization of American Social Science, 1865–1905* (Lexington: University of Kentucky Press, 1975); THOMAS HASKELL, *The Emergence of Professional Social Science*; MAGALI SARFATTI LARSON, *The Rise of Professionalism* (Berkeley: University of California Press, 1977). See also a valuable collection, *The Authority of Experts*, ed. Thomas Haskell (Bloomington: Indiana University Press, 1984).

10. ANDREW ABBOTT, *The System of Professions* (Chicago: University of Chicago Press, 1988).

11. EMILE DURKHEIM, *Professional Ethics and Civic Morals*, trans. Cornelia Brookfield (Glencoe, Ill.: Free Press, 1958); this highly favorable account of professionalism was first delivered as lectures at Bordeaux in the 1890s. In *The Acquisitive Society* (1922), R. H. TAWNEY also praises the professions as a fortress of disinterestedness in a rapacious society. The first critical view of professionalism was TALCOTT PARSONS' seminal essay 'The Professions and Social Structure' (1939), collected in *Essays in Sociological Theory* (Glencoe, Ill.: Free Press, 1954), pp. 34–49. For recent accounts of

professionalism, see DANIEL BELL, *The Coming of Post-Industrial Society* (New York: Basic Books, 1973); ALVIN GOULDNER, *The Future of Intellectuals and the Rise of the New Class* (New York: Seabury, 1979); IVAN ILLICH, *Disabling Professions* (London: M. Boyars, 1977).

12. See SANDRA GILBERT and SUSAN GUBAR, *The Madwoman in the Attic: The Woman Writer and the Nineteenth-Century Literary Imagination* (New Haven: Yale University Press, 1979), pp. 89–92; ANNETTE KOLODNY, 'A Map for Rereading'; JEAN KENNARD, 'Convention Coverage, or How to Read Your Own Life', *New Literary History*, 13 (1981): 69–88; PAULA TREICHLER, 'Escaping the Sentence', *Tulsa Studies in Women's Literature*, 3 (1984): 61–77; JUDITH FETTERLEY, 'Reading about Reading', in *Gender and Reading*, pp. 147–64. For critiques of this feminist orthodoxy, see JANICE HANEY-PERITZ, 'Monumental Feminism and Literature's Ancestral House', *Women's Studies*, 12 (1986): 113–28; and MARY JACOBUS, 'An Unnecessary Maze of Sign-Reading', in her *Reading Woman: Essays in Feminist Criticism* (New York: Columbia University Press, 1986), pp. 229–48.

13. See, for example, POLLY WYNN ALLEN, *Building Domestic Liberty: Charlotte Perkins Gilman's Architectural Feminism* (Amherst: University of Massachusetts Press, 1988); MARY A. HILL, *Charlotte Perkins Gilman: The Making of a Radical Feminist, 1860–1896* (Philadelphia: Temple University Press, 1980).

14. For an account of the scientific homemaking profession, see JULIE MATTHAE, *An Economic History of Women in America: Women's Work, the Sexual Division of Labor, and the Development of Capitalism* (New York: Schocken, 1982), pp. 157–67.

15. See DOLORES HAYDEN, *The Grand Domestic Revolution: A History of Feminist Designs for American Homes, Neighborhoods, and Cities* (Cambridge: MIT Press, 1981).

16. CHARLOTTE PERKINS GILMAN, *Women and Economics* (Boston: Small, Maynard, 1898), pp. 241–2.

17. CHARLOTTE PERKINS GILMAN, 'The Yellow Wallpaper', *The New England Magazine*, May 1892. Quotation from reprint (Old Westbury, NY: Feminist Press, 1973), 23–4.

18. A diagnosis is usually taken to be more scientific or more objective than a reading. Here, however, I emphasize the degree to which it is governed by interpretive conventions.

19. See WOLFGANG ISER, *The Implied Reader* (Baltimore: Johns Hopkins University Press, 1974), and *The Act of Reading* (Baltimore: Johns Hopkins University Press, 1978). My critique of Iser parallels ROBERT HOLUB, *Reception Theory* (London: Methuen, 1984). For a different critique (challenging Iser's distinction between the determinate and the indeterminate), see STANLEY FISH, 'Why No One is Afraid of Wolfgang Iser', *Diacritics*, 11 (March 1981): 2–13.

20. TONY BENNETT, 'Texts in History: The Determinations of Readings and Their Texts', in *Post-Structuralism and the Question of History*, ed. Derek Attridge, Geoff Bennington, and Robert Young (New York: Cambridge University Press, 1987), pp. 63–81; quotation from p. 74. For a helpful discussion of Iser and Bennett in the context of Bakhtin, see DAVID SHEPHERD, 'Bakhtin and the reader', in *Bakhtin and Cultural Theory*, ed. Ken Hirschkop and David Shepherd (Manchester: Manchester University Press, 1989), pp. 91–108.

21. This is, of course, the paradigm in *Discipline and Punish*, trans. Alan Sheridan (New York: Pantheon, 1979). For critiques of the structural determinism in Foucault and in New Historicism, see FRANK LENTRICCHIA, 'Foucault's Legacy: A New Historicism?' in *Ariel and the Police* (Madison: University of Wisconsin Press, 1988), pp. 86–102; LOUIS MONTROSE, 'Texts and Histories', in *Redrawing the Boundaries of Literary Studies in English*, ed. Giles Gunn and Stephen Greenblatt (New York: MLA, 1991); CAROLYN PORTER, 'Are We Being Historical Yet?' *South Atlantic Quarterly*, 87 (1988): 743–86; EDWARD SAID, *The World, the Text, and the Critic* (Cambridge: Harvard University Press, 1983).

22. Here I thank my students at Rutgers for their spirited (and skeptical) response to my New Historicist reading.

23. CHARLOTTE PERKINS GILMAN, 'Why I Wrote "The Yellow Wallpaper"', *Forerunner*, October 1913, reprinted in *The Charlotte Perkins Gilman Reader*, ed. Ann J. Lane (New York: Pantheon, 1980), p. 20.

24. CHARLOTTE PERKINS GILMAN 'Thoughts and Figgerings', December 1926, quoted in Allen, *Building Domestic Liberty*, p. 145.

25. *Bradwell v. Illinois*, 83 US 130. See LAWRENCE FRIEDMAN, *A History of American Law* (New York: Simon and Schuster, 1985), p. 639; NADINE TAUB and ELIZABETH M. SCHNEIDER, 'Perspectives on Women's Subordination and the Role of Law', in *The Politics of Law*, ed. David Kairys (New York: Pantheon, 1982), p. 125.

26. STARR, *Social Transformation of American Medicine*, p. 117.

27. RAYMOND WILLIAMS, *Marxism and Literature* (Oxford: Oxford University Press, 1977), pp. 121–7.

28. For a suggestive account of the genesis of agency through the noncoherence of discursive formations, see ANTHONY APPIAH, 'Tolerable Falsehoods: Agency and the Interests of Theory', in *Consequences of Theory: Selected Papers from the English Institute, 1987–88*, ed. Jonathan Arac and Barbara Johnson (Baltimore: Johns Hopkins University Press, 1991), pp. 63–90.

29. There is no occasion to discuss race in this paper, but for a stimulating analysis, see SUSAN S. LANSER, 'Feminist Criticism, "The Yellow Wallpaper", and the Politics of Color in America', *Feminist Studies*, 15 (1989): 415–41.

30. The well-known formulation, in its entirety, is 'the historicity of texts and the textuality of history'. See LOUIS MONTROSE, 'Renaissance Literary Studies and the Subject of History', *English Literary Renaissance*, 16 (1986): 5–12.

31. The 'containment' position is most forcefully articulated by STEPHEN GREENBLATT. See his 'Invisible Bullets: Renaissance Authority and Its Subversion', in *Political Shakespeare*, ed. Jonathan Dollimore and Alan Sinfield (Ithaca, 1985), pp. 18–47. For a critique of Greenblatt, see DONALD PEASE, 'Toward a Sociology of Literary Knowledge: Greenblatt, Colonialism, and the New Historicism', in *The Consequences of Theory*, pp. 108–53.

32. TORIL MOI, *Sexual/Textual Politics* (London: Methuen, 1985). For related discussions, see DIANA FUSS, *Essentially Speaking* (New York: Routledge, 1989), and RITA FELSKI, *Beyond Feminist Aesthetics* (Cambridge: Harvard University Press, 1989). See also *Differences*, I (Summer 1989), a special issue entitled 'The Essential Difference: Another Look at Essentialism'.

33. See, for example, the considerable difference between ELAINE SHOWALTER'S earlier book, *A Literature of Their Own* (Princeton: Princeton University Press, 1977) and her more recent work, *The Female Malady* (New York: Pantheon,

1985), or between her 'Feminist Criticism in the Wilderness', *Critical Inquiry*, 8 (1981): 179–206, and her 'Critical Cross-Dressing: Male Feminists and the Woman of the year', *Raritan*, 3 (1983): 130–49.

34. ANNETTE KOLODNY, 'A Map for Rereading', p. 57. Italics in original text.

35. For a persuasive defense of essentialist feminism on the ground of tactical necessity, see PAUL SMITH, *Discerning the Subject* (Minneapolis: University of Minnesota Press, 1988), pp. 132–51. In a different context, GAYATRI SPIVAK has also argued for a *strategic* alliance with essentialism in order to recover the subjectivity written out of conventional historiography. See her 'Subaltern Studies: Deconstructing Historiography', in *In Other Worlds* (New York: Methuen, 1988), pp. 197–221, especially pp. 206–7.

36. EVE KOSOFSKY SEDGWICK, *Between Men: English Literature and Male Homosocial Desire* (New York: Columbia University Press, 1985); ALICE JARDINE, *Gynesis: Configurations of Woman and Modernity* (Ithaca: Cornell University Press, 1985); JUDITH BUTLER, *Gender Trouble: Feminism and the Subversion of Identity* (New York: Routledge, 1990); MARY POOVEY, *Uneven Developments: The Ideological Work of Gender in Mid-Victorian England* (Illinois: University of Chicago Press, 1988).

37. For an interesting critique of *l'écriture féminine* as the metaphorization of difference (and the linking of metaphoricity to binarism), see DOMNA C. STANTON, 'Difference on Trial', in *The Poetics of Gender*, ed. Nancy K. Miller (New York: Columbia University Press, 1986), pp. 157–82.

38. The figure of 'internal difference' is of course a central post-structuralist postulate. For a feminist deployment of this figure (emphasizing class, but addressing the same problems of binarism), see JANE GALLOP, 'Annie Leclerc Writing a Letter, with Vermeer', in *The Poetics of Gender*, pp. 137–56.

39. JOAN WALLACH SCOTT, 'Gender: A Useful Category of Historical Analysis', *American Historical Review*, 81 (1986): 1053–75. See also JOAN KELLY, 'The Social Relations of the Sexes', in her *Women, History, and Theory* (Chicago: University of Chicago Press, 1984), pp. 1–18.

6 Labourers and Voyagers: From the Text to the Reader*

ROGER CHARTIER

One of the most recent developments in reading theory has been the call for a return to history. As the previous chapter suggests, a historicization of readers would avoid a problematic essentializing of 'the reader' and would recognize a necessary difference and diversity. While Dimock approaches the problem from the relatively abstract position of reading theory, however, in the following essay Roger Chartier, much of whose earlier work is concerned with the history of the book as a physical and social phenomenon, argues for research on reading as a material practice. This essay, inspired in part by the work of the historian and ethnologist Michel de Certeau (in particular by de Certeau's chapter on reading reprinted below), seeks to establish the parameters of and possibilities for a history of reading. Through a detailed examination of the implications of such research in a specific historical period (sixteenth- to eighteenth-century France), Chartier suggests possibilities for an analysis of reading practices (silent or aloud, private or public), and the relation of such practices to questions of location and gestures, the physical structure of books, technological developments in printing and distribution, and so on. Chartier positions such a study in relation to the quantitative history and sociology of the book which would elide the 'process by which a text takes on meaning' on the one hand, and to a phenomenological investigation of reading strategies which would elide the role of social and historical factors on the other. Chartier differs from most (literary) reading theorists by inserting a third element into the equation of text–reader: for Chartier, as for Jerome McGann (whose work on nineteenth- and twentieth-century English poetry has been so influential), the book, pamphlet, or other artifact – its material production as well as its distribution networks – should not be ignored in any properly historicized reading theory.

For other programmatic accounts of the possibilities for an integration of work on histories of the book with studies of reading, see

* Reprinted from *Diacritics*, **22**: 2 (1992): 49–61. Translated by J. A. González.

Chartier's essay 'The Practical Impact of Print' (1989), and Robert Darton, 'First Steps Toward a History of Reading' (1990); and see Cathy N. Davidson's *Revolution and the Word* (1986), for an example of the exploitation of such an approach by a literary scholar. Jerome McGann has independently developed a comparable theorization of the importance of audience and book production and dissemination with respect to English nineteenth- and twentieth-century literary texts: see, for example, *Social Values and Poetic Acts* (1988).

> Far from being writers – founders of their own place, heirs to the peasants of earlier ages now working on the soil of language, diggers of wells and builders of houses – readers are voyagers: they move across lands belonging to someone else, like nomads poaching their way across fields they did not write, despoiling the wealth of Egypt to enjoy it themselves. Writing accumulates, stocks up, resists time by the establishment of a place and multiplies its production through the expansionism of reproduction. Reading takes no measures against the erosion of time (one forgets oneself and also forgets), reading does not keep what it acquires, or it does so poorly, and each of the places through which it passes is a repetition of the lost paradise.
>
> (Michel de Certeau, *The Practice of Everyday Life*)

This magnificent text by Michel de Certeau, which contrasts writing (conservative, durable, and fixed) with readings (always on the order of the ephemeral) constitutes at the same time a necessary foundation and a disquieting challenge for any history that intends to inventory and account for a practice – reading – that rarely leaves traces, is scattered into an infinity of singular acts, and purposely frees itself from all the constraints seeking to subdue it. Such a project fundamentally rests on a double assumption: that reading is not already inscribed in the text, with no conceivable difference between the sense assigned to it (by the author, usage, criticism, and so forth) and the interpretation constructable by its readers; and that, correlatively, a text does not exist except for a reader who gives it signification:

> Whether it is a newspaper or Proust, the text has a meaning only through its readers; it changes along with them; it is ordered in accordance with codes of perception that it does not control. It becomes a text only in its relation to the exteriority of the reader, by an interplay of implication and ruses between two sorts of 'expectation' in combination: the expectation that organizes a readable space (a literality), and one that organizes a procedure necessary for the *actualization* of the work (a reading).
>
> (*Practice*, 170–1)[1]

The task of the historian is, then, to reconstruct the variations that differentiate the 'readable space' (the texts in their material and discursive forms) and those which govern the circumstances of their 'actualization' (the readings seen as concrete practices and interpretive procedures).

Based upon de Certeau's suggestions, I would like to indicate some of the stakes, problems, and conditions of possibility for such an historical project. Three poles, generally separated by academic tradition, define the space of this history: first, the analysis of texts, either canonical or ordinary, deciphered in their structures, themes, and aims; second, the history of books and, more generally, of all the objects and forms that carry out the circulation of writing; and finally, the study of practices which in various ways take hold of these objects or forms and produce usages and differentiated meanings. A fundamental question underlies this approach in associating textual criticism, bibliography, and cultural history. That is to understand how in the societies of the ancien régime between the sixteenth and eighteenth centuries the increasing circulation of printed writing transformed the modes of social interaction (*sociabilité*), permitted new ways of thinking, and modified power relations.

Hence the attention placed upon the manner in which (to use the terms of Paul Ricoeur) the encounter between 'the world of the text' and 'the world of the reader' functions (*Time and Narrative*, 3: 6). To reconstruct in its historical dimensions this process of the 'actualization' of texts above all requires us to realize that their meaning depends upon the forms through which they are received and appropriated by their readers (or listeners). Readers, in fact, never confront abstract, idealized texts detached from any materiality. They hold in their hands or perceive objects and forms whose structures and modalities govern their reading or hearing, and consequently the possible comprehension of the text read or heard. In contrast to a purely semantic definition of the text, which characterizes not only structuralist criticism in all its variants but also literary theories concerned with reconstructing the modes of reception of works, it is necessary to maintain that forms produce meaning, and that even a fixed text is invested with new meaning and being (*statut*) when the physical form through which it is presented for interpretation changes. We must also realize that reading is always a practice embodied in gestures, spaces, and habits. Far from the phenomenology of reading, which erases the concrete modality of the act of reading and characterizes it by its effects, postulated as universals, a history of modes of reading must identify the specific dispositions that distinguish communities of readers and traditions of reading. This approach supposes the recognition of a series of contrasts: to begin with, the distinctions between reading competencies. The fundamental but rough separation between the literate and the illiterate does not exhaust the possible differences in the relation to writing. Those who can read texts do not all read them in the same fashion. There is a wide gap' between the most skillful and the least competent readers – those who are obliged to read what they read aloud in order to understand it and who are at ease only with certain textual or typographical forms. Another contrast distinguishes between the norms and conventions of reading, defining for each community of readers the legitimate uses of the book, the forms of reading, and the instruments and procedures of interpretation. Finally, we have the contrast between the expectations and diverse interests that different groups of readers invest in the practice of reading. Upon these determining factors, which govern practice, depend the ways in which texts can be read – and read differently by readers who are equipped with different intellectual tools and maintain quite different relations to writing.

Michel de Certeau illustrated such an approach in describing the specific characteristics of the mystical reader: 'By "mystical readers" I have in mind all the procedures of reading which were suggested or practised in the field of solitary or collective experience designated in the sixteenth and seventeenth centuries as "illuminated", "mystical", or "spiritual"' ('La lecture' 67).[2] In the minor, marginal, and dispersed community that was mysticism's milieu, reading, determined by norms and habits, invested the book with novel functions: to replace the ecclesiastical institution considered to be inadequate; to make a certain kind of speech possible (that of the prayer, the communication with God, the *conversar*); and to indicate the practices through which spiritual experience is constructed. The mystical relation to the book can also be understood as a trajectory in which several 'moments' of reading succeed one another: the establishment of an otherness (*altérité*) which founds the subjective quest; the development of ecstasy (*jouissance*); the marking of bodies physically reacting to the digestion (*manducation*) of the text; and, at the extreme, the interruption of reading, the abandonment of the book, and detachment. Consequently to locate the network of practices and rules of reading specific to diverse communities of readers (spiritual, intellectual, professional, and so forth) is a primary task for any history concerned with understanding, in its differentiations, the pragmatic figure of the 'poaching' reader (*lecteur braconnier*) (see, for example, Jardine and Grafton).

But to read is always to read something. Certainly, to exist at all, the history of reading must be radically distinguished from the history of what is read: 'The reader emerges from the history of the book, in which he was for a long time undifferentiated or indistinct. . . The reader was taken as the effect of the book. Today he has become detached from the books of which he had seemed no more than a shadow. Suddenly this shadow has been released, has taken on a physiognomy, has acquired an independence' (de Certeau, 'La lecture', pp. 66–7). But this founding independence is not an arbitrary license. It is confined by the codes and conventions that govern the practices of a community. It is also confined by the discursive and material forms of the texts read. 'New readers make new texts, and their new meanings are a function of their new forms' (McKenzie, *Bibliography and the Sociology of Texts*, p. 20).

D. F. McKenzie thus points out with great acuity the double network of variations – variations of the dispositions of readers and variations of textual and formal devices – which must be taken into account in any history seeking to recover the shifting and plural meaning of texts. One can make use of this analysis in different ways: by locating the major contrasts distinguishing different modes of reading; by characterizing the most popular reading practices; or by paying attention to the publishing changes that offered old texts to new consumers, changes that made them more numerous and of more modest condition. Such a perspective translates a double dissatisfaction with the history of the book in France over the last twenty or thirty years, which has consistently taken as its objective to measure the unequal distribution of books in the different groups composing the society of the ancien régime. This led to the indispensable construction of factors revealing cultural divisions: for example, for a given location and time, the percentage of property inventories taken after death indicating the possession of books, the classification of collections according to the number of works they contain, or the thematic characterization of private libraries according to the proportion of different bibliographic categories present in them. From this perspective, to conceptualize reading in France between the sixteenth and eighteenth centuries was, above all, to put together series of quantitative data, to establish quantitative thresholds, and to locate how social differences were culturally translated.

This approach, pursued collectively (including by the author of this essay), produced a body of knowledge without which other inquiries would have been impossible. However, it poses a problem of its own. To begin with, it rests on a strictly sociographic conception which implicitly postulates that cultural separations are necessarily organized according to a preexisting social division. I believe it is necessary to challenge the analytic model which links differences in cultural practices with social oppositions constructed *a priori* – either on the scale of macroscopic contrasts (between the dominant and the dominated, between the elite and the people) or on a scale of finer differentiations (for example, between social groups hierarchized by distinctions of status or profession and levels of wealth).

Cultural separations are not necessarily ordered only according to a single grid of social divisions, conceived as determining the unequal possession of objects and the difference between behaviors. The perspective must be reversed to outline, first of all, the social areas where each corpus of texts and each variety of printed materials circulates. To start out thus from objects, and not from classes or groups, brings us to the realization that French sociocultural history has for too long been based on an incomplete conception of the social. In privileging only socioprofessional classifications, it has forgotten that other principles of differentiation, also fully social, could explain cultural divisions with greater pertinence. Thus there are also considerations of gender or generation, religious belief, community membership, academic or group traditions, and so on.

In another register, the history of the book in its social and serial definition sought to characterize cultural configurations according to categories of texts considered specific to them. Such an operation proves to be doubly reductive. For one thing, it simply equates the identification of differences to inequalities of distribution; and for another, it ignores the process by which a text takes on meaning for those who read it. Against these claims it is necessary to propose several modifications. The first of these situates the recognition of the most deeply embedded social divisions in the contrasting uses of shared material. More than we have tended to acknowledge, in the societies of the ancien régime it is the same texts which are taken up by readers from the popular classes and by those who are not. Sometimes readers of humble conditions owned books that were not particularly aimed at them (this was the case of Menocchio, the Friulian miller: of Jamerey Duval, the shepherd from Lorraine: and of Ménétra, the Parisian glazier: see Ginzburg, Hébrard, and Ménétra). Or sometimes creative and shrewd booksellers put within the reach of a broader clientele texts that previously had not circulated except in the narrow world of the wealthy and well read (as was the case with Castilian and Catalan *pliegos sueltos*, English chapbooks, or the collection known in France under the generic term Bibliothèque Bleue). What is essential, then, is to understand how the same texts could be diversely apprehended, handled, and understood.

The second modification is to reconstruct the networks of practices that organize the historically and socially differentiated modes of access to texts. Reading is not only an abstract operation of the intellect: it puts the body into play and is inscribed within a particular space, in a relation to the self or to others. This is why attention should particularly be paid to ways of reading that have been obliterated in our contemporary world: for example reading out loud in its double function – communicating that which is written to those who do not know how to decipher it, and binding together the interconnected forms of sociability which are all figures of the private sphere (the intimacy of the family, the conviviality of social life, the cooperation of scholars:

connivence lettré). A history of reading, then, cannot limit itself only to the genealogy of our contemporary manner of reading – in silence and by sight. It must equally, perhaps above all, take on the task of discovering forgotten gestures and habits that have now disappeared. The stakes are important because they reveal not only the remote peculiarity of traditionally shared practices, but also the specific structures of texts composed for uses that are no longer those of their readers today. Often in the sixteenth and seventeenth centuries, the implicit reading of a text, literary or not, was construed as a vocalization and its 'reader' as the auditor of read speech (*parole lectrice*). Thus addressed to the ear as much as the eye, the work played with forms and processes designed to submit the written word to the requirements of oral 'performance'. From the motifs of the *Quijote* to the structures of texts published in the Bibliothèque Bleue, there are numerous examples of this link maintained between the text and the voice (see Chartier, 'Leisure and Sociability').

'Whatever they may do, authors do not write books. Books are not written at all. They are manufactured by scribes and other artisans, by mechanics and other engineers, and by printing presses and other machines' (Stoddard, p. 4). This remark introduces the third modification that I would like to propose. Against the representation developed by literature itself and repeated by the most quantitative histories of the book, according to which the text exists in itself, separated from all materiality, we must insist that there is no text outside the material structure in which it is given to be read or heard. Thus there is no comprehension of writing, whatever it may be, which does not depend in part upon the forms in which it comes to its reader. Hence the necessary distinction between two groups of apparatuses: those which reveal strategies of writing and the intentions of the author, and those which are a result of the publishers' decisions or the constraints of the printing house. Authors do not write books. Rather they write texts which become objects copied, handwritten, etched, printed, and today computerized. This gap, which is rightly the space in which meaning is constructed, has too often been forgotten not only by classical literary history, which thinks of the work in itself as an abstract text for which the typographic forms are unimportant, but even by *Rezeptionstheorie*. Despite its desire to historicize the experience that readers have with works, *Rezeptionstheorie* postulates a pure and immediate relation between the 'signals' emitted by the text (which plays with accepted literary conventions) and the 'horizon of expectation' of the public to which they are addressed. In such a perspective the 'effect produced' does not depend at all upon the material forms the text takes.[3] Yet these forms contribute fully to shaping the anticipations of the reader *vis-à-vis* the text and to the production of new publics or innovative uses for it.

We thus return to the triangle with which we began, defined by the intricate relation between text, book, and reader. The variations of this relation outline some elementary figures in the connection between 'readable space' and 'actualization' of the text. The first variation considers a linguistically stable text presented in printed forms which themselves change. In studying the innovations occurring in the publication of the plays of William Congreve at the turn of the seventeenth and eighteenth centuries, McKenzie was able to demonstrate how some apparently insignificant formal transformations – the change from quarto to octavo formats, the numbering of scenes, the presence of an ornament between each scene, the list of the dramatis personae at the beginning of them, the marginal notation of the name of the character speaking, the indication of entrances and exits – had a major effect on the status of the works. A new readability was created by a format easier to handle and by a layout that reproduced in the book something of the movement of the actual production, thus breaking with the ancient conventions of printing plays with no rendering of their theatricality. A new manner of reading the same text resulted, but also a new horizon of reception. The forms used in the octavo edition of 1710, borrowed from those used in France for the edition of plays, gave an unofficial legitimacy to Congreve's plays, which from then on were inscribed in a classic canon. This is what could induce an author to refine his style in order to make the works conform to their new 'typographic' dignity (see McKenzie, 'Typography and Meaning'). Variations of the most formal modes of textual presentation can modify the register of reference and the mode of interpretation.

The same is true on a larger scale concerning the principal alteration of the layout in which texts were presented between the sixteenth and eighteenth centuries – what Henri-Jean Martin has termed 'the definitive triumph of white over black' (see Martin and Delmas, pp. 295–9): in other words, the opening up of the page through the multiplication of paragraphs that broke the uninterrupted continuity of the text common in the Renaissance and the indentations which, through varying the left margin, make the order of discourse immediately visible. A new reading of the same works or of the same genres was consequently suggested by their new publishers – a reading that fragments texts into small and separate units, an approach that reinforces the argument, whether intellectual or discursive, by a visual articulation of the page.

This textual segmentation (*découpage*) had fundamental implications when it was applied to sacred texts. The story of Locke's anxiety regarding the practice of dividing the text of the Bible into chapter and verse is well known. For him such a division presented a considerable risk of obliterating the powerful coherence of the Word of God. Referring to the Epistle of Paul, he thus noted that 'not only Common People take the Verses usually for distinct Aphorisms, but even Men of more advanc'd Knowledge in reading them, lose very much of the strength and force of the Coherence and the Light that depends on it'. The effects of such a division he thought disastrous, authorizing each sect or religious body to found its legitimacy on the fragments of the Scriptures that supported its views:

> If a Bible was printed as it should be, and as the several Parts of it were writ, in continued Discourse where the Argument is continued, I doubt not that the several Parties would complain of it, as an Innovation, and a dangerous Change in the publishing of those holy Books. . . . He [i.e., the member of a particular sect] need but be furnished with Verses of Sacred Scriptures, containing Words and Expressions that are but flexible . . . and his System that has appropriated them to the Orthodoxie of His Church, makes them immediately strong and irrefragable Arguments for his Opinion. This is the Benefit of loose Sentences and Scripture crumbled into Verses, which quickly turn into independent Aphorism.
> (Quoted in McKenzie, *Bibliography and the Sociology of Texts*, pp. 46–7)

The second figure in our triangle of relations is that in which the text passes from one published form to another order, transforming the text itself and constituting a new public. This is clearly the case with the body of texts that constitute the catalogue of the Bibliothèque Bleue. If this collection has occupied French historians for a long time, it is because it seems to furnish direct access to the 'popular culture' of the ancien régime, a culture supposedly expressed and nourished by texts distributed 'en masse' to the humblest readers.[4] But such is not the case for three essential reasons. To begin with, it is clear that the texts which formed the stock of French book peddlers were almost never written for this purpose. The Bibliothèque Bleue drew from the repertoire of already published texts those which appeared to be best suited to attract a large public. Hence two necessary precautions: first, not to take the texts put into the books included in the Bibliothèque Bleue as 'popular' in themselves, because in fact they belonged to a wide variety of genres drawn from learned literature; and second, to consider that these texts generally had already had a published existence, sometimes quite lengthy, before entering the repertoire of 'popular' books (*livres pour le plus grand nombre*). The study of titles in this 'popular' catalogue has moreover permitted registering how the most formal and material arrangements can inscribe in themselves the indices of cultural differentiation. Indeed the fundamental specificity of the Bibliothèque

Bleue is in the editorial interventions it imposed upon texts in order to make them readable by the large clientele at which they were aimed. All this work of adaptation – which shortened texts, simplified them, cut them up, and illustrated them – was determined according to the manner in which booksellers conceived the competencies and expectations of their customers. Thus the very structures of the book were governed by what the publishers thought to be the mode of reading of the clientele they were targeting.

Such a reading always required visible references, and this is my third assertion. Thus the anticipatory titles or the recapitulative summaries or even the wood engravings functioned as protocols of reading or sites of memory (*lieux de memoire*). Such a reading was comfortable only with brief, self-contained sequences, separated from one another – a reading that appears to have been satisfied with only minimal coherence. This manner of reading is not at all that of the lettered elite of the time – even if certain notables did not disdain to buy books from the Bibliothèque Bleue. These texts assumed their readers' foreknowledge. By the recurrence of highly coded forms, by the repetition of similar motifs from one title to another, and by the reuse of the same images, the knowledge of texts already encountered (either read or heard) was mobilized to help in the comprehension of new readings. The catalogue of the Bibliothèque Bleue thus organized a form of reading that was more recognition or recapitulation than discovery. It is therefore in the formal particularity of the Bibliothèque Bleue publications and in the modifications they impose on texts that they possess their 'popular' character.

In proposing this reevaluation of the Bibliothèque Bleue, my intention has been not only to better understand what was the single most powerful instrument of the acculturation to writing in ancien régime France.[5] It is also to argue that the detection of sociocultural differentiations and the study of formal and material devices, far from excluding one another, are necessarily linked. This is true not only because the forms are modeled on the expectations and competencies attributed to the public at which they are aimed, but above all because the works and objects produce the space of their social reception much more than they are produced by already concretized divisions. Recently Lawrence W. Levine provided a persuasive demonstration of this fact (see his 'William Shakespeare and the American People' and *Highbrow/Lowbrow*). Analyzing the manner in which the plays of Shakespeare were produced in America in the nineteenth century (that is to say, combined with other genres: melodrama, farce, circus, dance), he showed how this type of representation created a diverse public – 'popular' in the sense that it did not reduce down to just the lettered elite but actively participated in the production through its emotions and reactions. At the end of the century the strict separation established between genres, styles, and cultural sites dispersed this universal public, reserving a 'legitimate' Shakespeare for the few and relegating the other versions to the status of 'popular' entertainment. In establishing this 'bifurcated culture', transformations in the forms of presentation of a Shakespeare play (but also of symphony music, opera, or works of art) had a decisive role. Following a time of cultural mixing and sharing came another, in which the process of cultural distinction produced social separation. The traditional devices of representation in the American Shakespearean repertoire are thus of the same order as the 'typographic' transformations imposed by the publishers of the Bibliothèque Bleue upon the texts of which they took possession: both aim, in effect, to inscribe the text in a cultural matrix that was not its original destination, thereby permitting readings, understandings, and uses possibly disqualified by other intellectual practices.

These two cases lead us to the consideration of cultural differentiations not as the translation of already concretized and static divisions, but as the effect of a dynamic process. On the one hand, the transformation of forms and devices by which a text is presented authorizes new appropriations and consequently creates new publics for and uses of it. On the other hand, the sharing of the same objects by the whole of society gives rise to the search for new differences, suited to marking the divisions that were preserved. The trajectory of printed works in the French ancien régime bears witness to this situation. We could say that the distinctions between the manners of reading were progressively reinforced to the degree that printed works became less rare, less threatened by seizure, and more ordinary. Whereas the simple possession of a book had for a long time signified a cultural division in itself, with the conquests of printing it is, rather, specific reading attitudes and typographical objects which progressively take on this function. Against refined readings and carefully made books were henceforth counterposed hastily printed material and unskilled interpreters. But both groups, let us recall, often read the same texts, for which plural and contradictory significations were produced according to their contrasting uses. The question consequently becomes one of selection: why do certain texts lend themselves better than others to these continuing and recurrent uses (see Harlan)? Or at least, why do the makers (*faiseurs*) of books consider them capable of reaching a very diverse public? The answer lies in subtle relations between the structures of the works themselves, unequally suited to reappropriations, and the multiple determinations, as much institutional as formal, that establish their possible 'application' (in the phenomenological sense) to very different historical situations.

In the relation between the text, its printed form, and reading there is a third figure produced as soon as a text, fixed in its form and linguistically stable, is taken up by new readers who read differently from their predecessors. 'A book changes by the fact that it remains changeless while the world changes' (Bourdieu and Chartier, p. 236) – or, to make the proposition compatible with the scale of our reflection here, let us say, 'when its mode of being read changes'. The remark serves to justify the project of a history of the practices of reading, which attempts to mark the major contrasts that can give diverse meaning to the same text. It is surely time to reexamine three fundamental oppositions that have long been considered incontestable: to begin with, between a reading in which comprehension presupposes a required oral articulation, whether aloud or barely vocalized (*à basse voix*), and another species of reading that is purely visual (see Saenger, 'Silent Reading' and 'Physiologie de la lecture'). Let us recall (even if its chronology is questionable) a fundamental assertion of Michel de Certeau that associates the freedom of the reader with silent reading:

> In the last three centuries reading has become a gesture of the eye. It is no longer accompanied, as it used to be, by the murmur of vocal articulation, nor by the movement of a muscular mastication (*manducation*). To read without speaking the words or at least muttering them is a modern experience, unknown for millennia. In earlier times, the reader interiorized the text: he made his voice the body of the other; he was its actor. Today the text no longer imposes its own rhythm on the subject, it no longer manifests itself through the reader's voice. This withdrawal of the body, which is the condition of its autonomy, puts the text at a distance. It is the reader's *habeas corpus*.
>
> (*Practice of Everyday Life*, pp. 175–6; translation modified)

The second of these oppositions contrasts 'intensive' reading applied only to a few texts and sustained by hearing and memory with 'extensive' reading – consuming many texts, passing without constraint from one to another, granting little consecration (*sacralité*) to the object read (see Engelsing and Schön). Finally, the third of these oppositions is between the reading of intimacy, enclosure, and solitude – considered to be one of the essential foundations of the private sphere – and collective readings, whether orderly or unruly, in communal spaces (see Ariès, 'Introduction'; and Chartier, 'The Practical Impact of Writing').

In outlining a preliminary chronological thread, which marks as major transformations the progressive advances of silent reading in the Middle Ages and the entry into the world of extensive reading at the end of the eighteenth century, these now classic contrasts suggest several reflections. Some of these tend to complicate the oppositional pairs presented: shifting attention to the model's inaccuracies, complicating criteria that too rigidly differentiate styles of reading, reversing the image of an automatic connection between the collective and the 'popular' or between the elite and the private (see Darnton). Others invite the articulation of three series of transformations whose effects have often been imperfectly sorted out: first, the 'revolutions' that have occurred in the techniques of textual reproduction (with, most importantly, the passage from 'scribal culture' to 'print culture'); second, the changes in the forms of books themselves (the replacement of the *volumen* by the *codex* in the first centuries of the Christian era is the most fundamental; but others, certainly more subtle, alter the visual layout of the printed page between the sixteenth and eighteenth centuries – see Laufer); and finally, major alterations in reading abilities and in reading modes. These different evolutions do not proceed at the same pace and are not at all organized around the same turning points. The most interesting question posed to and by the history of reading today is without doubt that of the conjunction between these three sets of changes: technological, formal, and cultural.

The response we give to this question depends upon a re-evaluation of the trajectories and cultural divisions that characterize the society of the ancien régime. More than has been recognized, these were themselves ordered according to the role played by printed works. For a long time their distribution was measured by two restricted series of criteria: one, based upon the proportion of signatures, which sought to establish percentages of literacy and hence to estimate variations in the ability to read according to period, place, gender, and social situation; and another which, by inventorying the catalogues of libraries established by notaries or booksellers, sought to establish the circulation of books and the traditions of reading. But neither in ancien régime societies nor in our own can access to printing be reduced simply to the possession of books: not all books read are privately owned, and not all privately owned printed matter is in the form of books. Moreover written material occupies the very heart of the culture of the illiterate – in rituals, in public spaces, and in workplaces (see Chartier, *The Culture of Print*). Thanks to speech which deciphers it and to images which accentuate it, it is made accessible even to those who are incapable of reading or who cannot by themselves have more than a rudimentary understanding of the text. Rates of literacy, then, do not give a fair indication of familiarity with the written – particularly because in more traditional communities, where instruction in reading and instruction in writing were dissociated and successive, there were many individuals (especially among women) who left school knowing how to read, at least a little, but not how to write (see Spufford). Similarly, the private possession of books cannot adequately indicate the frequency with which printed texts were utilized by those who were too poor to have their own 'library'.

Even if it is impossible to establish the number of the reading-literate (*lisants*) who did not know how to set their names on paper, or how many possessed not a single book (at least none worth mentioning by a notary establishing the inventory of a decedent's possessions) but could still read posters and broadsheets, pamphlets and chapbooks, it is necessary to postulate that there were many such readers in order to comprehend the impact of print on the traditional forms of a culture that was still largely oral, gestural, and iconographic. The overlaps between the two modes of expression and communication are multiple: to begin with overlaps between writing and gesture, not only was writing at the center of everyday celebrations such as religious ceremonies, but numerous texts attempt to efface themselves as discourse and to produce, in practice, behavior conforming to social or religious norms. Such is the case, for example, of conduct books (*traités de civilité*), whose aim was to help individuals internalize the rules of worldly politesse or Christian decency (see Patrizi and Chartier). There is equally an interweaving between speech and writing, in two ways. First, texts intended by their author and, more often, by their publisher to reach the most popular audience often contain formulas or motifs that are themselves drawn from the oral tradition of tales and recitations. The writing styles in certain occasional pieces that plagiarize the speaking style of storytellers or the variations introduced in the fairy tales in the Bibliothèque Bleue, themselves originally drawn from written compilations, are good examples of the emergence of orality in print (see Chartier, 'The Hanged Woman Miraculously Saved' and Velay-Vallantin). Second, as mentioned above, a number of 'readers' do not understand texts except through the mediation of a voice. To understand the specificity of this relation to writing thus presumes that all reading is not necessarily individual, silent, and solitary but, on the contrary, marks the importance and diversity of a practice now largely lost – reading aloud.

From this initial assertion, which registers the powerful penetration of printed culture into the societies of the ancien régime, several others follow. It allows us to understand the importance given to writing, and the objects in which it is found, by the authorities whose intentions were to regulate behavior and to shape minds. Whence the pedagogical, acculturating, and disciplinary role attributed to texts placed in circulation for broad readerships; and the surveillance exercised over printing, subjected to a censor who was supposed to eliminate all that might endanger order, religion, or morals. Concerning these constraints, Michel de Certeau urges us to recognize both their power – all the stronger because of the strength of the institution that decreed them ('The creativity of the reader grows as the institution that controls him declines: *Practice of Everyday Life*, p. 172) – and their modalities, ranging from brutal prohibition to authorized interpretation, from exterior disciplines (administrative, judicial, inquisitorial, academic, and so forth) to the mechanisms which, in the book itself, seek to restrain the freedom of the reader.

Out of practices of writing and diverse treatments of printing, traditional texts constructed representations in which we can recognize the divisions that were considered decisive by the producers of books. These perceptions are fundamental because they found the strategies of writing and printing, regulated by the competencies and expectations of the different target audiences. They thereby acquire an efficacy of which the trace can be found in the protocols of explicit reading, in the forms given to typographic objects, or in the transformations that modified a text as soon as it was offered to new readers in a new published format. It is thus from these diverse representations of reading and from the dichotomies constructed in the modern age (between the reading of a text and the reading of an image, between literate reading and unskilled reading, between intimate reading and communal reading) that an attempt must be made to understand the agency and the uses of those printed texts, more modest than the book, but also more pervasive – texts ranging from individual images and posters (always accompanied by words) to occasional pieces and pamphlets like those found in the Bibliothèque Bleue (often illustrated with images). The representations of traditional ways of reading and of their differences from each other – revealed on the practical level by the transformations of printed materials (*mises en imprimé*) or in their normative purposes (*finalité*) by their literary, pictorial, or autobiographical stagings (*mises en scène*) – constitute the essential data for an archeology of reading practices. Yet while they may articulate the contrasts most apparent to the minds of their contemporaries, they should not be allowed to mask other divisions which may have been less clearly perceived. For example, it is certain that there are many practices that reverse the very terms of the frequently described opposition between readings in bourgeois or aristocratic solitude on the one hand, and mass communal readings on the other. Indeed, reading aloud (for others to listen to) remained an enduring, unifying element in elite society, and, conversely, printing penetrated to the very heart of intimate popular culture, capturing in unpretentious objects (not all of which were books) the traces of an important moment of existence, the memory of an emotion, the sign of an identity. Contrary to classic imagery – in fact, a product of the modern age – 'the people' are not always plural, and it is necessary to rediscover in their secret solitude the modest practices of those who cut out images of occasional works, colored printed etchings, and read books from the Bibliothèque Bleue for their personal pleasure.

Attached to a particular country (France between the sixteenth and eighteenth centuries) and having chosen a specific problem (the effects of the penetration of printed works into popular culture – *la culture du plus grand nombre*), the approach suggested in this text (and at work in several others) attempts to make functional two propositions of Michel de Certeau. The first reminds us, against all the reductions that cancel out the creative and inventive force of practices, that reading is never totally constrained and that it cannot be recursively deduced from the texts to which it is applied. The second emphasizes that the tactics of readers, infiltrating the 'special space' (*lieu propre*) produced by the strategies of writing, obey certain rules, logics, and models. Thus is articulated the founding paradox of any history of reading, which must postulate the freedom of a practice of which, broadly, it can only grasp the determinations. To construct communities of readers as 'interpretive communities' (to use the expression of Stanley Fish), to detect how material forms affect meaning, to locate social difference more in real practices than in statistical distributions – such are the paths outlined in our attempt to understand historically this 'silent production' which is the activity of reading.

Notes

The translator and editors gratefully acknowledge support for the translation of this essay provided by the Center for Cultural Studies, University of California, Santa Cruz.

1. On the reading–writing duo in this book see the article by ANNE-MARIE CHARTIER and JEAN HÉBRARD, 'L'invention du quotidien, une lecture, des usages', *Le Débat*, **49** (March–April 1988): 97–108.

2. The suggestions in this essay are reconsidered in one of MICHEL DE CERTEAU's major works, *La Fable mystique* (Paris: Gallimard, 1982), in particular the third part, 'La Scène de l'énonciation' (pp. 209–73). This work has recently been translated into English: *The Mystic Fable*, trans. Michael B. Smith (Chicago: University of Chicago Press, 1992).

3. For a programmatic definition of *Rezeptionstheorie, see* HANS ROBERT JAUSS, *Literaturgeschichte als Provokation* (Frankfurt-am-Main: Suhrkamp, 1974).

4. The fundamental but contested study on this issue is by ROBERT MANDROU, *De la culture populaire aux XVIIe et XVIIIe siècles.* Among the criticisms addressed to this book is DE CERTEAU. 'La beauté du mort'; reconsidered in DE CERTEAU, *La Culture au pluriel* (pp. 49–80).

5. See CHARTIER, 'The Bibliothèque Bleue and Popular Reading' and 'The Literature of Roguery in the Bibliothèque Bleue' in *The Cultural Uses of Print in Early Modern France* (pp. 240–64 and pp. 265–342).

Works cited

ARIÈS, PHILIPPE 'Introduction', *Passions of the Renaissance*. Vol. 3 of *A History of Private Life*. Ed. Roger Chartier. Cambridge: Harvard University Press, 1989, pp. 1–11.

BOURDIEU, PIERRE and ROGER CHARTIER 'La Lecture: Une pratique culturelle', *Pratiques de la lecture*. Ed. Roger Chartier. Marseille: Rivages, 1985.

CERTEAU, MICHEL DE *La Culture au pluriel*. 1974. 2nd edn Paris: Bourgois, 1980.

—'La Lecture absolue (Théorie et pratique des mystiques chrétiens: XVIe–XVIIe siècles)', *Problèmes actuels de la lecture*. Ed. Lucien Dällenbach and Jean Ricardou. Paris: Clancier-Guénaud, 1982.

— *The Practice of Everyday Life*. Trans. Steven F. Rendall. Berkeley: University of California Press, 1984.

CERTEAU, MICHEL DE, DOMINIQUE JULIA and JACQUES REVEL 'La Beauté du mort: Le concept de "culture populaire"', *Politique aujourd'hui* (December 1970): 3–23.

CHARTIER, ROGER (ed.) *The Culture of Print: Power and the Uses of Print in Early Modern Europe*. Cambridge: Polity; Ithaca: Cornell University Press, 1989.

— *The Cultural Uses of Print in Early Modern France*. Princeton: Princeton University Press, 1987.

— 'The Hanged Woman Miraculously Saved: An Occasional', *Culture of Print*, pp. 59–91.

— 'Leisure and Sociability: Reading Aloud in Early Modern Europe', *Urban Life in the Renaissance*. Ed. S. Zimmermann and R.F.E Weissman. Newark: University of Delaware Press; London: Associated University Press, 1989.

— 'The Practical Impact of Writing', *Passions of the Renaissance*. Vol. 3 of *A History of Private Life*. Ed. Roger Chartier. Cambridge: Harvard University Press, 1989.

DARNTON, ROBERT 'First Steps toward a History of Reading', *Australian Journal of French Studies*, **23**, 1 (1986): 5–30.

ENGELSING, ROLF 'Die Perioden de Lesergeschichte in die Neuzeit. Das statistische Ausmass und die soziokulturelle Debeutung der Lektüre', *Archiv für Geschichte des Buchwesen*, **10** (1970): 945–1002.

GINZBURG, CARLO *The Cheese and the Worms: the Cosmos of a Sixteenth-Century Miller*. Trans. John and Anne Tedeschi. Baltimore: Johns Hopkins University Press, 1980.

HARLAN, DAVID 'Intellectual History and the Return of Literature', *American Historical Review*, **94** (June 1989): 581–609.

HÉBRARD, JEAN 'Comment Valentin Jamerey-Duval apprit-il à lire? L'autodidaxie exemplaire?' *Pratiques de la lecture*. Ed. Roger Chartier. Marseille: Rivages, 1985.

JARDINE, LISA and ANTHONY GRAFTON '"Studied for Actions": How Gabriel Harvey Read his Livy', *Past and Present*, 129 (November 1990): 30–78.

LAUFER, ROGER 'L'espace visuel du livre ancien', Martin and Chartier, 1, pp. 478–97.

— 'Les espaces du livre', Martin and Chartier, 2: 128–39.

LEVINE, LAWRENCE W. *Highbrow/Lowbrow: The Emergence of Cultural Hierarchy in America*. Cambridge: Harvard University Press, 1988.

—'William Shakespeare and the American People: A Study in Cultural Transformation', *American Historical Review*, 89 (February 1984): 34–66.

MANDROU, ROBERT *De la culture populaire aux XVIIe et XVIIIe siècles: La bibliothèque bleue de Troyes*. 1964. Paris: Stock, 1974.

MARTIN, HENRI-JEAN and BRUNO DELMAS *Histoire et pouvoirs de l'écrit*. Paris: Perrin, 1988.

MARTIN, HENRI-JEAN and ROGER CHARTIER (eds) *Histoire de l'Edition française*. 2 vols, Paris: Promodis, 1982–84.

MCKENZIE, D.F. *Bibliography and the Sociology of Texts*. Panizzi Lectures, 1985. London: British Library, 1986.

—'Typography and Meaning: The Case of William Congreve', *Buch und Buchandel in Europa im achtzehnten Jahrhundert*. Ed. Giles Barber and Bernhard Fabian. Hamburg: Ernest Hauswedell, 1981.

MÉNÉTRA, JACQUES-LOUIS *Journal de ma vie: Jacques-Louis Ménétra, compagnon vitrier au 18e siècle*. Ed. Daniel Roche. Paris: Montalba, 1982.

PATRIZI, GIORGIO 'Il libro del Cortegiano e la trattatistica sul comportamento', *La prosa*. Part 2 of *Le Forme del testo*. Vol. 3 of *Letteratura italiana*. Torino: Einaudi, 1984: pp. 855–90.

PATRIZI, GIORGIO and ROGER CHARTIER 'From Texts to Manners: a Concept and its Books: *Civilité* between Aristocratic Distinction and Popular Appropriation' Chartier, *Cultural Uses of Print*, pp. 71–109.

RICOEUR, PAUL *Time and Narrative*. Trans. Kathleen McLaughlin and David Pellauer. 3 vols. Chicago: University of Chicago Press, 1984–88.

SAENGER, PAUL 'Physiologie de la lecture et séparation des mots', *Annales E.S.C.* (1989): 939–52.

—'Silent Reading: Its Impact on Late Medieval Script and Society', *Viator*, 13 (1982): 367–414.

SCHÖN, ERICH *Der Verlust der Sinnlichkeit oder Die Verwandlungen des Lesers: Mentalitätswandel um 1800*. Stuttgart: Klett-Cotta, 1987.

SPUFFORD, MARGARET 'First Steps in Literacy: The Reading and Writing Experiences of the Humblest Seventeenth-Century Autobiographers', *Social History*, 4, 3 (1979): 407–35.

STODDARD, ROGER E. 'Morphology and the Book from an American Perspective', *Printing History*, 9, 1 (1987): 2–14.

VELAY-VALLANTIN, CATHERINE 'Tales as a Mirror: Perrault in the Bibliothèque Bleue', Chartier, *Culture of Print*, pp. 92–135.

7   Reading as Poaching*

MICHEL DE CERTEAU

The following chapter is from *The Practice of Everyday Life* (1984), in which Michel de Certeau discusses the tactics of apparently power-less consumers – tactics involved in such 'ordinary' activities as re-membering, telling stories, talking, dwelling, cooking and reading. De Certeau is interested in the ways in which ordinary men and women – as opposed to experts, the clerisy, professionals – are able to transform, to re-use, to reappropriate and even to reinvent the func-tion and form of the product for which they act as apparently passive consumers. In terms of reading, de Certeau's ethnographic and socio-logical investigation of reading tactics seeks to dissolve the distinction between literary and non-literary reading and to suggest ways in which non-professional, non-clerical readings and meanings are con-stituted. In an evocative metaphor, de Certeau figures reading as an act of 'poaching' to suggest an unauthorized appropriation of the proper, of the property, of texts. For de Certeau, reading involves tac-tics of wandering, of improvisation: for him, it constitutes an 'ephem-eral dance' across textual space, an illicit, even secretive reinvention of the text – reading as resistance. In this way, de Certeau seeks to de-scribe a politicization of reading which has already and necessarily occurred, a liberation of the text and of reading from the 'strong-box' of meaning, of *author*ized reading.

By the time of his death, in 1986, de Certeau's work, which itself constantly transgresses disciplinary borders, had become widely in-fluential in many academic fields, including history, sociology, eth-nography, literary and cultural studies, and so on. See the recent special issue of *Diacritics* (22: 2, summer 1992) on de Certeau's work; on reading, in particular, see Chartier's essay (Chapter 6). The impli-cations of de Certeau's work in *The Practice of Everyday Life* for literary studies have been most fully exploited by Ross Chambers in his re-cent book *Room for Maneuver* (1991).

---

* Reprinted from *The Practice of Everyday Life*, trans. Steven Rendall (Berkeley: University of California Press, 1984), pp. 165–76.

> To arrest the meanings of words once and for all, that is what Terror
> wants.
>
> (Jean-François Lyotard, *Rudiments païens*)

Some time ago, Alvin Toffler announced the birth of a 'new species' of
humanity, engendered by mass artistic consumption. This
species-in-formation, migrating and devouring its way through the
pastures of the media, is supposed to be defined by its 'self mobility'.[1] It
returns to the nomadic ways of ancient times, but now hunts in artificial
steppes and forests.

This prophetic analysis bears, however, only on the masses that
consume 'art'. An inquiry made in 1974 by a French government agency
concerned with cultural activities[2] shows to what extent this production
only benefits an elite. Between 1967 (the date of a previous inquiry made
by another agency, the INSEE) and 1974, public monies invested in the
creation and development of cultural centers reinforced the already
existing cultural inequalities among French people. They multiplied the
places of expression and symbolization, but, in fact, the same categories
profit from this expansion: culture, like money, 'goes only to the rich'.
The masses rarely enter these gardens of art. But they are caught and
collected in the nets of the media, by television (capturing nine out of ten
people in France), by newspapers (eight out of ten), by books (seven out
of ten, of whom two read a great deal and, according to another survey
made in autumn 1978, five read more than they used to),[3] etc. Instead of
an increasing nomadism, we thus find a 'reduction' and a confinement:
consumption, organized by this expansionist grid takes on the
appearance of something done by sheep progressively immobilized and
'handled' as a result of the growing mobility of the media as they
conquer space. The consumers settle down, the media keep on the move.
The only freedom supposed to be left to the masses is that of grazing on
the ration of simulacra the system distributes to each individual.

This is precisely the idea I oppose: such an image of consumers is
unacceptable.

The ideology of 'informing' through books

This image of the 'public' is not usually made explicit. It is nonetheless
implicit in the 'producers' ' claim to *inform* the population, that is, to
'give form' to social practices. Even protests against the vulgarization/
vulgarity of the media often depend on an analogous pedagogical claim;
inclined to believe that its own cultural models are necessary for the
people in order to educate their minds and elevate their hearts, the elite

upset about the 'low level' of journalism or television always assumes that the public is moulded by the products imposed on it. To assume that is to misunderstand the act of 'consumption'. This misunderstanding assumes that 'assimilating' necessarily means 'becoming similar to' what one absorbs, and not 'making something similar' to what one is, making it one's own, appropriating or reappropriating it. Between these two possible meanings, a choice must be made, and first of all on the basis of a story whose horizon has to be outlined. 'Once upon a time. . . .'

In the eighteenth century, the ideology of the Enlightenment claimed that the book was capable of reforming society, that educational popularization could transform manners and customs, that an elite's products could, if they were sufficiently widespread, remodel a whole nation. This myth of Education[4] inscribed a theory of consumption in the structures of cultural politics. To be sure, by the logic of technical and economic development that it mobilized, this politics was led to the present system that inverts the ideology that formerly sought to spread 'Enlightenment'. The means of diffusion are now dominating the ideas they diffuse. The medium is replacing the message. The 'pedagogical' procedures for which the educational system was the support have developed to the point of abandoning as useless or destroying the professional 'body' that perfected them over the span of two centuries: today, they make up the apparatus which, by realizing the ancient dream of enclosing *all* citizens and *each one* in particular, gradually destroys the goal, the convictions, and the educational institutions of the Enlightenment. In short, it is as though the *form* of Education's establishment had been too fully realized, by eliminating the very *content* that made it possible and which from that point on loses its social utility. But all through this evolution, the idea of producing a society by a 'scriptural' system has continued to have as its corollary the conviction that although the public is more or less resistant, it is moulded by (verbal or iconic) writing, that it becomes similar to what it receives, and that it is *imprinted* by and like the text which is imposed on it.

This text was formerly found at school. Today, the text is society itself. It takes urbanistic, industrial, commercial, or televised forms. But the mutation that caused the transition from educational archeology to the technocracy of the media did not touch the assumption that consumption is essentially passive – an assumption that is precisely what should be examined. On the contrary, this mutation actually reinforced this assumption: the massive installation of standardized teaching has made the intersubjective relationships of traditional apprenticeship impossible; the 'informing' technicians have thus been changed, through the systematization of enterprises, into bureaucrats cooped up in their specialities and increasingly ignorant of users; productivist logic itself, by isolating producers, has led them to suppose that there is no creativity among consumers; a reciprocal blindness, generated by this system, has ended up making both technicians and producers believe that initiative takes place only in technical laboratories. Even the analysis of the repression exercised by the mechanisms of this system of disciplinary enclosure continues to assume that the public is passive, 'informed', processed, marked, and has no historical role.

The efficiency of production implies the inertia of consumption. It produces the ideology of consumption-as-a-receptacle. The result of class ideology and technical blindness, this legend is necessary for the system that distinguishes and privileges authors, educators, revolutionaries, in a word, 'producers', in contrast with those who do not produce. By challenging 'consumption' as it is conceived and (of course) confirmed by these 'authorial' enterprises, we may be able to discover creative activity where it has been denied that any exists, and to relativize the exorbitant claim that *a certain kind* of production (real enough, but not the only kind) can set out to produce history by 'informing' the whole of a country.

A misunderstood activity: reading

Reading is only one aspect of consumption, but a fundamental one. In a society that is increasingly written, organized by the power of modifying things and of reforming structures on the basis of scriptural models (whether scientific, economic, or political), transformed little by little into combined 'texts' (be they administrative, urban, industrial, etc.), the binominal set production–consumption can often be replaced by its general equivalent and indicator, the binominal set writing–reading. The power established by the will to rewrite history (a will that is by turns reformist, scientific, revolutionary, or pedagogical) on the basis of scriptural operations that are at first carried out in a circumscribed field, has as its corollary a major division between reading and writing.

'Modernization, modernity itself, is writing', says François Furet. The generalization of writing has in fact brought about the replacement of custom by abstract law, the substitution of the state for traditional authorities, and the disintegration of the group to the advantage of the individual. This transformation took place under the sign of a 'cross-breeding' of two distinct elements, the written and the oral. Furet and Ozouf's recent study has indeed demonstrated the existence, in the less educated parts of France, of a 'vast semi-literacy, centered on reading, instigated by the Church and by families, and aimed chiefly at girls'.[5] Only the schools have joined, with a link that has often remained extremely fragile, the ability to read and the ability to write. These abilities were long separated, up until late in the nineteenth century, and even today, the adult life of many of those who have been to school very quickly dissociates 'just reading' and writing; and we must thus ask ourselves how reading proceeds where it is married with writing.

Research on the psycho-linguistics of comprehension[6] distinguishes between 'the lexical act' and the 'scriptural act' in reading. It shows that the schoolchild learns to read by a process that *parallels* his learning to decipher; learning to read is not a *result* of learning to decipher: *reading* meaning and *deciphering* letters correspond to two different activities, even if they intersect. In other words, cultural memory (acquired through listening, through oral tradition) alone makes possible and gradually enriches the strategies of semantic questioning whose expectations the deciphering of a written text refines, clarifies, or corrects. From the child to the scientist, reading is preceded and made possible by oral communication, which constitutes the multifarious 'authority' that texts almost never cite. It is as though the construction of meanings, which takes the form of an expectation (waiting for something) or an anticipation (making hypotheses) linked to an oral transmission, was the initial block of stone that the decoding of graphic materials progressively sculpted, invalidated, verified, detailed, in order to make way for acts of reading. The graph only shapes and carves the anticipation.

In spite of the work that has uncovered an autonomy of the practice of reading underneath scriptural imperialism, a *de facto* situation has been created by more than three centuries of history. The social and technical functioning of contemporary culture hierarchizes these two activities. To write is to produce the text; to read is to receive it from someone else without putting one's own mark on it, without remaking it. In that regard, the reading of the catechism or of the Scriptures that the clergy used to recommend to girls and mothers, by forbidding these Vestals of an untouchable sacred text to write continues today in the 'reading' of the television programs offered to 'consumers' who cannot trace their own writing on the screen where the production of the Other – of 'culture' – appears. 'The link existing between reading and the Church'[7] is reproduced in the relation between reading and the church of the media. In this mode, the construction of the social text by professional intellectuals (*clercs*) still seems to correspond to its 'reception' by the faithful who are supposed to be satisfied to reproduce the models elaborated by the manipulators of language.

What has to be put in question is unfortunately not this division of labor (it is only too real), but the assimilation of reading to passivity. In fact, to read is to wander through an imposed system (that of the text, analogous to the constructed order of a city or of a supermarket). Recent analyses show that 'every reading modifies its object',[8] that (as Borges already pointed out) 'one literature differs from another less by its text than by the way in which it is read',[9] and that a system of verbal or iconic signs is a reservoir of forms to which the reader must give a meaning. If then 'the book is a result (a construction) produced by the reader',[10] one must consider the operation of the latter as a sort of *lectio*, the production proper to the 'reader' (*'lecteur'*).[11] The reader takes neither the position of the author nor an author's position. He invents in texts something different from what they 'intended'. He detaches them from their (lost or accessory) origin. He combines their fragments and creates something un-known in the space organized by their capacity for allowing an indefinite plurality of meanings. Is this 'reading' activity reserved for the literary critic (always privileged in studies of reading), that is, once again, for a category of professional intellectuals (*clercs*), or can it be extended to all cultural consumers? Such is the question to which history, sociology, or educational theory ought to give us the rudiments of an answer.

Unfortunately, the many works on reading provide only partial clarifications on this point or depend on the experience of literary people. Research has been primarily concerned with the teaching of reading.[12] It has not ventured very far into the fields of history and ethnology, because of the lack of traces left behind by a practice that slips through all sorts of 'writings' that have yet to be clearly determined (for example, one "reads" a landscape the way one reads a text).[13] Investigations of ordinary reading are more common in sociology, but generally statistical in type: they are more concerned with calculating the correlations between objects read, social groups, and places frequented than with analyzing the very operation of reading, its modalities and its typology.[14]

There remains the literary domain, which is particularly rich today (from Barthes to Riffaterre or Jauss), once again privileged by writing but highly specialized: 'writers' shift the 'joy of reading' in a direction where it is articulated on an art of writing and on a pleasure of re-reading. In that domain, however, whether before or after Barthes, deviations and creativities are narrated that play with the expectations, tricks, and normativities of the 'work read'; there theoretical models that can account for it are already elaborated.[15] In spite of all this, the story of man's travels through his own texts remains in large measure unknown.

'Literal' meaning, a product of a social elite

From analyses that follow the activity of reading in its detours, drifts across the page, metamorphoses and anamorphoses of the text produced by the travelling eye, imaginary or meditative flights taking off from a few words, overlappings of spaces on the militarily organized surfaces of the text, and ephemeral dances, it is at least clear, as a first result, that one cannot maintain the division separating the readable text (a book, image, etc.) from the act of reading. Whether it is a question of newspapers or Proust, the text has a meaning only through its readers; it changes along with them; it is ordered in accord with codes of perception that it does not control. It becomes a text only in its relation to the exteriority of the reader, by an interplay of implications and ruses between two sorts of 'expectation' in combination; the expectation that organizes a *readable* space (a literality), and one that organizes a procedure necessary for the *actualization* of the work (a reading).[16]

It is a strange fact that the principle of this reading activity was formulated by Descartes more than three hundred years ago, in discussing contemporary research on combinative systems and on the example of ciphers (*chiffres*) or coded texts:

> And if someone, in order to decode a cipher written with ordinary letters, thinks of reading a B everywhere he finds an A, and reading a C where he finds a B, and thus to substitute for each letter the one that follows it in alphabetic order and if, reading in this way, he finds words that have a meaning, he will not doubt that he has discovered the true meaning of this cipher in this way, even though it could very well be that the person who wrote it meant something quite different, giving a different meaning to each letter. . . .[17]

The operation of encoding, which is articulated on signifiers, produces the meaning, which is thus not defined by something deposited in the text, by an 'intention', or by an activity on the part of the author.

What is then the origin of the Great Wall of China that circumscribes a 'proper' in the text, isolates its semantic autonomy from everything else, and makes it the secret order of a 'work'? Who builds this barrier constituting the text as a sort of island that no reader can ever reach? This fiction condemns consumers to subjection because they are always going to be guilty of infidelity or ignorance when confronted by the mute 'riches' of the treasury thus set aside. The fiction of the 'treasury' hidden in the work, a sort of strong-box full of meaning, is obviously not based on the productivity of the reader, but on the *social institution* that overdetermines his relation with the text.[18] Reading is as it were overprinted by a relationship of forces (between teachers and pupils, or between producers and consumers) whose instrument it becomes. The use made of the book by privileged readers constitutes it as a secret of which they are the 'true' interpreters. It interposes a frontier between the text and its readers that can be crossed only if one has a passport delivered by these official interpreters, who transform their own reading (which is *also* a legitimate one) into an orthodox 'literality' that makes other (equally legitimate) readings either heretical (not 'in conformity' with the meaning of the text) or insignificant (to be forgotten). From this point of view, 'literal' meaning is the index and the result of a social power, that of an elite. By its very nature available to a plural reading, the text becomes a cultural weapon, a private hunting reserve, the pretext for a law that legitimizes as 'literal' the interpretation given by *socially* authorized professionals and intellectuals (*clercs*).

Moreover, if the reader's expression of his freedom through the text is tolerated among intellectuals (*clercs*) (only someone like Barthes can take this liberty), it is on the other hand denied students (who are scornfully driven or cleverly coaxed back to the meaning 'accepted' by their teachers) or the public (who are carefully told 'what is to be thought' and whose inventions are considered negligible and quickly silenced).

It is thus social hierarchization that conceals the reality of the practice of reading or makes it unrecognizable. Formerly, the Church, which instituted a social division between its intellectual clerks and the 'faithful', ensured the Scriptures the status of a 'Letter' that was supposed to be independent of its readers and, in fact, possessed by its exegetes: the autonomy of the text was the reproduction of sociocultural relationships within the institution whose officials determined what parts of it should be read. When the institution began to weaken, the reciprocity between the text and its readers (which the institution hid) appeared, as if by withdrawing the Church had opened to view the indefinite plurality of the 'writings' produced by readings. The creativity of the reader grows as the institution that controlled it declines. This process, visible from the Reformation onward, already disturbed the pastors of the seventeenth century. Today, it is the socio-political mechanisms of the schools, the press, or television that isolate the text controlled by the teacher or the producer from its readers. But behind the theatrical décor of this new orthodoxy is hidden (as in earlier ages)[19] the silent, transgressive, ironic or poetic activity of readers (or television viewers) who maintain their reserve in private and without the knowledge of the 'masters'.

Reading is thus situated at the point where *social* stratification (class relationships) and *poetic* operations (the practitioner's constructions of a text) intersect: a social hierarchization seeks to make the reader conform to the 'information' distributed by an elite (or semi-elite); reading operations manipulate the reader by insinuating their inventiveness into the cracks in a cultural orthodoxy. One of these two stories conceals what is not in conformity with the 'masters' and makes it invisible to them; the other disseminates it in the networks of private life. They thus both collaborate in making reading into an unknown out of which emerge, on the one hand, only the experience of the *literate* readers (theatricalized and dominating), and on the other, rare and partial, like bubbles rising from the depths of the water, the indices of a *common* poetics.

An 'exercise in ubiquity', that 'impertinent absence'

The autonomy of the reader depends on a transformation of the social relationships that overdetermine his relation to texts. This transformation is a necessary task. This revolution would be no more than another totalitarianism on the part of an elite claiming for itself the right to conceal different modes of conduct and substituting a new normative education for the previous one, were it not that we can count on the *fact* that there *already* exists, though it is surreptitious or even repressed, an experience other than that of passivity. A politics of reading must thus be articulated on an analysis that, describing practices that have long been in effect, makes them politicizable. Even pointing out a few aspects of the operation of reading will already indicate how it eludes the law of information.

'I read and I daydream... My reading is thus a sort of impertinent absence. Is reading an exercise in ubiquity?'[20] An initial, indeed initiatory, experience: to read is to be elsewhere, where *they* are not, in another world;[21] it is to constitute a secret scene, a place one can enter and leave when one wishes; to create dark corners into which no one can see within an existence subjected to technocratic transparency and that implacable light that, in Genet's work, materializes the hell of social alienation. Marguerite Duras has noted: 'Perhaps one always reads in the dark.... Reading depends on the obscurity of the night. Even if one reads in broad daylight, outside, darkness gathers around the book.'[22]

The reader produces gardens that miniaturize and collate a world, like a Robinson Crusoe discovering an island; but he, too, is 'possessed' by his own fooling and jesting that introduces plurality and difference into the written system of a society and a text. He is thus a novelist. He deterritorializes himself, oscillating in a nowhere between what he invents and what changes him. Sometimes, in fact, like a hunter in the forest, he spots the written quarry, follows a trail, laughs, plays tricks, or else like a gambler, lets himself be taken in by it. Sometimes he loses the fictive securities of reality when he reads: his escapades exile him from the assurances that give the self its location on the social checkerboard. *Who* reads, in fact? Is it I, or some part of me? 'It isn't *I* as a truth, but I as uncertainty about myself, reading these texts that lead to perdition. The more I read them, the less I understand them, and everything is going from bad to worse.'[23]

This is a common experience, if one believes testimony that cannot be quantified or quoted, and not only that of 'learned' readers. This experience is shared by the readers of *True Romances, Farm Journal* and *The Butcher and Grocery Clerk's Journal*, no matter how popularized or technical the spaces traversed by the Amazon or Ulysses of everyday life.

Far from being writers – founders of their own place, heirs of the peasants of earlier ages now working on the soil of language, diggers of wells and builders of houses – readers are travellers; they move across lands belonging to someone else, like nomads poaching their way across fields they did not write, despoiling the wealth of Egypt to enjoy it themselves. Writing accumulates, stocks up, resists time by the establishment of a place and multiplies its production through the expansionism of reproduction. Reading takes no measures against the erosion of time (one forgets oneself *and* also forgets), it does not keep what it acquires, or it does so poorly, and each of the places through which it passes is a repetition of the lost paradise.

Indeed, reading has no place: Barthes reads Proust in Stendhal's text;[24] the television viewer reads the passing away of his childhood in the news reports. One viewer says about the program she saw the previous evening: 'It was stupid and yet I sat there all the same.' What place captivated her, which was and yet was not that of the image seen? It is the same with the reader: his place is not *here* or *there*, one or the other, but neither the one nor the other, simultaneously inside and outside, dissolving both by mixing them together, associating texts like funerary statues that he awakens and hosts, but never owns. In that way, he also escapes from the law of each text in particular, and from that of the social milieu.

Spaces for games and tricks

In order to characterize this activity of reading, one can resort to several models. It can be considered as a form of the *bricolage* Lévi-Strauss analyzes as a feature of 'the savage mind', that is, an arrangement made with 'the materials at hand', a production 'that has no relationship to a project', and which readjusts 'the residues of previous construction and destruction'.[25] But unlike Lévi-Strauss's 'mythological universes', if this production also arranges events, it does not compose a unified set: it is another kind of 'mythology' dispersed in time, a sequence of temporal fragments not joined together but disseminated through repetitions and different modes of enjoyment, in memories and successive knowledges.

Another model: the subtle art whose theory was elaborated by medieval poets and romancers who insinuate innovation into the text itself, into the terms of a tradition. Highly refined procedures allow countless differences to filter into the authorized writing that serves them as a framework, but whose law does not determine their operation. These poetic ruses, which are not linked to the creation of a proper (written) place of their own, are maintained over the centuries right up to contemporary reading, and the latter is just as agile in practicing diversions and metaphorizations that sometimes are hardly even indicated by a 'pooh!' interjected by the reader.

The studies carried out in Bochum elaborating a *Rezeptionsästhetik* (an esthetics of reception) and a *Handlungstheorie* (a theory of action) also provide different models based on the relations between textual tactics and the 'expectations' and successive hypotheses of the receiver who considers a drama or a novel as a premeditated action.26 This play of textual productions in relation to what the reader's expectations make him produce in the course of his progress through the story is presented, to be sure, with a weighty conceptual apparatus; but it introduces dances between readers and texts in a place where, on a depressing stage, an orthodox doctrine had erected the statue of 'the work' surrounded by consumers who were either conformers or ignorant people.

Through these investigations and many others, we are directed toward a reading no longer characterized merely by an 'impertinent absence', but by advances and retreats, tactics and games played with the text. This process comes and goes, alternately captivated (but by what? what is it which arises both in the reader and in the text?), playful, protesting, fugitive.

We should try to rediscover the movements of this reading within the body itself, which seems to stay docile and silent but mines the reading in its own way: from the nooks of all sorts of 'reading rooms' (including lavatories) emerge subconscious gestures, grumblings, tics, stretchings, rustlings, unexpected noises, in short a wild orchestration of the body.[27] But elsewhere, at its most elementary level, reading has become, over the past three centuries, a visual poem. It is no longer accompanied, as it used to be, by the murmur of a vocal articulation nor by the movement of a muscular manducation. To read without uttering the words aloud or at least mumbling them is a 'modern' experience, unknown for millennia. In earlier times, the reader interiorized the text; he made his voice the body of the other; he was its actor. Today, the text no longer imposes its own rhythm on the subject, it no longer manifests itself through the reader's voice. This withdrawal of the body, which is the condition of its autonomy, is a distancing of the text. It is the reader's *habeas corpus*.

Because the body withdraws itself from the text in order henceforth to come into contact with it only through the mobility of the eye,[28] the geographical configuration of the text organizes the activity of the reader less and less. Reading frees itself from the soil that determined it. It detaches itself from that soil. The autonomy of the eye suspends the body's complicities with the text; it unmoors it from the scriptural place; it makes the written text an ob-ject and it increases the reader's possibilities of moving about. One index of this: the methods of speed reading.[29] Just as the airplane makes possible a growing independence with respect to the constraints imposed by geographical organization, the techniques of speed reading obtain, through the rarefaction of the eye's stopping points, an acceleration of its movements across the page, an autonomy in relation to the determinations of the text and a multiplication of the spaces covered. Emancipated from places, the reading body is freer in its movements. It thus transcribes in its attitudes every subject's ability to convert the text through reading and to 'run it' the way one runs traffic lights.

In justifying the reader's impertinence, I have neglected many aspects. Barthes distinguished three types of reading: the one that stops at the pleasure afforded by words, the one that rushes on to the end and 'faints with expectation', and the one that cultivates the desire to write:[30] erotic, hunting, and initiatory modes of reading. There are others, in dreams, battle, autodidacticism, etc., that we cannot consider here. In any event, the reader's increased autonomy does not project him, for the media extend their power over his imagination, that is, over everything he lets emerge from himself into the nets of the text – his fears, his dreams, his fantasized and lacking authorities. This is what the powers work on that make out of 'facts' and 'figures' a rhetoric whose target is precisely this surrendered intimacy.

But whereas the scientific apparatus (ours) is led to share the illusion of the powers it necessarily supports, that is, to assume that the masses are transformed by the conquests and victories of expansionist production, it is always good to remind ourselves that we mustn't take people for fools.

Notes

1. ALVIN TOFFLER, *The Culture Consumers* (Baltimore: Penguin, 1965), pp. 33–52, on the basis of Emanuel Demby's research.

2. *Pratiques culturelles des Français* (Paris: Secrétariat d'Etat à la Culture, S.E.R., 1974, 2 vols).

3. According to a survey by LOUIS-HARRIS (September–October 1978), the number of readers in France grew 17% over the past twenty years: there is the same percentage of people who read a great deal (22%), but the percentage of people who read a little or a moderate amount has increased. See JANICK JOSSIN, in *L'Express* for 11 November 1978, pp. 151–62.

4. See JEAN EHRARD, *L'Idée de nature en France pendant la première moitié du XVIIIe siècle* (Paris: SEPVEN, 1963), pp. 753–67.

5. FRANÇOIS FURET and JACQUES OZOUF, *Lire et écrire. L'Alphabétisation des Français de Calvin à Jules Ferry* (Paris: Minuit, 1977), I, pp. 349–69, 199–228.

6. See for example J. MEHLER and G. NOIZET, *Textes pour une psycholinguistique* (La Haye: Mouton, 1974); and also JEAN HÉBRARD, 'Ecole et alphabétisation au XIXe siècle,' Colloque 'Lire et écrire', MSH, Paris, June 1979.

7. FURET and OZOUF, *Lire et écrire*, p. 213.

8. MICHEL CHARLES, *Rhétorique de la lecture* (Paris: Seuil, 1977), p. 83.

9. JORGE LUIS BORGES, quoted by GÉRARD GENETTE, *Figures* (Paris: Seuil, 1966), p. 123.

10. CHARLES, *Rhétorique de la lecture*, p. 61.

11. As is well known, 'lector' was, in the Middle Ages, the title of a kind of University Professor.

12. See especially *Recherches actuelles sur l'enseignement de la lecture*, ed. ALAIN BENTOLILA (Paris: Retz CEPL, 1976); JEAN FOUCAMBERT and J. ANDRÉ, *La Manière d'être lecteur. Apprentissage et enseignement de la lecture, de la maternelle au CM2* (Paris: SERMAP OCDL, 1976); LAURENCE LENTIN, *Du parler au lire. Interaction entre l'adulte et l'enfant* (Paris: ESF, 1977); etc. To these should be added at least a portion of the abundant American literature: JEANNE STERNLICHT CHALL, *Learning to Read, the Great Debate . . . 1910–1965* (New York: McGraw-Hill, 1967); DOLORES DURKIN, *Teaching Them to Read* (Boston: Allyn & Bacon, 1970); ELEANOR JACK GIBSON and HARRY LEVIN, *The Psychology of Reading* (Cambridge, Mass.: MIT, 1975); MILFRED ROBECK and JOHN A. R. WILSON, *Psychology of Reading: Foundations of Instruction* (New York: John Wiley, 1973); *Reading Disabilities. An International Perspective*, ed. LESTER and MURIEL TARNOPOL (Baltimore: University Park Press, 1976); etc., along with three important journals: *Journal of Reading*, since 1957 (Purdue University, Department of English), *The Reading Teacher*, since 1953 (Chicago International Reading Association), *Reading Research Quarterly*, since 1965 (Newark, Delaware, International Reading Association).

13. See the bibliography in FURET and OZOUF, *Lire et écrire*, II, pp. 358–72, to which we can add MITFORD MCLEOD MATHEWS, *Teaching to Read, Historically Considered* (Chicago: University of Chicago Press, 1966). JACK GOODY's studies (*Literacy in a Traditional Society* [Cambridge: Cambridge University Press, 1968] and *The Domestication of the Savage Mind* [Cambridge: Cambridge University Press, 1977], etc.) open several paths toward an ethnohistorical analysis.

14. In addition to statistical investigations, see J. CHARPENTREAU et al., *Le Livre et la lecture en France* (Paris: Editions ouvrières, 1968).

15. ROLAND BARTHES, of course: *Le Plaisir du texte* (Paris: Seuil, 1973), *The Pleasure of the Text*, trans. R. MILLER (New York: Hill and Wang, 1975), and 'Sur la Lecture,' *Le Français aujourd'hui*, No. 32 (January 1976), pp. 11–18. See, somewhat at random, in addition to the works already cited, TONY DUVERT,

'La Lecture introuvable,' *Minuit*, No. 1 (November 1972), 2–21; O. MANNONI, *Clefs pour l'imaginaire* (Paris: Seuil, 1969), pp. 202–17; MICHEL MOUGENOT, 'Lecture/écriture,' *Le Français aujourd'hui*, No. 30 (May 1975); VICTOR N. SMIRNOFF, 'L'Oeuvre lue,' *Nouvelle revue de psychanalyse*, No. 1 (1970), 49–57; TZVETAN TODOROV, *Poétique de la prose* (Paris: Seuil, 1971), p. 241 et seq.; JEAN VERRIER, 'La Ficelle,' *Poétique*, No. 30 (April 1977); *Littérature*, No. 7 (October 1972); *Esprit*, December 1974, and January 1976; etc.

16. See, for example, MICHEL CHARLES' 'propositions' in his *Rhétorique de la lecture*.

17. DESCARTES, *Principia*, IV, p. 205

18. PIERRE KUENTZ, 'Le tête à texte,' *Esprit*, December 1974, pp. 946–62, and 'L'Envers du texte,' *Littérature*, No. 7 (October 1972).

19. Some documents, unfortunately all too rare, shed light on the autonomy of the trajectories, interpretations, and convictions of Catholic readers of the Bible. See, on the subject of his 'farmer' father, RÉTIF DE LA BRETONNE, *La Vie de mon père* (1778) (Paris: Garnier, 1970), pp. 29, 131–2, etc.

20. GUY ROSOLATO, *Essais sur le symbolique* (Paris: Gallimard, 1969), 288.

21. THERESA DE AVILA considered reading to be a form of prayer, the discovery of another space in which desire could be articulated. Countless other authors of spiritual works think the same, and so do children.

22. MARGUERITE DURAS, *Le Camion* (Paris: Minuit, 1977), and 'Entretien à Michèle Porte', quoted in *Sorcières*, No. 11 (January 1978), 47.

23. JACQUES SOJCHER, 'Le Professeur de philosophie,' *Revue de l'Université de Bruxelles*, No. 3–4 (1976), pp. 428–9.

24. BARTHES, *Le Plaisir du texte*, p. 58.

25. CLAUDE LÉVI-STRAUSS, *La Pensée sauvage* (Paris: Plon, 1962), pp. 3–47; *The Savage Mind* (Chicago: University of Chicago Press, 1966). In the reader's 'bricolage,' the elements that are re-employed, all being drawn from official and accepted bodies of material, can cause one to believe that there is nothing new in reading.

26. See in particular the works of HANS ULRICH GUMBRECHT ('Die Dramenschliessende Sprachhandlung im Aristotelischen Theater und ihre Problematisierung bei Marivaux') and of KARLHEINZ STIERLE ('Das Liebesgeständnis in Racines *Phèdre* und das Verhältnis von (Sprach-)Handlung und Tat'), in *Poetica* (Bochum), 1976; etc.

27. GEORGES PEREC had discussed this very well in 'Lire: Esquisse sociophysiologique,' *Esprit*, January 1976, 9–20.

28. It is nonetheless known that the muscles that contract the vocal cords and constrict the glottis remain active in reading.

29. See FRANÇOIS RICHAUDEAU, *La Lisibilité* (Paris: Retz CEPL, 1969); or GEORGES RÉMOND, 'Apprendre la lecture silencieuse à l'ecole primaire,' in BENTOLILA, *La manière d'être lecteur*, pp. 147–61.

30. BARTHES, 'Sur la lecture,' pp. 15–16.

8 Wilde's Hard Labour and the Birth of Gay Reading*

WAYNE KOESTENBAUM

While the 1980s and early 1990s saw a redescription of reading in terms of gender together with a rehistoricization and politicization of approaches to reading of the kind suggested by Dimock's essay (see Chapter 5), during the same period gay and lesbian approaches to lit-' erature, criticism and theory have developed through the work of theorists such as Jonathan Dollimore and Eve Kosofsky Sedgwick. Wayne Koestenbaum's essay attempts to map such concerns on to the question of reading. What would be involved in 'gay reading'? Is it possible to determine such an act (is it an act?), or would such a determination restrict the subversive potential of its oppositions? How would it be possible to avoid reductive, essentializing assertions of gay identity in this discussion? Gay reading, Koestenbaum argues, would constitute an exemplary politics of resistance and self-construction: such reading would approach canonical works differently, for the inscription of gay desire 'felt not by author but by reader'. But Koestenbaum also suggests that this very identity – the 'gay reader' – might itself be said to be historically constituted and constructed *in reading* – and, in particular, through a reading of two inaugural gay texts, Oscar Wilde's *De Profundis* (1897) and 'The Ballad of Reading Gaol' (1898): 'the reader becomes gay... by reading Wilde'.

For other explorations of gay reading, see Joseph Chadwick, 'Toward Gay Reading: Robert Glück's "Reader"' in Anthony Easthope and John O. Thompson, eds., *Contemporary Poetry Meets Modern Theory* (Hemel Hempstead: Harvester Wheatsheaf, 1991), pp. 40–52; and Roland Barthes, *The Pleasure of the Text* (1975). For recent work on Wilde and on the history of gay writing and reading more generally, see Jonathan Dollimore's *Sexual Dissidence: Augustine to Wilde, Freud to Foucault* (Oxford: Oxford University Press, 1991); for a rather different approach to questions of 'homosocial' – and homophobic – reading,

---

* Reprinted from JOSEPH A. BOONE and MICHAEL CADDEN (eds), *Engendering Men: The Question of Male Feminist Criticism* (New York: Routledge, 1990), pp. 176–89.

see Eve Kosofsky Sedgwick, *Epistemology of the Closet* (Hemel Hempstead: Harvester Wheatsheaf, 1991).

'Gay reading' as a critical term may seem indefensible. Potentially oppressive, it is attractive only if considered part of a reverse discourse, elective and not imposed. Since recent histories of sexuality have shown that gay identity evolved from classifying, medical, and legal impulses, I threaten to gild the lily of homosexuality's roots in punishment by invoking, in this essay, an interpretive community founded on desire for the same gender.[1] Embracing without thought of consequence the dominant culture's assumption that sexualities are, like social security numbers, valid nodes of power and control, I risk submitting to a dangerously comfortable essentialism – as if gayness transcended gender, class, race, nationality, or epoch.

Although the notion of a 'gay reader' may be fraught, I want to construct such a reader. The interpretive position I describe may be occupied by a woman, but it is most historically precise to speak of it as a gay man's. By referring only to men, I oversimplify. And yet this urge to warp evidence to fit the perimeters of wish is itself part of my subject: I acquiesce to 'camp', to the grand urge to make irresponsible claims in the name of a self that, dreading erasure, writes itself in too bold a hand. Exaggerated masquerade helps the drag queen invent 'identity'; he broadcasts an imagined and essential self through luridness, paint, and posing. My description of a limited point of view – mine – as if it were universal, shares with the drag queen a taste for absolute gesture, a desire to wear socially constructed identities (showgirl, secretary, prostitute, diva) as if they were god-given and natural.

Male feminist criticism means to articulate maleness as strange, outcast, and impermissible; gayness *is* outcast, and so I may discuss my reading of Oscar Wilde without apologizing for its partiality. Hedging bets – 'what I describe here applies only to a small group of privileged gay men' – capitulates to homophobia. Assuming the prerogatives of *écriture féminine*, I will map gay reading as if it were a continent, though it may be only a peninsula.

The (male twentieth-century first-world) gay reader, like the female spectator, knows the rewards of looking from the outside in. He reads resistantly for inscriptions of his condition, for texts that will confirm a social and private identity founded on a desire for other men – an urge strong enough that it seems a vocation and defines him and his kind as a separate world. Reading becomes a hunt for histories that deliberately foreknow or unwittingly trace a desire felt not by author but by reader, who is most acute when searching for signs of himself.

Two critics have begun to describe such a reader. Roland Barthes, under the guise of methodology-as-eros (*S/Z*), asks what other gay critics have been shy to answer: are there undermining and refiguring styles of reading that have either an imagined or actual connection to gay desires?[2] And D.A. Miller, in *The Novel and the Police*, closes with an essay on *David Copperfield* that playfully gestures toward David Miller reading Dickens: the importance of being David.[3]

On the one hand, I am invoking something as pedestrian as gay male reader–response criticism. (How do specific gay men read? What difference does it make if we postulate a gay male reader?) On the other, more provocative, hand, I am hypothesizing that there are connections between gay identity and prison (both are enclosures established by social codes) and that a certain kind of involved, implicated reader is a gay man in the prison of his identity: the way we read now, our hunger to place ourselves in texts, began, in part, with Oscar Wilde in Reading Gaol, sentenced in 1895 to two years of 'hard labour' for 'gross indecency' with men. In the letter he wrote from prison to his lover, Lord Alfred Douglas (Bosie), 'In Carcere et Vinculis' (posthumously titled *De Profundis*), and in the poem he wrote after release, 'The Ballad of Reading Gaol', Wilde gestured toward such a gay male reader and suggested that 'gay identity' is constructed through reading, although once it has been located on the page, it glows like an essence that already existed *before* a reader's glance brought it to life.

It is strange that Oscar Wilde, hardly addicted to eternal verities, invented an essentialist gay reader. Recent studies of Wilde by Ed Cohen, Jonathan Dollimore, and Regenia Gagnier, among others, have shown Wilde's detachment from the intrinsic paradisaical 'nature' that thrilled André Gide; a gay Satan, radically reversing the dominant logos, Wilde was precursor to such postmodernists as Andy Warhol.[4] Wilde, like Warhol, understood publicity to be modern art's preeminent genre and saw himself as part of a literary and cultural marketplace; he recognized that mechanical reproduction was the empowering, if sometimes disenfranchising, fact of his age. When art can be copied, writes Walter Benjamin, the 'aura' of an original is lost. Wilde, however, reclaimed aura for gay purposes by redefining mechanical reproduction *as* aura and insisting that the copy bears the original's transcendence.[5] Dollimore argues that Wilde, in his prison writings, retreated from anti-essentialism into the quietism of earnestness; on the contrary, I claim that, in *De Profundis* and 'The Ballad of Reading Gaol', Wilde posits an essential 'gay identity' in order to develop gay writing and gay reading as reverse discourses.

Obsessed with copying, cannily undermining essences, Wilde entertained the glittering, seductive, and centerless play of surfaces and refused to take essences earnestly. Though he celebrated the aura's degradation, Wilde, in fact, did not pledge strict allegiance to the copy; his texts acknowledge their status as reproductions, but they also feign, or contain, an aura. And the aura that Wilde's prison writings hide, beneath the sparkle of the secondhand, the derivative, and the stereotyped, is a 'gay' essence. Because his imprisonment created, in a suffering instant, modern gayness – enough so that homosexuals became, in E.M. Forster's memorable phrase, 'unspeakables of the Oscar Wilde sort'[6] – Wilde in jail could hardly avoid the knowledge that his name had become, like an instantly memorable advertising logo for a new product, the aura of gayness.

Although the 'gayness' in a text may be merely an illusion of essence, a trope, a reflection, not a tangibility, the reader's hunger for textual gayness *as if it were real* is no different than the longing of any reader in a world saturated with copies for the original. Wilde took seriously this longing and satisfied it. He invented a reader who finds palpable gayness by unearthing Wilde's spirit – his figure – from the text's letter. Though essentialist, this postulated 'gay reader' never abandons historical knowledge, never forgets that an actual man, Oscar Wilde, did two years of hard labor in prison; this reader (whether holding a work of Wilde's or a later gay text) is always searching for 'Oscar Wilde' as the origin of an imprisoned indecency that contemporary gay men must recognize as their own. Wilde justified his incarceration by imagining a new kind of elucidator/disciple, in love with him enough to accord his 'nature' – his sexuality – the status of an essence. Wilde's imprisonment taught a century the costs of being gay; the letter he wrote in prison preaches the rewards of using gayness to form a reverse discourse based on reading, a *vita nuova* founded, ironically, on the very name of his jail.

De Profundis: the gaol of reading

De Profundis, like many novels, warns that tragedies come from misreading, miswriting, or mishandling letters; but Wilde's letter is unique among self-conscious epistles because its writer and its implied reader are gay. This document asks: what difference does one new term – *gay* – make in reading a letter?

The 'you' supplicated and denounced in *De Profundis* is Bosie (Wilde's lover) and the reader of the posthumously published letter. Bosie was a specific recalcitrant gay reader. Wilde, addressing him, made him emblematic. The fact that gay identity was born from Wilde's trial forces us to take his scene of reading between Bosie and Wilde seriously and to generalize from Bosie's position to the stance of post-Wilde gay readers. According to *De Profundis*, the reader is a young, attractive, indolent boy implored to perform something – to address the writer. The reader is a traitor, a boy who has been intimate with a famous man and has abused that privilege.[7] Not every reader of *De Profundis* is a lazy, indifferent ephebe. But Bosie's silence seems representative: the gay reader as imagined by Wilde is a querulous wordless presence, a renegade disciple, a disloyal fan, whose lack of fealty and whose silence make the writer write.

Bosie's silence forces Wilde to compose:

> Dear Bosie, – After long and fruitless waiting I have determined to write to you myself, as much for your sake as for mine, as I would not like to think that I had passed through two long years of imprisonment without ever having received a single line from you, or any news or message even, except such as gave me pain.[8]

Wilde's entire miraculous *De Profundis* is an answer to an unwritten letter, to a desired text's absence – as if he were indirectly bemoaning the absence of a tradition of gay *belles-lettres* to which he can respond. Wilde sends his epistle into the void that precedes the invention of gay writing.

If Bosie's silence infuriates Wilde, the youth's greater sin is that he has *tried* to write: Bosie, whom Wilde calls 'the true author of the hideous tragedy' (p. 130), has dared to publish the elder man's private love letters in the *Mercure de France* and to dedicate a volume of verse to him. The gay reader projected by *De Profundis* hubristically overreaches and claims a writer's prerogatives. Overinterpreting, throwing himself, like the hysteric, too fully into what he reads, he crosses, without the writer's permission, the boundary between private and public; throughout the letter, Wilde anxiously repairs those veils of privacy that he spent his career methodically rending. He denounces Bosie's use of the 'open postcard' – as if in response to the indignity of having letters read in court and seeing them treated not as mediated representations but as damning realities. Ronald Firbank composed his novels on postcards – an emblematic space for openly gay writing; unlike the closet of sealed envelopes, postcards preclude privacy. Wilde, jailed, regretted the exposed page that seemed to unincarcerated Firbank a source of play. *De Profundis* is unhappy to resemble a postcard, open to the censoring eyes of prison officials, and inscribed with the message 'Wish you were here.'

In prison, Wilde was permitted to read before he was permitted to write.[9] The book lists that he gave the gaol officials do more than document his longing for imaginative liberty. They confirm that reading, as an act of will and pleasure, may take writing's place and that certain styles of reading, performed under strict, punitive circumstances (whether the prison or the closet), *are* writing and counteract servitude. Wilde's prison reading stands for elucidations that take place inside the closet. It is fair to treat Reading Gaol as figurative as well as literal, for Wilde himself turned it into trope: 'on the day of my release, I shall be

merely passing from one prison into another'.[10] Thus the paradigmatic
gay reader sketched by *De Profundis* is not simply Bosie, but the
imprisoned writer, reduced by jailkeepers to mere reading and learning
to find in the reader's position the seeds of a finer disobedience. 'Better
than Wordsworth himself I know what Wordsworth meant' (p. 152), says
Wilde, and 'if I may not write beautiful books, I may at least read
beautiful books' (p. 153). The fear that *De Profundis* will never reach its
intended reader or that language itself is fated by its elusive differential
nature never to span the distance between speaker and listener
empowers one to read beautiful books but not write them and to read
beauty into them – to read even an ugly book as if it were beautiful.

De Profundis separates into two tonalities. The first is manic and
particular: Wilde recites Bosie's sins, and compiles a minute, exacting
history of various letters – their transmission, receipt, and
consequence. He spends much of *De Profundis* recounting 'revolting
and loathsome letters' (p. 103), 'no less loathsome letters' (p. 105),
'one of your most offensive letters' (p. 107), 'one of the violent letters
you wrote to me on the point' (p. 107), 'some equally unpleasant
telegrams' (p. 108), 'passionate telegrams' (p. 111), 'a most pathetic
and charming letter' (p. 119), 'a letter of fantastic literary conceits'
(p. 121), 'dreadful letters, abusive telegrams, and insulting postcards'
(p. 124). Wilde claims, in fact, that he was imprisoned as a result of
writing Bosie a 'charming letter' (p. 120). These letters evoke the
world of mechanical reproduction – of repetitions so painful and
numbing that Wilde in prison faces a shadow 'that wakes me up at
night to tell me the same story over and over till its wearisome
iteration makes all sleep abandon me till dawn: at dawn it begins
again' (p. 125). This reiterative Wilde is a prisoner who has stumbled,
newly stereotyped as gay, into literature's bloody arena, uncertain
what to say, uncertain who is listening – acknowledging, by his
confusion, that being, or becoming, gay changes everything textual
and makes letter-writing a different act.

The second tonality is the blurred realm of the aura. Wilde compares
himself to Christ and forgives Bosie. The two lovers hardly require
letters because nothing separates them – as if Wilde's fanciful dictum
'There was no difference at all between the lives of others and one's
own life' (p. 170) had come true. When the gap between writer and
reader vanishes, so does the gap between word and meaning; Wilde
seeks signs thoroughly drenched with their referents – like a divinity's
words untranslated, 'the actual terms, the *ipsissima verba*, used by
Christ' (p. 174). Wilde wants a reader, like an enamored fan, to winnow
De Profundis for traces of the writer's original mark. His ideal gay
reader is like Bette Davis's vulture/protégé, Eve Harrington, who,
loving the star, ruins her. The Wildean gay reader is a fan who longs to

sleep with the beloved writer and who reads in order to wear, figuratively, the author's outfits.

Towards the end of *De Profundis*, Wilde describes his own page as a body. Indeed, *De Profundis* is a scarified body, whose every bleeding wound the reader should suck for the ichor of the writer's aura. If the woman has been compared to the blank page,[11] then the Wildean gay male may be called a wounded, stabbed page – a St Sebastian marked by arrows, redeemed by gaping gashes. (Affairs between United States congressmen and their adolescent male pages is a more recent instance of the word 'page' bearing homerotic freight.) Wilde, describing *De Profundis*, invites the reader-as-Bosie to enjoy the gashed male textual body:

> I cannot reconstruct my letter or rewrite it. You must take it as it stands, blotted in many places with tears, in some with the signs of passion or pain, and make it out as best you can, blots, corrections, and all. As for the corrections and errata, I have made them in order that my words should be an absolute expression of my thoughts, and err neither through surplusage nor through being inadequate. . . . As it stands, at any rate, my letter has its definite meaning behind every phrase. There is in it nothing of rhetoric. Whenever there is erasion or substitution, however slight, however elaborate, it is because I am seeking to render my real impression, to find for my mood its exact equivalent. Whatever is first in feeling comes away last in form.
>
> (pp. 197–8)

Wilde, describing the flawed, tear-smudged letter, asks for the reader's forgiveness, but knows that erasures and emendations attest to originality. No mere copy, the letter is an authentic prison document. Its blots are signs of aura that the reader should treasure as stigmata. Thus Wilde succumbs to or invents Pound's modernist poetics of absolute rhythm – where every phrase faithfully represents, in a one-to-one correspondence, some essential emotion.

But is the page the writer's body or the reader's? The letter's rheumy accuracy portrays not its writer, but Bosie, its reader: 'If you have read this letter carefully as you should have done you have met yourself face to face' (p. 197). The reader is invited to study *De Profundis* in order to see himself – his moral ugliness – more clearly. The text as mirror is a portrait of the reader as a young man, and its true subject is the reader's body experiencing Wilde's white-hot mark:

> you will let the reading of this terrible letter – for such I know it is – prove to you as important a crisis and turning-point of your life as

the writing of it is to me. Your pale face used to flush easily with wine or pleasure. If, as you read what is here written, it from time to time becomes scorched as though by a furnace blast, with shame, it will be all the better for you.

(p. 130)

The lacerated page is Bosie's body, licked by the flames of Wilde's faithful portraiture.

In sum, *De Profundis* is a liminal, revolutionary document, a primary invocation to a historically constituted gay reader; it is the first text that Wilde wrote after he had been publicly branded as gay and one of the first texts ever written with the knowledge that it would be seen as the work of an 'exposed' gay man. *De Profundis*, though composed in a prison cell, is uncloseted. Handing over its no longer secret preference, it coins a new gesture: it asks to be read as a document of a gay man's position and supposes that its canniest reader will be gay. Written as a private letter destined to be published posthumously, the epistle's central, burning problematic is the obsolescent distinction between public and private, the regrettable death of the division between commercial and domestic, open postcard and sealed missive.

Privacy lost, Wilde is reduced to the anonymous status of a letter: 'I myself, at that time, had no name at all. In the great prison where I was then incarcerated, I was merely the figure and *letter* of a little cell in a long gallery; one of a thousand lifeless numbers, as of a thousand lifeless lives' (p. 136; emphasis added). A letter is a private communication between writer and reader. But it is also a piece of alphabet – an *A*, for example, as in *The Scarlet Letter*, where *letter* implied, as it did for Wilde, a stigma, a fixed, blazoned identity, legible to strangers. Every reader of Wilde necessarily accuses him, remarks his sin. But the gay reader, himself scarlet, sees that the scarlet *A* means something other than its proscribed, punitive denotation.

When placed beside *figure, letter* refers to literality – the letter of the law. The question of letter in *De Profundis* is, finally, how literally we should take Bosie: Wilde's angry invocation to his lover is the document's loudest rhetorical gesture, and yet is the letter solely directed at the real, historical boyfriend? Isn't Bosie simply the disobedient lacuna where the post-Wilde gay reader finds himself – a reader who exists, in the first place, *because* a typology of homosexuality arose from Wilde's trial? *Letter* also denotes a bit of typeface, used to print. *De Profundis* balances the two meanings of *letter* – a communication between writer and reader, and a puncturing, imprinting fragment of typeface that can replicate itself, that generates unoriginal and inauthentic copies, but that has the power to wound the reader's conscience by reminding him of his own essential nature.

The reproduction of Wilde's prison writings

Wilde gave fetishistic attention to the typing, printing, and publication of 'The Ballad of Reading Gaol' and *De Profundis*. His fastidious, mannered interest in surface as opposed to depth seems to contradict my claim that certain texts possess gay 'essences' that a reader can intuit and interpret. However, I would argue that Wilde's self-conscious commodification of his prison experience deepens, rather than flattens, the figure of his suffering. Attention to type, to publication, to the mechanics of a letter's spread, to language as a series of differences drifting away from a phantasmal source, needn't drain 'life' from the image or negate an essential 'gay identity'. By commodifying his prison experience, Wilde tried to perpetuate, through the mechanics of modern publicity and publication, 'imprisoned homosexuality' as an essential identity. 'Gay reading' can live inside the copy as if it were the original because it has the knack of finding nature or essence within the copy reproduced unnaturally, by cloning.

Clone, a disparaging term for muscled gay men who dress and groom themselves stereotypically, signifies a mechanically reproduced masculinity inhabited as if it were real. One can acquire reality only by faking it. Men can acquire masculinity only by mimicking it. Because the word *clone* evokes laboratories, it also subtly derides a gay male's nonprocreative sexuality; it defines homosexuality as replication of the same. Gay men may father children, but homosexuality has often seemed equal to mechanical, not sexual, reproduction. Against this assumption that gay men are, at best, Petri dishes, gay criticism needs to develop a theory of typing or copying that wipes the tarnish off clones. Mechanical reproduction is *not* second-rate: there is nothing wrong with becoming a clone, wanting to be famous for fifteen minutes, striving to be sexy through mimicry, or commodifying one's life, body, and work. To consider replication degrading is, literally, homophobic: *afraid of the same*. If the patriarchal male pen is, figuratively, a fertilizing penis, let us enjoy the fact that the gay male instrument of textual dissemination may well be a xerox machine – or, in Wilde's time, a typewriter.

Indeed, *type* refers both to typeface and, in French, to a guy, a chap, a fellow. How do guys resemble typeface? When a man looks like a man, he possesses a reproducible, imitable essence of 'maleness'. Wilde, aware of masculinity and language as replicable properties, was obsessed with the word *type*. In his dialogue 'The Decay of Lying', he wrote that 'a great artist invents a type, and Life tries to copy it, to reproduce it in a popular form, like an enterprising publisher'.[12] In *De Profundis*, Wilde describes Christ as having 'the essentials of the supreme romantic type' (p. 176) and condemns Lord Alfred Douglas as 'a very complete specimen of a very modern type' (p. 198); further, he admonishes Bosie, 'you had better quote from it. It is set up in type' (p. 209). Of course, Wilde was 'stereo*typed*' (p. 105) as a homosexual, and even descrbed himself as 'a specially typical example' of degeneration's 'fatal law'.[13] Wilde was content to be a type of the homosexual not because he enjoyed being stigmatized, but because he wished to puncture the future, to influence.[14]

To print successfully, moveable type must be, like Wilde's sexuality, inverted: the *Chicago Manual of Style* defines *type* as 'individual bits of metal with the images of letters cast in reverse on their ends'.[15] Letters, like *De Profundis*, have most hope of influencing when they come from reversal (of fortune, of sexual preference). Type makes impressions on a page: it is striking that Wilde should have titled several poems 'Impressions' and that, after his death, Robert Ross should have remarked that 'Wilde left curiously different impressions on professing judges.'[16] Wilde's concern with 'type' conceals a skewed query into the etiology of homosexuality (is it imprinted or chosen?) and the radical claim that one typesets, as it were, the page of one's own psyche.

With 'The Ballad of Reading Gaol', Wilde monitored exactness and density of type and complained particularly about the weak impression made by his pseudonym, 'C.3.3'. Leonard Smithers, the publisher, wrote to Wilde:

> It has been a somewhat awkward title page to set with satisfaction, and even now, owing to the lightness of the impression of the 'C.3.3.' it does not look perfectly satisfactory. But this will be set quite right when the sheet is properly made ready for the press, which is a matter which takes several hours careful coaxing of the type to accomplish properly.[17]

Wilde was equally fastidious about the copying and typing of *De Profundis*. Exclaiming that Ross 'must read it carefully and *copy it out carefully every word* for me', he longed to see the work typed.[18] Giving Ross the manuscript, Wilde was particular about the typewriter as the crucible through which this text must pass: 'the only thing to do is to be thoroughly modern and have it typewritten'.[19] Wilde mockingly described the typewriter as feminine: 'I assure you that the typewriting machine, when played with expression, is not more annoying than the piano when played by a sister or near relation. Indeed many among those most devoted to domesticity prefer it.'[20] It is significant that Wilde should call for a woman – and a modern contraption associated with female labor – to commit to print his messianic message. Homosexuality, in its earlier incarnation as sodomy, implied an alienation from procreative sex; and yet Wilde was a father, although he lost title to his children and to his literary estate while in prison. Oddly, his son,

Vyvyan Holland, whom we might call an original and not a mechanically reproduced impression, became the custodian of what he terms 'the original (if I may so call it) carbon copy' of *De Profundis*.[21] Wilde's son, Vyvyan, continues his father's struggle, through *De Profundis*, to redefine the meaning of reproduction. Even Wilde's punishment – called 'hard labour' by the law – conceals a verdict on the relationship between homosexuality and reproduction. Parliament effected a pun: Wilde's labor gave birth to nothing. His punishment, which was literally oakum-picking, seems a metaphor for capitalism's alienated labor, for modern publication (mechanical reproduction), and for the 'barrenness' of gay sex.

De Profundis invents a gay reader berated by the text into equivalence with the writer; appropriately, Wilde's contemporaries considered it a durance to read his prison works. Editions of 'The Ballad of Reading Gaol' depicted the book as a jail. The leather cover of a 1937 limited edition reproduced a prison wall, down to the grilled window; a 1907 American edition, on its cover, invited the public to 'Read the Greatest Tragical Poem in Literature', as if of first importance were not the poem itself but the reader's entrance into its imprisoning magnitude. This cover's mysterious insignia – a spirit lamp – implied that reading the poem might magically bring Wilde back.[22] When in 1907 Doubleday advertised its 'Patrons' Edition De Luxe of Oscar Wilde', it lured the reader into an even more punitive proximity to the text: 'Your name will be beautifully engrossed on the title page of the first volume of the set you own . . . To be identified with one's books has always been the truest mark of the book-lover. . . . It associates one more closely with the Masters one loves.'[23] Reading a beloved author's books, one is pressed like Bosie, into typeface, name sadistically 'engrossed' on the book's cover – as in Kafka's story 'In the Penal Colony', where letters are written on the prisoner's flesh. Wilde, angry that Bosie dedicated a book to him, understood that being tattooed on another man's page could be torment. Doubleday's 1907 edition pursues suggestions made by *De Profundis* itself – that the reader is no ordinary passive spectator, but a disciple whose body must sympathetically take on the writer's pains.

When parts of *De Profundis* were published after Wilde's death, readers fell under the spell of a man who seemed legibly alive. His readers obeyed the logic of 'type', of cloning: they felt compelled to read Wilde twice. Laurence Housman wrote of *De Profundis*, 'I read it once with great and almost entire admiration, and am now reading it again.'[24] This repetition was exactly what Wilde, in the letter, demanded of Bosie: 'you must read this letter right through', must 'read the letter over and over again till it kills your vanity' (pp. 97–8). A reviewer in the *Times Literary Supplement* commented that 'everything which Wilde says of Christ in this little book is worth reading and considering and reading again'.[25] By reading Wilde twice, readers engineered his resurrection: according to one reviewer, Wilde was a 'revisiting shade of immortal Glamour' that fell 'athwart every part of the poem'.[26] Wilde's shade appeared to the automatic writer and medium Hester Travers Smith, who recorded Wilde's after-death pronouncements in her book, *Oscar Wilde from Purgatory*, and even André Gide was visited by the dead master in seances.[27] A homophobic reviewer of *De Profundis*, who commented 'I refuse to forget that [Wilde] is most fearfully alive',[28] inadvertently revealed that modern gayness may be defined as Wilde's posthumous persistence, and that the gay reader is constituted by the prison of *imitatio Oscar* – by the compulsion to fill Wilde's shoes. Leonard Smithers, first publisher of the 'Ballad', continued until 1907 (seven years after Wilde's death) to use the date 1899 for new printings of the poem[29] – evading a new copyright and century, maintaining Wilde's perpetual presence, and feigning that every copy, further removed from Wilde's living, tear-stained page, retained some intrinsic connection to the original. But Wilde understood that cloning – mechanical reproduction – was useful to gay identity. When a difficult, new, rarefied, illegal pleasure repeatedly appears, it grows familiar; it enters the dictionary. Reading a copy of 'The Ballad of Reading Gaol' is like caressing a saint's bone and feeling it to be the calcified origin of one's own seemingly immutable 'gay identity' – rock-hard, contingent, textual.

'The Ballad of Reading Gaol': the interpreted cock

The gay reader is not merely a responder to printed matter. He is a commiserator. In Wilde's 'The Ballad of Reading Gaol', the last thing he wrote for publication, there are two criminals. One is Wilde, in prison. He speaks of himself infrequently: 'And I trembled as I groped my way / Into my numbered tomb.'[30] He usually reverts to the plural ('We sewed the sacks, we broke the stones, / We turned the dusty drill', (p. 238), a 'we' of prisoners united by the oppression of repetitive tasks and by a shared discursive position: they are each remonstrated to feel empathy with a greater, more emblematic criminal in their midst – a Christlike 'He', whose execution they mourn. (This 'He' is a man Wilde saw executed in Reading Gaol – Charles Thomas Wooldridge, who had murdered his wife, slitting her throat three times.[31] Does a pact between gay male writer and reader depend on erasing the slain wife and justifying her death? Women are missing from my paradigm of gay male reading. Has something actual and feminine been figuratively slain to make room for this bucolic practice of gay male interpretation? Or is this

parenthetical shudder homophobic?) If Wilde is the first criminal, the
second is C.T.W., to whom the Ballad is dedicated. As Wilde mourns
C.T.W., we, reading the poem, mourn Wilde, our greatest 'He'. Thus the
poem does for gay community what a mass does for Christendom: it
enacts, in little, the spectacle that started the 'church'. 'God's son died
for all' (p. 247): Wilde died for the sins of us outcast men. Gay
community begins around the vicarious experience of a Passion: the
reader becomes gay – joins a community of outcast men – by reading
Wilde, as Wilde became gay by commiserating with C.T.W. Cloned, the
reader is remade in the image of the convict's type; cloning is not a
lonely experience, because confessing outcast status enfolds one in a
nation of others who are also like Wilde.

Reading the poem, we cross the space between ourselves and Wilde,
as Wilde, commiserating, closed the gap between himself and C.T.W. The
poem's subject is the distance between two outcast men, Wilde and the
reader, who collide by crossing: 'Like two doomed ships that pass in
storm / We had crossed each other's way' (p. 236). Wilde and the reader,
after all, are alike: 'A prison wall was round us both, / Two outcast men
we were' (p. 236). Both reader and writer are potentially criminals: 'Yet
each man kills the thing he loves, / By each let this be heard' (p. 232).
The words on Wilde's grave at Père-Lachaisse come from the 'Ballad':

> And alien tears will fill for him
>   Pity's long-broken urn,
> For his mourners will be outcast men,
>   And outcasts always mourn.

(p. 248)

These lines predict the constituency of mourners who will arrive there
and read the memorial as a mirror; this inscription projects gay identity
forming around Wilde's emblematic imprisonment. The chiasmus in the
lines 'For his *mourners* will be *outcast* men, / And *outcasts* always *mourn*'
– the way that the two words, *mourners* and *outcasts*, change relative
places from one line to the next – further reflects gay identity's
formation. The outcast identity grows to be independent of and prior to
the act of mourning that originally constituted it: reading Wilde's grave
creates a gay subjectivity empowered to read the grave. This chiasmus is
the *cross* on which Wilde expired, a Calvary. Post-Wilde gay readers
discover they are gay as if it were a fact already there, when it is
precisely their mourning of Wilde, their acknowledgment of a likeness,
that guides them toward that identity.

The verb *read* is a homonym for the color *red*, a word prominent in the
Ballad. The poem's title, 'The Ballad of *Reading* Gaol', underscores, by
macabre exploited coincidence, this homonym, which conflates Christ's

blood, communion wine, Wilde's suffering in Reading Gaol, and our reading of the poem. The poem plays with the word: 'For none of us can tell to what *red* Hell / His sightless soul may stray' (p. 236); 'He did not wear his scarlet coat, / For blood and wine are *red*' (p. 231); 'He does not bend his head to hear / The Burial Office *read*' (p. 233); 'The grey cock crew, the *red* cock crew, / But never came the day' (p. 240); 'God's dreadful dawn was *red*' (p. 242); 'In *Reading* Gaol by *Reading* Town / There is a pit of shame' (p. 252). The two meanings, red and read, most palpably intersect here: 'The man in *red* who *reads* the Law' (p. 251). Does the man who reads the Law write it, too, or just absently intone what another man has decreed? Wilde discovers the possibility of reading the Law against itself – through reading, opening up a rift within the Law and finding a sexual surprise.[32]

The surprise is Wilde's resurrection: the persistence of his reputation and of the homosexual 'type' molded in his image.

> For three long years they will not sow
> 　Or root or seedling there:
> For three long years the unblessed spot
> 　Will sterile be and bare,
> And look upon the wondering sky
> 　With unreproachful stare.
>
> (p. 246)

For a mythic three years (Christ died at thirty-three, and Wilde was prisoner C.3.3), no signs of him will appear above his outcast grave; his legacy will be 'sterile' – unreproductive. But then, he predicts his own return; he imagines his revarnished reputation, as well as a new self-designation arising – the ability to choose 'outcast' as a pleasing identity. With a new identity comes a new language, an eccentric prison argot at which 'the Ballad' marvels:

> I never saw a man who looked
> 　With such a wistful eye
> Upon that little tent of blue
> 　Which prisoners call the sky . . .
>
> (p. 231)

Prisoners, as if perversely, affix the word *sky* to a paltry tent of *blue* – a word infused, at the turn of the century, with gay meanings;[33] outcast men name the objects of their world unconventionally, and it is Wilde's fall and hard labor that gave birth to this new, potentially enfranchising, lexicon.

Here, Wilde describes the 'reading' that will sprout from his fall, making it, like Satan's in *Paradise Lost*, fortunate:

> Out of his mouth a red, red rose!
>   Out of his heart a white!
> For who can say by what strange way,
>   Christ brings His will to light,
> Since the barren staff the pilgrim bore
>   Bloomed in the great Pope's sight?
>
> (p. 246–7)

Reading arose: the rose that comes out of his mouth is red, and we must read it. What rises from Wilde's mouth, from Wilde's work, is the possibility of a barren typology – 'homosexual' – bringing about new ways of assigning meaning. In *De Profundis*, Wilde said that 'everything to be true must become a religion' (p. 154). For gayness to be more than a mere lifestyle or recreational choice – for it to be an encyclopedia, a geography, a wealth of routes and signs – it must acknowledge its own capacious interpretive mannerisms as more than manner, as matter; it must recognize that gay men, at least since Wilde, have known themselves through mourning and cloning – noting a likeness between the plights of two outcasts. Outcast identity is particularly incarcerating, but any identity is a prison – an enclosure, whether fashion or flesh, over which we have little control, but that helps us to read.

I dwell on 'reading', of course, because I am a literary critic – interested in styles of interpretation that accommodate readers like myself. My glance at Wilde in Reading Gaol takes place within the limited frame of a revisionary literary critical project. But reading is more than a private traffic with printed matter. It is an engagement, achieved through the imagination, across a distance; a tightly knit affair between a speaker and a listener; a survivor's gesture of reconnaissance and affection toward the past. Reading is mourning – a community forming around a likeness, around a death or a fall. In 'The Ballad', Wilde wrote, 'The red cock crew': he meant that the cock was red. But I mean something else: the read cock. The cock is Wilde's. And we must interpret it; we must try to read what his cock cries. The read cock – the interpreted penis – elucidated desire – *gay identity as Wilde imagined it* – is something worth reading, interpreting, inventing. If Wilde did not write it, let us write it for him.

Notes

1. See the several volumes of MICHEL FOUCAULT's *History of Sexuality*, particularly *Volume 1: An Introduction*, trans. Robert Hurley (New York: Random House, 1980). See also JOHN D'EMILIO, *Sexual Politics, Sexual Communities: The Making of a Homosexual Minority in the United States, 1940–1970* (Chicago: University of Chicago Press, 1983), and JEFFREY WEEKS, *Sexuality and Its Discontents: Meanings, Myths, and Modern Sexualities* (London: Routledge & Kegan Paul, 1985).

2. ROLAND BARTHES, *S/Z: An Essay*, trans. Richard Miller (New York: Farrar, Straus and Giroux, 1988).

3. D.A. MILLER, *The Novel and the Police* (Berkeley: University of California Press, 1988).

4. See ED COHEN, 'Writing Gone Wilde: Homoerotic Desire in the Closet of Representation', *PMLA*, **102**, 5 (October 1987): 801–13; JONATHAN DOLLIMORE, 'Different Desires: Subjectivity and Transgression in Wilde and Gide', *Genders*, **2** (July 1988): 24–41; REGENIA GAGNIER, *Idylls of the Marketplace: Oscar Wilde and the Victorian Public* (Stanford: Stanford University Press, 1986). I have had the privilege of reading important unpublished work on Wilde and on gay theory by Christopher Craft, Bruce Hainley, Patrick Horrigan, Michael Lucey, and Eve Kosofsky Sedgwick; I am grateful, as well, to the students in my 1988 undergraduate seminar at Yale on gay and lesbian literature.

5. See WALTER BENJAMIN, 'The Work of Art in the Age of Mechanical Reproduction', in *Illuminations* (New York: Schocken Books, 1969), pp. 217–52.

6. E.M. FORSTER, *Maurice* (New York: W.W. Norton, 1987), p. 156.

7. This reader resembles Proust's Albertine. Wilde, like Marcel, turned fear of infidelity into a prose-engendering germ.

8. OSCAR WILDE, 'De Profundis', in *De Profundis and Other Writings*, ed. Hesketh Pearson (Harmondsworth: Penguin, 1986), p. 97. Further references appear in my text.

9. See RICHARD ELLMANN, *Oscar Wilde* (New York: Knopf, 1988), pp. 508–9.

10. Quoted in ROBERT ROSS, 'Preface', in Oscar Wilde, *De Profundis* (London: Methuen, 1905), p. vii.

11. SUSAN GUBAR, '"The Blank Page" and the Issues of Female Creativity', in Elizabeth Abel (ed.), *Writing and Sexual Difference* (Chicago: University of Chicago Press, 1982), pp. 73–94.

12. OSCAR WILDE, 'The Decay of Lying', in WILDE, *De Profundis*, p. 74.

13. Oscar Wilde's petition, written in Reading Gaol, to the Secretary of State for the Home Department; quoted in H. MONTGOMERY HYDE, *Oscar Wilde: The Aftermath* (London: Methuen, 1963), p. 71.

14. Typing – defined as the ability to make a fatal impression on a lover or on the next generation – resembles the poetics of infection that dominates homophobic constructions of AIDS: sexual magnetism as a contagion.

15. *The Chicago Manual of Style*, 13th edn (Chicago: University of Chicago Press, 1982), p. 587.

16. ROBERT ROSS, 'Preface', p. ix.

17. Quoted in HYDE, *Oscar Wilde*, p. 173.

18. Ibid., p. 89.
19. Quoted in ibid., p. 90.
20. Quoted in ibid., p. 90.
21. VYVYAN HOLLAND, 'Introduction', in WILDE, *De Profundis and Other Writings*, p. 91.
22. ABRAHAM HORODISCH, *Oscar Wilde's 'Ballad of Reading Gaol': A Bibliographic Study* (New York: Aldus, 1954), pp. 84, 59.
23. 'The Story of Oscar Wilde', Advertising brochure for the Patrons' Edition De Luxe of Oscar Wilde (New York: Doubleday, Page).
24. Karl Beckson (ed.), *Oscar Wilde: The Critical Heritage* (London: Routledge & Kegan Paul, 1970), p. 243.
25. Ibid., p. 247.
26. Ibid., p. 222.
27. HESTER TRAVERS SMITH, *Oscar Wilde From Purgatory* (New York: Henry Holt, n.d.), p. 97.
28. *Oscar Wilde: The Critical Heritage*, p. 322.
29. See HORODISCH, *Oscar Wilde's 'Ballad of Reading Gaol'*, p. 14.
30. 'The Ballad of Reading Gaol', in WILDE, *De Profundis and Other Writings*, p. 239. Page numbers will appear in my text.
31. ELLMANN, *Oscar Wilde*, pp. 503–4.
32. The *red* room, in which CHARLOTTE BRONTË's Jane Eyre is locked for hitting John *Reed* over the head when he forbade her to *read* one of his books is another exemplary conflation of redness and reading.
33. See JOHN ADDINGTON SYMONDS, *In the Key of Blue and Other Prose Essays* (London: Elkin Mathews, 1893).

9   Renewing the Practice of Reading, or Freud's Unprecedented Lesson*

SHOSHANA FELMAN

One of the most important influences on Anglo-American literary criticism and theory during the 1980s and 1990s has been the work of the French psychoanalyst Jacques Lacan. Shoshana Felman's brief chapter discusses the implications of Lacanian psychoanalysis for reading theory, and suggests ways in which psychoanalysis has 'transform[ed] the procedures, strategies, and techniques available to the interpreter'. According to Felman, we are still trying to assimilate the lessons of Freud via the lessons of Lacan and to explore their repercussions for notions of and possibilities for reading theory. Felman suggests that conventional ideas about the operation of psychoanalytic reading or interpretation tend to rely on the detection of a subtext, the unconscious of the text. By contrast, Felman suggests that Lacanian analysis, while recognising such a 'difference that inhabits language', also asserts that the unconscious is not just that which is read, but also *that which reads*': 'the very constitution of psychoanalysis', Felman declares, 'is the outcome, in Lacan's eyes, of an unprecedented, prodigious act of reading'. Felman briefly suggests ways in which a recognition of the unconscious as a reader would produce a revolutionary notion of (analytic) reading as differential and dialogic.

For more on this topic, see Felman, *What Does a Woman Want?* (1993). See also Elizabeth Wright, 'The Reader in Analysis' (1991) for another brief essay on the implications of Lacan's work for reading theory; and see Jacobus's essay, above, for an exemplary psychoanalytic reading.

I would like to address, in the light of Lacan's radical rethinking of the crucial psychoanalytic issue of interpretation, the general question – both practical and theoretical – of the relationship between psychoanalysis and reading. In theory: What insight does psychoanalysis provide into the very nature of interpretation? In

* Reprinted from *Jacques Lacan and the Adventure of Insight: Psychoanalysis in Contemporary Culture* (Cambridge, Mass.: Harvard University Press, 1987), pp. 19–25.

practice: How has psychoanalysis modified the nature and the possibilities of reading by drastically transforming the procedures, strategies, and techniques available to the interpreter?

An exemplary lesson of reading

In 1968 the French philosopher Louis Althusser wrote of Lacan:

> It is to the intransigent, lucid – and for many years solitary – theoretical effort of Jacques Lacan that we owe today this result [a new understanding of the mechanisms of the discourse of the unconscious], which has drastically transformed our way of reading Freud. At a time when what Lacan has given us that was so radically new begins to pass into the public domain and when everyone can use it, in his own way, to his profit, I would like to make a point of acknowledging our debt toward his exemplary lesson of reading, the effects of which, as we shall see, go well beyond its original object.[1]

While fully subscribing to Althusser's acknowledgment, I would suggest that we can by no means take it for granted that Lacan's 'exemplary lesson of reading' has in any way been *learned*, let alone assimilated, even by those of us who are familiar with his work, those who have been immersed in the (French) public domain that has so eagerly appropriated his concepts and words. A lesson – any lesson – cannot simply be confused with the words, the terminology it uses to articulate itself. A reading lesson is, precisely, not a statement; it is a performance. It is not theory, it is practice, a practice that derives – as such – its worth from its efficiency, not from its exemplarity; a practice, therefore, that can be exemplary only in so far as it is understood to be a model or a paradigm, not for imitation but for (self) transformation. The passage of Lacan's original terminology into the public domain that has indeed appropriated it for a variety of usages and profits, far from ensuring an understanding of the lesson, in effect blocks such understanding, serves itself as a defense against the lesson. For, as was the case with Freud, it is not in words that the lesson can be learned, but in the body, in one's life.

It is true that words are what we read; and in this case we have to read Lacan's words, from which we have to learn how to read. But language for Lacan (even his own) is something altogether other than a list of terms to be mastered. It is rather something like a list of terms we should be transformed by, a list of terms into which to write, or to translate, ourselves.

The American philosopher Richard Rorty writes that 'we are in for another few hundred years of getting adjusted to the availability of the psychoanalytic vocabulary'.[2] By way of agreeing with this statement, I would suggest that we are in for another few hundred years of getting adjusted to the availability of Lacan's lesson of reading; a lesson that itself is an attempt toward, precisely, the adjustment or translation of our modes of thinking and of operating to the still unassimilated radicality of the Freudian revolution.

In acknowledging my own debt to Lacan's exemplary lesson of reading, I can only try to be a teacher of this lesson in so far as I am its student: I can offer only my own reading of Lacan's unformulated theory of reading, through an analysis of Lacan's practice as a reader and of what constitutes what I take to be the path-breaking originality of this practice. But this analysis should itself be viewed as but a step in the effort, that is, in the far from finished process, of adjusting my own ways of thinking and of operating (of adjusting my own ways of reading) to the availability of both the Lacanian and the Freudian insights. I will try, in other words, to read Lacan's lesson of reading not just in my statement about what Lacan is doing when he reads, when he articulates a reading, but in my own way of articulating such a statement, in my own practice as reader.

A theory of practice

What is the relationship between psychoanalysis and reading in Lacan's particular perspective on the matter?

'It is obvious', says Lacan, 'that in analytic discourse, what is at stake is nothing other than what can be read; what can be read beyond what the subject has been incited to say'.[3] 'What is at stake in analytic discourse is always this – to what is uttered as a signifier [by the patient], you [analysts] give another reading than what it means'.[4] In these two quotations that describe the practice of psychoanalysis, 'reading' refers to the analyst's activity of interpreting, and the emphasis is on the displacement operated by the interpreting: the analyst is called upon to interpret the excess in the patient's discourse – what the patient says *beyond* what he has been incited to say, beyond the current motivation of the situation; and the analytic meaning is then a displacement of the meaning of the patient's discourse, since it consists in giving what has been pronounced *another reading*. The analytic reading is thus essentially the reading of a difference that inhabits language, a kind of mapping in the subject's discourse of its points of disagreement with, or difference from, itself.

This, however, is still by and large the conventional view of the role of reading in analysis. Lacan's view is more radical than that. For the activity of reading is not just the analyst's, it is also the analysand's: interpreting is what takes place *on both sides* of the analytic situation. The unconscious, in Lacan's eyes, is not simply the object of psychoanalytical investigation, but its subject. The unconscious, in other words, is not simply *that which must be read* but also, and perhaps primarily, *that which reads*. The unconscious is a reader. What this implies most radically is that whoever reads, interprets out of his unconscious, is an analysand, even when the interpreting is done from the position of the analyst.

> The analyst's interpretation merely reflects the fact that the unconscious, if it is what I say it is, namely, a play of the signifier, the unconscious has already in its formations – dreams, slips of tongue or pen, jokes or symptoms – *proceeded by interpretation*. The Other is already there in the very opening, however evanescent, of the unconscious.
>
> (S XI, p. 118)

> At the other extreme [of analytical experience], there is interpretation . . . Interpretation at its term points to desire, with which, in a certain sense, it is identical. When all is said and done, desire is interpretation itself.
>
> (S XI, p. 161)

Unconscious desire proceeds by interpretation; interpretation proceeds by unconscious desire. The unconscious is a reader. The reader is therefore, on some level, always an analysand – an analysand who 'knows what he means' but whose interpretation can be given *another reading* than what it means. This is what analytic discourse is all about.

> In analytic discourse, you presume the subject of the unconscious to be capable of reading. This is what this whole affair of the unconscious amounts to. Not only do you presume him to be capable of reading, but you presume him to be capable of learning how to read.
>
> (S XX, p. 38)

It is because the unconscious is a reader capable of learning – capable, that is, of learning how to read – that psychoanalysis came into being: the very constitution of psychoanalysis is the outcome, in Lacan's eyes, of an unprecedented, prodigious act of reading. This is how Lacan accounts for the very discovery of the unconscious:

> [Freud's] first interest was in hysteria . . . . He spent a lot of time listening, and while he was listening, there resulted something paradoxical, a *reading*. It was while listening to hysterics that he *read* that there was an unconscious. That is, something he could only construct, and in which he himself was implicated; he was implicated in it in the sense that, to his great astonishment, he noticed that he could not avoid participating in what the hysteric was telling him, and that he felt affected by it. Naturally, everything in the resulting rules in which he established the practice of psychoanalysis is designed to counteract this consequence, to conduct things in such a way as to avoid being affected.[5]

Freud as reader

Freud's discovery of the unconscious is the outcome of his reading of the hysterical discourse of his patients, of his being capable of reading in the hysterical discourse of the Other his own unconscious. The discovery of the unconscious is therefore Freud's discovery, within the discourse of the other, of what was actively reading within himself: his discovery, or his reading, of what was reading – in what was being read. Freud's discovery, for Lacan, thus consists not – as it is conventionally understood – of the revelation of a new *meaning* (the unconscious) but of the practical discovery of a new *way of reading*.

In what ways is this unprecedented Freudian act of reading, this inaugural emergence of analytic reading, revolutionary?

(1) Even though Freud's insight springs from a discovery of *what is reading* (his own unconscious) in *what is being read* (the discourse of the hysteric), even though the reading hinges on the reader's own involvement in the subject matter (his 'implication' in the symptom observed), the reading is by no means introspective. What Freud reads in the hysteric is not his own resemblance but, rather, his own difference from himself: the reading necessarily passes through the Other, and in the Other, reads not identity (other or same), but difference and self-difference.

(2) Dialogue is not an accident, a contingency of the reading, but its structuring condition of possibility. The reading is revolutionary in that it is essentially, constitutively dialogic. It is grounded in a division; it cannot be synthesized, summed up in a monologue.

(3) 'It was while listening to the hysterics that [Freud] read that there was an unconscious. That is, something he could only construct.' The unconscious is not, in effect, 'discovered'; it is *constructed*: it is not given to be observed, a substance out there that has finally come under the microscope; it is a theoretical construction. The reading is, in other words, of such a nature that it cannot be direct, intuitive; it is constitutively mediated by a hypothesis; it necessitates a theory. But the reading is not theory: it is practice, a practical procedure, partially blind to what it does but which proves to be efficient. The theoretical construction of the unconscious is what, after the fact, is constructed to account for the efficiency of the practice. But the practice, the partially unconscious analytic reading practice, always inescapably precedes the theory. There is a constitutive belatedness of the theory over the practice, the theory always trying to catch up with what it was that the practice, or the reading, was really doing. This belated repetition of the theoretical construction can, however, only partially and asymptotically recover the *primal scene* of analytic reading.

In the perspective of this Lacanian conception of the absolute primacy of Freud's analytic *reading practice* and its precedence over his theory, we might say that Freud's theory of the unconscious is indeed itself nothing other than Freud's constant effort to adjust his own modes of thinking to the availability of his own exemplary lesson of reading.

After Freud

Given this grasp of what we may now call Freud's primal scene of reading, Lacan's own analytic theory and practice – his theoretical and practical lesson of reading – turns on this crucial analytic question: what does it mean to be a reader? The question, asked in constant reference to Freud's practice, to Freud's text accounting for his practice, and to Lacan's own analytic practice, comprises three more questions:

(1) What was Freud in effect *doing* as a reader (as a reader of his patients, of the symptom, of his dreams, of literary texts, of his own practice, of his own theoretical constructions)?
(2) What does it mean to be a reader *of* Freud?
(3) What does it mean to be a reader *after* Freud?

These three questions are themselves not so much formulated theoretically as they are pragmatically thought out in each Lacanian reading.

Notes

1. LOUIS ALTHUSSER and ETIENNE BALIBAR, *Lire le capital* (Paris: Petite Collection Maspéro, 1971), p. 13; my translation.

2. RICHARD RORTY, 'Freud, Morality, and Hermeneutics', in *New Literary History*, **12** (Autumn 1980): 177

3 JACQUES LACAN, *Le Séminaire, Livre XX: Encore* (Paris: Seuil, 1975), p. 29: hereafter cited in the text as *S*, XX. All translations from *Le Séminaire* are by Shoshana Felman (Ed.).

4. JACQUES LACAN, *Le Séminaire, Livre XI: Les Quatre Concepts fondamentaux de la psychanalyse* (Paris: Seuil, 1973), p. 116: hereafter cited in the text as *S*, XI (Ed.).

5. Transcribed from a recording of Lacan's talk at the Kanzer Seminar, Yale University, 24 November 1975, translated by Barbara Johnson; my italics. As a rule, italics in quoted passages are mine unless otherwise indicated.

10 Reading*

MAURICE BLANCHOT

'Reading Maurice Blanchot differs from all other reading experiences.
One begins by being seduced by the limpidity of a language that allows for no discontinuities or inconsistencies. Blanchot is, in a way,
the clearest, the most lucid of writers: he steadily borders on the inex-
pressible and approaches the extreme of ambiguity, but always recognizes them for what they are.' Paul de Man's description of reading
the French novelist and critic Maurice Blanchot (from *Blindness and
Insight*, 1983, p. 62) also captures something of what reading is *for*
Blanchot. The following essay is the first section from a two-part consideration of reading and interpretation from *L'Espace littéraire* (1955).
In this essay Blanchot considers the *literariness* of a certain reading.
Blanchot's intense, lyrical meditation on reading resists the reductive-
ness of a crude identification of the 'reader' with a stable subject, or of
reading with the production of a single meaning. For Blanchot, rather
than an affirmation of identity, reading involves a dissolution of the
reader's sense of self. For Blanchot, reading is a creative but anonymous act: 'The reading of a poem is the poem itself' (*The Space of Literature*, English translation, 1982: p. 198).

Blanchot's criticism and fictional writings, until recently relatively
little known to Anglo-American criticism, have nevertheless been influential for post-structuralist critics such as Paul de Man, Geoffrey Hartman, and J. Hillis Miller. In addition to de Man's essay on
Blanchot in *Blindness and Insight*, see Timothy Clark, *Derrida, Heidegger, Blanchot: Sources of Derrida's Notion and Practice of Literature* (Cambridge: Cambridge University Press, 1992), Chapter 2, and his essay
'Reading in Blanchot', in Bennett (ed.), *Reading Reading* (1993).

Reading: we are not surprised to find admissions like this in a writer's
travel diary: 'Always such dread at the moment of writing . . .' and when

---

* Reprinted from *The Gaze of Orpheus and Other Literary Essays*, trans. Lydia Davis (New
York: Station Hill Press, 1981), pp. 91–8.

Lomazzo talks about the horror that seized Leonardo every time he tried to paint, we can understand this, too, we feel we could understand it.

But if a person confided to us, 'I am always anxious at the moment of reading', or another could not read except at rare, special times, or another would disrupt his whole life, renounce the world, forego work and happiness in the world, in order to open the way for himself to a few moments of reading, we would undoubtedly place him alongside Pierre Janet's patient who was reluctant to read because, she said, 'when a book is read it becomes dirty'.

The person who enjoys simply listening to music becomes a musician as he listens, and the same kind of thing happens when someone looks at paintings. The world of music and the world of painting can be entered by anyone who has the key to them. That key is the 'gift', and the gift is the enchantment and understanding of a certain taste. Lovers of music and lovers of painting are people who openly display their preference like a delectable ailment that isolates them and makes them proud. The others modestly recognize the fact that they have no ear. One must be gifted to hear and to see. This gift is a closed space – the concert hall, the museum – with which one surrounds oneself in order to enjoy a clandestine pleasure. People who do not have the gift remain outside, people who have it go in and out as they please. Naturally, music is loved only on Sunday; this god is no more demanding than the other.

Reading does not even require any gift, and it refutes that recourse to a natural privilege. No one is gifted – not the author, not the reader – and anyone who feels he is gifted primarily feels he is not gifted, feels that he is infinitely unequipped, that he lacks the power attributed to him, and just as being an 'artist' means not knowing there is already an art, not knowing there is already a world, so reading, seeing, and hearing works of art demands more ignorance than knowledge, it demands a knowledge filled with immense ignorance, and a gift that is not given beforehand, a gift that is received, secured and lost each time in self-forgetfulness. Each picture, each piece of music presents us with the organ we need in order to receive it, 'gives' us the eye and the ear we need in order to see it and hear it. Non-musicians are people who decide in the very beginning to reject the possibility of hearing, they hide from it as though suspiciously closing themselves off from a threat or an irritation. André Breton repudiates music, because he wants to preserve within himself his right to hear the discordant essence of language, its nonmusical music, and Kafka, who constantly recognizes that he is more closed to music than anyone else in the world, manages to regard this defect as one of his strong points: 'I am really strong, I have one particular strength, and that is – to characterize it in a brief and unclear manner – my non-musical being.'

Usually someone who does not like music cannot tolerate it at all, just as a man who finds a Picasso painting repellent excludes it with a violent hatred, as though he felt directly threatened by it. The fact that he hasn't even looked at the picture says nothing against his good faith. It is not in his power to look at it. Not looking at it does not put him in the wrong, it is a form of his sincerity, his correct presentiment of the force that is closing his eyes. 'I refuse to look at that.' 'I could not live with that before my eyes.' These formulations define the hidden reality of the work of art – its absolute intolerance – more powerfully than the art lover's suspect complacencies. It is quite true that one cannot live with a picture before one's eyes.

The plastic work of art has a certain advantage over the verbal work of art in that it renders more manifest the exclusive void within which the work apparently wants to remain, far from everyone's gaze. Rodin's 'The Kiss' allows itself to be looked at and even thrives on being looked at; his 'Balzac' is without gaze, a closed and sleeping thing, absorbed in itself to such a degree that it disappears. This decisive separation, which sculpture takes as its element and which sets out another, rebellious space in the center of space – sets out a space that is at once hidden, visible, and shielded, perhaps immutable, perhaps without repose – this protected violence, before which we always feel out of place, does not seem to be present in books. The statue that is unearthed and displayed for everyone's admiration does not expect anything, does not receive anything, seems rather to have been torn from its place. But isn't it true that the book that has been exhumed, the manuscript that is taken out of a jar and enters the broad daylight of reading, is born all over again through an impressive piece of luck? What is a book that no one reads? Something that has not yet been written. Reading, then, is not writing the book again but causing the book to write itself or *be* written – this time without the writer as intermediary, without anyone writing it. The reader does not add himself to the book, but his tendency is first to unburden it of any author, and something very hasty in his approach, the very futile shadow that passes across the pages and leaves them intact, everything that makes the reading appear superfluous, and even the reader's lack of attention, the slightness of his interest, all his infinite lightness affirms the book's new lightness: the book has become a book without an author, without the seriousness, the labor, the heavy pangs, the weight of a whole life that has been poured into it – an experience that is sometimes terrible, always dangerous, an experience the reader effaces and, because of his providential lightness, considers to be nothing.

Although he does not know it, the reader is involved in a profound struggle with the author: no matter how much intimacy remains today between the book and the writer, no matter how directly the author's figure, presence, and history are illuminated by the circumstances of publication – circumstances that are not accidental but that may be already slightly anachronistic – in spite of this, every reading in which consideration of the writer seems to play such a large role is an impeachment that obliterates him in order to give the work back to itself, to its anonymous presence, to the violent, impersonal affirmation that it is. The reader himself is always fundamentally anonymous, he is any reader, unique but transparent. Instead of adding his name to the book (as our fathers did in the past), he rather erases all names by his nameless presence, by that modest, passive, interchangeable, insignificant gaze under whose gentle pressure the book appears written, at one remove from everything and everyone.

Reading transforms a book the same way the sea and the wind transform the works of men: the result is a smoother stone, a fragment that has fallen from heaven, without any past, without any future, and that we do not wonder about as we look at it. Reading endows the book with the kind of sudden existence that the statue 'seems' to take from the chisel alone: the isolation that hides it from eyes that see it, the proud remoteness, the orphan wisdom that drives off the sculptor just as much as it does the look that tries to sculpt it again. In some sense the book needs the reader in order to become a statue, it needs the reader in order to assert itself as a thing without an author and also without a reader. What reading brings to it is not first of all a more human truth; but neither does it make the book into something inhuman, an 'object', a pure compact presence, fruit from the depths unripened by our sun. It simply 'makes' the book – the work – become a work beyond the person who produced it, beyond the experience expressed in it and even beyond all the artistic resources that various traditions have made available. The nature of reading, its singularity, illuminates the singular meaning of the verb 'to make' in the expression 'it makes the work become a work'. Here the word 'make' does not indicate a productive activity: reading does not make anything, does not add anything; it lets be what is; it is freedom – not the kind of freedom that gives being or takes it away, but a liberty that receives, consents, says yes, can only say yes, and in the space opened by this yes, allows the work's amazing decision to be affirmed: that it is – and nothing more.

'Lazare, veni foras.'

Reading that accepts the work for what it is and in so doing unburdens it of its author, does not consist of replacing the author by a reader, a fully existent person, who has a history, a profession, a religion, and is even well read, someone who, on the basis of all that, would begin a dialogue with the other person, the one who wrote the book. Reading is not a conversation, it does not discuss, it does not question. It never asks the book – and certainly not the author – 'What exactly did you mean? Well, what truth are you offering me?' True reading never challenges the true book: but it is not a form of submission to the 'text' either. Only the non-literary book is presented as a stoutly woven web of determined significations, as an entity made up of real affirmations: before it is read by anyone, the non-literary book has already been read by everyone, and it is this preliminary reading that guarantees it a secure existence. But the book whose source is art has no guarantee in the world, and when it is read, it has never been read before; it only attains its presence as a work in the space opened by this unique reading, each time the first reading and each time the only reading.

This is the source of the strange freedom exemplified by reading, literary reading. It is free movement, if it is not subject to anything, if it does not depend on anything already present. The book is undoubtedly there – not only in its reality as paper and print, but also in its nature as a book, this fabric of stable significations, this affirmation that it owes to a pre-established language, and also this precinct formed around it by the community of all readers, which already includes me even though I have not read it, and also made up of all other books, which, like angels with interlaced wings, watch closely over the unknown volume, because if even one book is threatened, a dangerous breach is opened in the world's library. And so the book is there, but the work is still hidden, perhaps radically absent, in any case disguised, obscured by the obviousness of the book behind which it awaits the liberating decision, the *Lazare, veni foras.*

The mission of reading seems to be to cause this stone to fall: to make it transparent, to dissolve it with the penetration of a gaze which enthusiastically goes beyond it. There is something dizzying about reading, or at least about the outset of reading, that resembles the irrational impulse by which we try to open eyes that are already closed, open them to life; this impulse is connected to desire, which is a leap, an infinite leap, just as inspiration is a leap: I want to *read* what has nevertheless not been written. But there is more, and what makes the 'miracle' of reading – which perhaps enlightens us concerning the meaning of all thaumaturgy – even more singular is that here the stone and the tomb not only contain a cadaverous emptiness that must be animated, but they also constitute the presence – hidden though it is – of what must appear. To roll the stone, to move it away, is certainly something marvellous, but we accomplish it each instant in our everyday language, and we converse each instant with this Lazarus, who has been dead for three days, or perhaps forever, and who, beneath his tightly woven bandages, is sustained by the most elegant conventions, and answers us and talks to us in our very hearts. But what responds to the appeal of literary reading is not a door falling or becoming transparent or even becoming a little thinner; rather, it is a rougher kind of stone, more tightly sealed, crushing – a vast deluge of stone that shakes the earth and the sky.

Such is the particular nature of this 'opening', which is what reading is made up of: only what is more tightly closed opens; only what has been borne as an oppressive nothingness without consistency can be admitted into the lightness of a free and happy Yes. And this does not tie the poetic work to the search for an obscurity that would confound everyday understanding. It merely establishes a violent rupture between the book that is there and the work that is never there beforehand, between the book that is the concealed work and the work that cannot affirm itself except in the thickness – thickness made present – of this concealment: it establishes a violent rupture, and the passage from a world in which everything has some degree of meaning, in which there is darkness and light, to a space where nothing has any meaning yet, properly speaking, but to which, even so, everything that has meaning returns as to its own origin.

But these remarks would also risk deceiving us, if they seemed to say that reading was the work of clearing a way from one language to another, or a bold step requiring initiative, effort, and the conquest of obstacles. The approach to reading may be a difficult kind of happiness, but reading is the easiest thing in the world, it is freedom without work, a pure Yes blossoming in the immediate.

The light, innocent Yes of reading

Reading, in the sense of literary reading, is not even a pure movement of comprehension, the kind of understanding that tries to sustain meaning by setting it in motion again. Reading is situated beyond comprehension or short of comprehension. Nor is reading exactly an appeal that the unique work that should disclose itself in reading reveal itself behind the appearance of common speech, behind the book that belongs to everyone. No doubt there is some sort of appeal, but it can only come from the work itself, it is a silent appeal that imposes silence in the midst of the general noise, an appeal the reader hears only as he responds to it, that deflects the reader from his habitual relations and turns him towards the space near which reading bides and becomes an approach, a delighted reception of the generosity of the work, a reception that raises the book to the work that it is, through the same rapture that raises the work to being and turns the reception into a ravishment, the ravishment in which the work is articulated. Reading is this abode and it has the simplicity of the light and transparent Yes that is this abode. Even if it demands that the reader enter a zone in which he has no air and the ground is hidden from him, even if, beyond these stormy approaches, reading seems to be a kind of participation in the open violence that is the work, in itself reading is a tranquil and silent presence, the pacified center of excess, the silent Yes that lies at the heart of every storm.

The freedom of this Yes – which is present, ravished, and transparent – is the essence of reading. Because of this, reading stands in contrast to that aspect of the work which, through the experience of creation, approaches absence, the torments of the infinite, the empty depths of something that never begins or ends – a movement that exposes the creator to the threat of essential solitude, that delivers him to the interminable.

In this sense, reading is more positive than creation, more creative, although it does not produce anything. It shares in the decision, it has the lightness, the irresponsibility, the innocence of the decision. It does nothing and everything is accomplished. For Kafka there was dread, there were unfinished stories, the torment of a wasted life, of a mission betrayed, every day turned into an exile, every night exiled from sleep, and finally, there was the certainty that '*The Metamorphosis* is unreadable, radically flawed.' But for Kafka's reader, the dread turns into ease and happiness, the torment over faults is transfigured into innocence, and in each scrap of text there is delight in fullness, certainty of completion, a revelation of the unique, inevitable, unpredictable work. This is the essence of reading, of the light Yes which – far more effectively than the creator's dark struggle with chaos, in which he seeks to disappear so as to master it – evokes the divine share of creation.

This is why an author's grievances against the reader often seem misplaced. Montesquieu writes, 'I am asking a favor that I am afraid no one will grant me: and that is not to judge twenty years' work in a moment's reading; to approve or condemn the entire book and not just a few sentences', and he is asking something that artists are often sorry they do not have, as they think with bitterness how their works are the victims of a casual reading, a distracted glance, a careless ear: such effort, such sacrifice, such care, such calculation, a life of solitude, centuries of mediation and seeking – all this is appraised, judged and annihilated by the ignorant decision of the first person to come along, by a chance mood. And when Valéry worries about today's uncultivated reader who demands that facility accompany his reading, this worry may be justified, but the culture of an attentive reader, the scruples of a reading filled with devotion, an almost religious reading, one that has become a sort of cult, would not change anything; it would create even more serious dangers, because although the lightness of a casual reader,

dancing quickly around the text, may not be true lightness, it has no
consequences and holds a certain promise: it proclaims the happiness
and innocence of reading, which may in fact be a dance with an invisible
partner in a separate space, a joyful, wild dance with the 'tomb'.
Lightness from which we must not hope for the impulse of a graver
concern, because where we have lightness, gravity is not lacking.

11 The Resistance to Theory*

PAUL DE MAN

In Anglo-American criticism, the most powerful and influential expo-
nent of that particular practice and theorization of reading designated
by the term 'deconstruction' has been Paul de Man. For de Man, the
work of reading is inescapably a work of theorization. In *Allegories of
Reading* (1979), de Man suggests that reading is itself theorized in and
by literary and other texts so as to produce repetitions, in reading, of
the text's figurations of reading. The chapter reprinted below, from
The Resistance to Theory, is extracted from an essay in which de Man
considers the question of what it is about literary theory 'that is so
threatening that it provokes such strong resistances and attacks'. In
the first part of the essay, not reprinted here, de Man concludes that
'resistance may be a built-in constituent' of the discourse of literary
theory: he suggests that, rather than simply a response to the radical
disturbance of deconstruction, attacks on theory, 'are the displaced
symptoms of a resistance inherent in the theoretical enterprise itself' –
that is to say, to 'language about language'. As de Man argues, below,
such resistance is in fact a resistance in reading, 'to the rhetorical or
tropological dimension of language'. De Man suggests that reading is
'a negative process, in which the grammatical cognition is undone, at
all times, by its rhetorical displacement'. It is from this basis that
de Man presents reader-response criticism as itself a form of resistance to reading. Such theory, de Man argues, elides 'the problematization of the phenomenalism of reading' in its attempts to produce a
grammar or hermeneutics of reading which takes no account of the
'residue of indetermination' left by figuration, by language.

See also de Man's *Allegories of Reading* (1979) and his Introduction to
Hans Robert Jauss's *Toward an Aesthetic of Reception* (1982). For essays
on de Man's work, see Waters and Godzich (eds), *Reading de Man
Reading* (1989), and Miller's essay (Chapter 12).

---

* Reprinted from *The Resistance to Theory* (Manchester: Manchester University Press,
1986), pp. 12–20.

We return, then, to the original question in an attempt to broaden the discussion enough to inscribe the polemics inside the question rather than having them determine it. The resistance to theory is a resistance to the use of language about language. It is therefore a resistance to language itself or to the possibility that language contains factors or functions that cannot be reduced to intuition. But we seem to assume all too readily that, when we refer to something called 'language', we know what it is we are talking about, although there is probably no word to be found in the language that is as overdetermined, self-evasive, disfigured and disfiguring as 'language'. Even if we choose to consider it at a safe remove from any theoretical model, in the pragmatic history of 'language', not as a concept, but as a didactic assignment that no human being can bypass, we soon find ourselves confronted by theoretical enigmas. The most familiar and general of all linguistic models, the classical *trivium*, which considers the sciences of language as consisting of grammar, rhetoric, and logic (or dialectics), is in fact a set of unresolved tensions powerful enough to have generated an infinitely prolonged discourse of endless frustration of which contemporary literary theory, even at its most self-assured, is one more chapter. The difficulties extend to the internal articulations between the constituent parts as well as the articulation of the field of language with the knowledge of the world in general, the link between the *trivium* and the *quadrivium*, which covers the non-verbal sciences of number (arithmetic), of space (geometry), of motion (astronomy), and of time (music). In the history of philosophy, this link is traditionally, as well as substantially, accomplished by way of logic, the area where the rigor of the linguistic discourse about itself matches up with the rigor of the mathematical discourse about the world. Seventeenth-century epistemology, for instance, at the moment when the relationship between philosophy and mathematics is particularly close, holds up the language of what it calls geometry (*mos geometricus*), and which in fact includes the homogeneous concatenation between space, time and number, as the sole model of coherence and economy. Reasoning *more geometrico* is said to be 'almost the only mode of reasoning that is infallible, because it is the only one to adhere to the true method, whereas all other ones are by natural necessity in a degree of confusion of which only geometrical minds can be aware'.[1] This is a clear instance of the interconnection between a science of the phenomenal world and a science of language conceived as definitional logic, the precondition for a correct axiomatic-deductive, synthetic reasoning. The possibility of thus circulating freely between logic and mathematics has its own complex and problematic history as well as its contemporary equivalences with a different logic and a different mathematics. What matters for our present argument is that this articulation of the sciences of language with the mathematical sciences represents a particularly compelling version of a continuity between a theory of language, as logic, and the knowledge of the phenomenal world to which mathematics gives access. In such a system, the place of aesthetics is preordained and by no means alien, provided the priority of logic, in the model of the *trivium*, is not being questioned. For even if one assumes, for the sake of argument and against a great deal of historical evidence, that the link between logic and the natural sciences is secure, this leaves open the question, within the confines of the *trivium* itself, of the relationship between grammar, rhetoric and logic. And this is the point at which literariness, the use of language that foregrounds the rhetorical over the grammatical and the logical function, intervenes as a decisive but unsettling element which, in a variety of modes and aspects, disrupts the inner balance of the model and, consequently, its outward extension to the non-verbal world as well.

Logic and grammar seem to have a natural enough affinity for each other and, in the tradition of Cartesian linguistics, the grammarians of Port-Royal experienced little difficulty at being logicians as well. The same claim persists today in very different methods and terminologies that nevertheless maintain the same orientation toward the universality that logic shares with science. Replying to those who oppose the singularity of specific texts to the scientific generality of the semiotic project, A.J. Greimas disputes the right to use the dignity of 'grammar' to describe a reading that would not be committed to universality. Those who have doubts about the semiotic method, he writes, 'postulate the necessity of constructing a grammar for each particular text. But the essence (*le propre*) of a grammar is its ability to account for a large number of texts, and the metaphorical use of the term . . . fails to hide the fact that one has, in fact, given up on the semiotic project.'[2] There is no doubt that what is here prudently called 'a large number' implies the hope at least of a future model that would in fact be applicable to the generation of all texts. Again, it is not our present purpose to discuss the validity of this methodological optimism, but merely to offer it as an instance of the persistent symbiosis between grammar and logic. It is clear that, for Greimas as for the entire tradition to which he belongs, the grammatical and the logical functions of language are coextensive. Grammar is an isotope of logic.

It follows that, as long as it remains grounded in grammar, any theory of language, including a literary one, does not threaten what we hold to be the underlying principle of all cognitive and aesthetic linguistic systems. Grammar stands in the service of logic which, in turn, allows for the passage to the knowledge of the world. The study of grammar, the first of the *artes liberales*, is the necessary precondition for scientific and humanistic knowledge. As long as it leaves this principle intact, there is nothing threatening about literary theory. The continuity between theory and phenomenalism is asserted and preserved by the system itself. Difficulties occur only when it is no longer possible to ignore the epistemological thrust of the rhetorical dimension of discourse, that is, when it is no longer possible to keep it in its place as a mere adjunct, a mere ornament within the semantic function.

The uncertain relationship between grammar and rhetoric (as opposed to that between grammar and logic) is apparent, in the history of the *trivium*, in the uncertain status of figures of speech or tropes, a component of language that straddles the disputed borderlines between the two areas. Tropes used to be part of the study of grammar but were also considered to be the semantic agent of the specific function (or effect) that rhetoric performs as persuasion as well as meaning. Tropes, unlike grammar, pertain primordially to language. They are text-producing functions that are not necessarily patterned on a non-verbal entity, whereas grammar is by definition capable of extra-linguistic generalization. The latent tension between rhetoric and grammar precipitates out in the problem of reading, the process that necessarily partakes of both. It turns out that the resistance to theory is in fact a resistance to reading, a resistance that is perhaps at its most effective, in contemporary studies, in the methodologies that call themselves theories of reading but nevertheless avoid the function they claim as their object.

What is meant when we assert that the study of literary texts is necessarily dependent on an act of reading, or when we claim that this act is being systematically avoided? Certainly more than the tautology that one has to have read at least some parts, however small, of a text (or read some part, however small, of a text about this text) in order to be able to make a statement about it. Common as it may be, criticism by hearsay is only rarely held up as exemplary. To stress the by no means self-evident necessity of reading implies at least two things. First of all, it implies that literature is not a transparent message in which it can be taken for granted that the distinction between the message and the means of communication is clearly established. Second, and more problematically, it implies that the grammatical decoding of a text leaves a residue of indetermination that has to be, but cannot be, resolved by grammatical means, however extensively conceived. The extension of grammar to include para-figural dimensions is in fact the most remarkable and debatable strategy of contemporary semiology, especially in the study of syntagmatic and narrative structures. The codification of contextual elements well beyond the syntactical limits of the sentence leads to the systematic study of metaphrastic dimensions and has considerably refined and expanded the knowledge of textual codes. It is equally clear, however, that this extension is always strategically directed towards the replacement of rhetorical figures by grammatical codes. This tendency to replace a rhetorical by a grammatical terminology (to speak of hypotaxis, for instance, to designate anamorphic or metonymic tropes) is part of an explicit program, a program that is entirely admirable in its intent since it tends towards the mastering and the clarification of meaning. The replacement of a hermeneutic by a semiotic model, of interpretation by decoding, would represent, in view of the baffling historical instability of textual meanings (including, of course, those of canonical texts), a considerable progress. Much of the hesitation associated with 'reading' could thus be dispelled.

The argument can be made, however, that no grammatical decoding, however refined, could claim to reach the determining figural dimensions of a text. There are elements in all texts that are by no means ungrammatical, but whose semantic function is not grammatically definable, neither in themselves nor in context. Do we have to interpret the genitive in the title of Keats' unfinished epic *The Fall of Hyperion* as meaning 'Hyperion's Fall', the case story of the defeat of an older by a newer power, the very recognizable story from which Keats indeed started out but from which he increasingly strayed away, or as 'Hyperion Falling', the much less specific but more disquieting evocation of an actual process of falling, regardless of its beginning, its end or the identity of the entity to whom it befalls to be falling? This story is indeed told in the later fragment entitled *The Fall of Hyperion*, but it is told about a character who resembles Apollo rather than Hyperion, the same Apollo who, in the first version (called *Hyperion*), should definitely be triumphantly standing rather than falling if Keats had not been compelled to interrupt, for no apparent reason, the story of Apollo's triumph. Does the title tell us that Hyperion is fallen and that Apollo stands, or does it tell us that Hyperion and Apollo (and Keats, whom it is hard to distinguish, at times, from Apollo) are interchangeable in that all of them are necessarily and constantly falling? Both readings are grammatically correct, but it is impossible to decide from the context (the ensuing narrative) which version is the right one. The narrative context suits neither and both at the same time, and one is tempted to suggest that the fact that Keats was unable to complete either version manifests the impossibility, for him as for us, of reading his own title. One could then read the word 'Hyperion' in the title *The Fall of Hyperion* figurally, or, if one wishes, intertextually, as referring not to the historical or mythological character but as referring to the title of Keats' own earlier text (*Hyperion*). But are we then telling the story of the failure of the first text as the success of the second, the Fall of *Hyperion* as the Triumph of *The Fall of Hyperion*? Manifestly, yes, but not quite, since the second text also fails to be concluded. Or are we telling the story of why all texts, as texts, can always be said to be falling? Manifestly yes, but not quite, either, since the story of the fall of the first version, as told in the second, applies to the first version only and could not legitimately be read as meaning also the fall of *The Fall of Hyperion*. The undecidability involves the figural or literal status of the proper name Hyperion as well as of the verb falling, and is thus a matter of figuration and not of grammar. In 'Hyperion's Fall', the word 'fall' is plainly figural, the representation of a figural fall, and we, as readers, read this fall standing up. But in 'Hyperion Falling', this is not so clearly the case, for if Hyperion can be Apollo and Apollo can be Keats, then he can also be us and his figural (or symbolic) fall becomes his and our literal falling as well. The difference between the two readings is itself structured as a trope. And it matters a great deal how we read the title, as an exercise not only in semantics, but in what the text actually does to us. Faced with the ineluctable necessity to come to a decision, no grammatical or logical analysis can help us out. Just as Keats had to break off his narrative, the reader has to break off his understanding at the very moment when he is most directly engaged and summoned by the text. One could hardly expect to find solace in this 'fearful symmetry' between the author's and reader's plight since, at this point, the symmetry is no longer a formal but an actual trap, and the question no longer 'merely' theoretical.

This undoing of theory, this disturbance of the stable cognitive field that extends from grammar to logic to a general science of man and of the phenomenal world, can in its turn be made into a theoretical project of rhetorical analysis that will reveal the inadequacy of grammatical models of non-reading. Rhetoric, by its actively negative relationship to grammar and to logic, certainly undoes the claims of the *trivium* (and by extension, of language) to be an epistemologically stable construct. The resistance to theory is a resistance to the rhetorical or tropological dimension of language, a dimension which is perhaps more explicitly in the foreground in literature (broadly conceived) than in other verbal manifestations or – to be somewhat less vague – which can be revealed in any verbal event when it is read textually. Since grammar as well as figuration is an integral part of reading, it follows that reading will be a negative process in which the grammatical cognition is undone, at all times, by its rhetorical displacement. The model of the *trivium* contains within itself the pseudo-dialectic of its own undoing and its history tells the story of this dialectic.

This conclusion allows for a somewhat more systematic description of the contemporary theoretical scene. This scene is dominated by an increased stress on reading as a theoretical problem or, as it is sometimes erroneously phrased, by an increased stress on the reception rather than on the production of texts. It is in this area that the most fruitful exchanges have come about between writers and journals of various countries and that the most interesting dialogue has developed between literary theory and other disciplines, in the arts as well as in linguistics, philosophy and the social sciences. A straightforward *report* on the present state of literary theory in the United States would have to stress the emphasis on reading, a direction which is already present, moreover, in the New Critical tradition of the forties and the fifties. The methods are now more technical, but the contemporary interest in a poetics of literature is clearly linked, traditionally enough, to the problems of reading. And since the models that are being used certainly are no longer *simply* intentional and centered on an identifiable self, nor *simply* hermeneutic in the postulation of a single originary, pre-figural and absolute text, it would appear that this concentration on reading would lead to the rediscovery of the theoretical difficulties associated with rhetoric. This is indeed the case, to some extent; but not quite. Perhaps the most instructive aspect of contemporary theory is the refinement of the techniques by which the threat inherent in rhetorical analysis is being avoided at the very moment when the efficacy of these techniques has progressed so far that the rhetorical obstacles to understanding can no longer be mistranslated in thematic and phenomenal commonplaces. The resistance to theory which, as we saw, is a resistance to reading, appears in its most rigorous and theoretically elaborated form among the theoreticians of reading who dominate the contemporary theoretical scene.

It would be a relatively easy, though lengthy, process to show that this is so for theoreticians of reading who, like Greimas or, on a more refined level, Riffaterre or, in a very different mode, H.R. Jauss or Wolfgang Iser – all of whom have a definite, though sometimes occult, influence on literary theory in this country – are committed to the use of grammatical models or, in the case of *Rezeptionsästhetik*, to traditional hermeneutic models that do not allow for the problematization of the phenomenalism of reading and therefore remain uncritically confined within a theory of literature rooted in aesthetics. Such an argument would be easy to make because, once a reader has become aware of the rhetorical dimensions of a text, he will not be amiss in finding textual instances that are irreducible to grammar or to historically determined meaning, provided only he is willing to acknowledge what he is bound to notice. The problem quickly becomes the more baffling one of having to account for the shared reluctance to acknowledge the obvious. But the argument would be lengthy because it has to involve a textual analysis that cannot avoid being somewhat elaborate; one can succinctly suggest the grammatical indetermination of a title such as *The Fall of Hyperion*, but to confront such an undecidable enigma with the critical reception and reading of Keats' text requires some space.

The demonstration is less easy (though perhaps less ponderous) in the case of the theoreticians of reading whose avoidance of rhetoric takes another turn. We have witnessed, in recent years, a strong interest in certain elements in language whose function is not only not dependent on any form of phenomenalism but on any form of cognition as well, and which thus excludes, or postpones, the consideration of tropes, ideologies, etc., from a reading that would be primarily performative. In some cases, a link is reintroduced between performance, grammar, logic, and stable referential meaning, and the resulting theories (as in the case of Ohmann) are not in essence distinct from those of avowed grammarians or semioticians. But the most astute practitioners of a speech-act theory of reading avoid this relapse and rightly insist on the necessity to keep the actual performance of speech acts, which is conventional rather than cognitive, separate from its causes and effects – to keep, in their terminology, the illocutionary force separate from its perlocutionary function. Rhetoric, understood as persuasion, is forcefully banished (like Coriolanus) from the performative moment and exiled in the affective area of perlocution. Stanley Fish, in a masterful essay, convincingly makes this point.[3] What awakens one's suspicion about this conclusion is that it relegates persuasion, which is indeed inseparable from rhetoric, to a purely affective and intentional realm and makes no allowance for modes of persuasion which are no less rhetorical and no less at work in literary texts, but which are of the order of persuasion by *proof* rather than persuasion by seduction. Thus to empty rhetoric of its epistemological impact is possible only because its tropological, figural functions are being bypassed. It is as if, to return for a moment to the model of the *trivium*, rhetoric could be isolated from the generality that grammar and logic have in common and considered as a mere correlative of an illocutionary power. The equation of rhetoric with psychology rather than with epistemology opens up dreary prospects of pragmatic banality, all the drearier if compared to the brilliance of the performative analysis. Speech-act theories of reading in fact repeat, in a much more effective way, the grammatization of the *trivium* at the expense of rhetoric. For the characterization of the performative as sheer convention reduces it in effect to a grammatical code among others. The relationship between trope and performance is actually closer but more disruptive than what is here being proposed. Nor is this relationship properly captured by reference to a supposedly 'creative' aspect of performance, a notion with which Fish rightly takes issue. The performative power of language can be called positional, which differs considerably from conventional as well as from 'creatively' (or, in the technical sense, intentionally) constitutive. Speech-act oriented theories of reading read only to the extent that they prepare the way for the rhetorical reading they avoid.

But the same is still true even if a 'truly' rhetorical reading that would stay clear of any undue phenomenalization or of any undue grammatical or performative codification of the text could be conceived – something which is not necessarily impossible and for which the aims and methods of literary theory should certainly strive. Such a reading would indeed appear as the methodical undoing of the grammatical construct and, in its systematic disarticulation of the *trivium*, will be theoretically sound as well as effective. Technically correct rhetorical readings may be boring, monotonous, predictable and unpleasant, but they are irrefutable. They are also totalizing (and potentially totalitarian) for since the structures and functions they expose do not lead to the knowledge of an entity (such as language) but are an unreliable process of knowledge production that prevents all entities, including linguistic entities, from coming into discourse as such, they are indeed universals, consistently defective models of language's impossibility to be a model language. They are, always in theory, the most elastic theoretical and dialectical model to end all models and they can rightly claim to contain within their own defective selves all the other defective models of reading-avoidance, referential, semiological, grammatical, performative, logical, or whatever. They are theory and not theory at the same time, the universal theory of the impossibility of theory. To the extent however that they are theory, that is to say teachable, generalizable and highly responsive to systematization, rhetorical readings, like the other kinds, still avoid and resist the reading they advocate. Nothing can overcome the resistance to theory since theory *is* itself this resistance. The loftier the aims and the better the methods of literary theory, the less possible it becomes. Yet literary theory is not in danger of going under; it cannot help but flourish, and the more it is resisted, the more it flourishes, since the language it speaks is the language of self-resistance. What remains impossible to decide is whether this flourishing is a triumph or a fall.

Notes

1. BLAISE PASCAL, 'De l'esprit géométrique et de l'art de persuader', in *Oeuvres complètes*, ed. L. Lafuma (Paris: Seuil, 1963), pp. 349ff.

2. A.J. GREIMAS, *Du Sens* (Paris: Seuil, 1970), p. 13.

3. STANLEY FISH, 'How to Do Things with Austin and Searle: Speech Act Theory and Literary Criticism', in *Modern Language Notes* 91 (1976): 983–1025. See especially p. 1008.

12 Reading Unreadability: de Man*

J. HILLIS MILLER

In his book *The Ethics of Reading* (1987), J. Hillis Miller explores what 'the ethics of reading' might involve, how it might be possible to read such a phrase. Through readings of texts by Kant, de Man, George Eliot, Anthony Trollope and Henry James, Miller argues that the moment of reading may properly be said to be 'ethical', to be a response which is both responsive to the text and itself responsible. As Miller points out in the chapter reprinted here, such a description of reading may sound strange since we are used to thinking of reading as an epistemological operation, one concerned with knowledge, understanding, or meaning, rather than with ethics. In fact, however, Miller's sense of the ethics of reading goes to the heart of debates over the question of interpretation and the authority of and for reading. Miller's sense of an ethics of reading involves the possibility of 'a response to an irresistible demand', a response which is also, at the same time, and necessarily, 'free'. Miller's complex reading of de Man puts a certain twist on this paradoxical description of reading, in that, as suggested in the previous essay, reading for de Man involves a certain impossibility – the impossibility of reading. Essentially, this would involve a repetition in reading of a necessary, inescapable failure to read which is figured in the text itself. Reading, in this sense, is itself unreadable.

See Miller's *Versions of Pygmalion* (1990) for an elaboration of the ethics of reading; see also 'The Authority of Reading: An Interview with J. Hillis Miller', in J. Hillis Miller, *Hawthorne and History: Defacing It* (Oxford, 1991); in *Protocols of Reading* (1989), Robert Scholes launches a spirited attack on Miller's *The Ethics of Reading*.

Allegories are always ethical, the term ethical designating the structural interference of two distinct value systems. In this sense, ethics has nothing to do with the will (thwarted or free) of a subject, nor *a fortiori*, with a relationship between subjects. The ethical

---

* Reprinted from *The Ethics of Reading: Kant, de Man, Eliot, Trollope, James, and Benjamin* (New York: Columbia University Press, 1987), pp. 41–59.

category is imperative (i.e, a category rather than a value) to the
extent that it is linguistic and not subjective. Morality is a version of
the same language aporia that gave rise to such concepts as 'man' or
'love' or 'self', and not the cause or the consequence of such
concepts. The passage to an ethical tonality does not result from a
transcendental imperative but is the referential (and therefore
unreliable) version of a linguistic confusion. Ethics (or, one should
say, ethicity) is a discursive mode among others.

(Paul de Man)[1]

Every construction, every system – that is, every text – has within
itself the ignorance of its own exterior as the rupture of its coherence
which it cannot account for.

(Hans-Jost Frey)[2]

This chapter attempts to 'read' the passage I have cited from *Allegories of
Reading* (in defiance of Paul de Man's assertion that a critical text, as
soon as it is taken as a text, is as 'unreadable' as any other text). What
de Man means by 'unreadable', something far different from widespread
notions that it has to do with the 'indeterminacy' of the meaning of the
text, will be one of my concerns. My choice of the question of 'ethics' in
de Man is meant to further my investigation of what it might mean to
speak of an 'ethics of reading' through the reading of an example drawn
from literary criticism or 'theory', after the example from philosophy
and before the properly 'literary' ones from Trollope, Eliot, and James.
My choice is also intended to confront frequent charges that de Man's
work is 'nihilistic', undermines the value of all humanistic study, reduces
the work of interpretation to the free play of arbitrary imposition of
meaning, finds in each text only what it went there to look for, and so on.
What de Man actually says is so far from all this is that it is a kind of
puzzle to figure out how such ideas about his work have got around and
pass current as valid intellectual coinage. Perhaps such ideas are just
that, clichés passed from hand to hand by those who have never
bothered to read de Man's work, no easy task, as I began by admitting.

'My' passage comes in the essay in *Allegories of Reading* entitled
'Allegory (*Julie*)'. This essay follows the one entitled 'Self (*Pygmalion*)',
and comes just before the one entitled 'Allegory of Reading (*Profession de
foi*)'. Other essays, in turn, come before and after each of those. My
extract, in short, is abstracted from an intricate sequence of discursive
and narrative argumentation in *Allegories of Reading* as a whole. The
sequence of essays in that book is by no means arbitrary, haphazard, or
merely chronological according to the order of writing, though exactly
what story the book 'as a whole' tells is another question. In any case,
the act of abstraction I have performed in my initial citation is both

necessary and at the same time illegitimate, unauthorized, as is always the case in such cases. The critic must make citations or refer to them, but cannot cite, for example, the whole of *Allegories of Reading*. Nevertheless, the citation cut off from its context takes on a different meaning, becomes a son with no father, defenselessly wandering the world, more likely to be vulnerable to my misreading.

Beyond that difficulty, presumably de Man's dictum that 'a totally enlightened language, regardless of whether it conceives of itself as a consciousness or not, is unable to control the recurrence, in its readers as well as in itself, of the errors it exposes' (*AR*, p. 219) applies as much to the text of *Allegories of Reading* as to any other text, in a familiar recursive movement like that of the Cretan liar, disqualifying the affirmation in the act of making it. Moreover, what de Man says about the reader must apply also to me. I too must be unable to avoid repeating the errors I think I have seen and mastered by my reading of *Allegories of Reading*. That does not bode well for my fulfillment of the blithe promise to 'read' a passage by de Man I made in my first sentence. I shall return later on to the question of just how this recurrence of error occurs in de Man and in me as a reader of de Man. Of course that final lucidity will in principle contain its own blind spot requiring a further elucidation and exposure of error, and so on, *ad infinitum*, with always a remainder of opacity. One should not underestimate, however, the productive illumination produced as one moves through these various stages of reading, as I shall now try to do.

By 'the ethics of reading', the reader will remember, I mean that aspect of the act of reading in which there is a response to the text that is both necessitated, in the sense that it is a response to an irresistible demand, and free, in the sense that I must take responsibility for my response and for the further effects, 'inter-personal', institutional, social, political, or historical, of my act of reading, for example as that act takes the form of teaching or of published commentary on a given text. What happens when I read *must* happen, but I must acknowledge it as *my* act of reading, though just what the 'I' is or becomes in this transaction is another question. To say that there is a properly ethical dimension to the act of reading sounds odd, as I have said. It would seem that the act of reading as such must have little to do with ethics, even though the text read may make thematic statements which have ethical import, which is not at all the same thing. Reading itself would seem to be epistemological, cognitive, a matter of 'getting the text right', respecting it in that sense, not a matter involving moral obligation.

Even less would Paul de Man's particular 'theory' of reading seem likely to have an ethical dimension. Epistemological categories, categories of truth and falsehood, enlightenment and delusion, insight and blindness, seem to control the admirable rigor of his essays. The

category of ethics or, as he says, 'ethicity', does, however, somewhat
surprisingly, appear at crucial moments in de Man's essays, for example
in 'my' passage. The category of ethicity is one version of that insistence
on a necessary referential, pragmatic function of language which
distinguishes de Man's work from certain forms of structuralism or
semiotics. It also gives the lie to those who claim 'deconstruction' asserts
the 'free play' of language in the void, abstracted from all practical,
social, or political effect. Of de Man one can say what he himself says of
Rousseau:

> his radical critique of referential meaning never implied that the
> referential function of language could in any way be avoided,
> bracketed, or reduced to being just one contingent linguistic
> property among others, as is postulated, for example, in
> contemporary semiology which, like all post-Kantian formalisms,
> could not exist without this postulate.
>
> (*AR*, p. 207)

Ethicity is for de Man associated with the categories of politics and
history, though these three modes of what he calls 'materiality' are not
the same. My goal here is to account for the presence of the word 'ethics'
in de Man's vocabulary, and to present thereby a salient example within
contemporary literary theory of an ethics of reading.

'Ethicity', like other forms of reference to the extralinguistic by way of
the linguistic, occurs for de Man not at the beginning as a basis for
language, and not at the end, as a final triumphant return to reality
validating language, but in the midst of an intricate sequence, the
sequentiality of which is of course only a fiction, a convenience for
thinking as a narrative what in fact always occurs in the tangle of an 'all
at once' mixing tropological, allegorical, referential, ethical, political, and
historical dimensions. The passage I began by citing and propose in this
chapter to try to 'read' follows in *Allegories of Reading* on the page after
one of de Man's most succinct formulations of his paradigmatic model
for the narrative pattern into which all texts fall:

> The paradigm for all texts consists of a figure (or a system of
> figures) and its deconstruction. But since this model cannot be
> closed off by a final reading, it engenders, in its turn, a
> supplementary figural superposition which narrates the
> unreadability of the prior narration. As distinguished from primary
> deconstructive narratives centered on figures and ultimately always
> on metaphor, we can call such narratives to the second (or the third)
> degree *allegories*.
>
> (*AR*, p. 205)

This formulation is by no means immediately transparent in meaning. I have elsewhere attempted to read it in detail.[3] What is most important here is the fact that the ethical moment, for de Man, occurs toward the end of this intricate sequence, as primary evidence of a text's inability to read itself, to benefit from its own wisdom. First comes the assertion of an unjustified and aberrant metaphor, then the 'deconstruction' of that metaphor, the revelation of its aberrancy, then the 'allegory', that is, the expression in a veiled form of the impossibility of reading that revelation of aberrancy. One form that repetition of the first error takes is the mode of referentiality that de Man calls 'ethicity'.

The first feature of the ethical for de Man, then, is that it is an aspect not of the first narrative of metaphorical denomination, nor of the second narrative of the deconstruction of that aberrant act of denomination, but of the 'third' narrative of the failure to read which de Man calls 'allegory'. Says de Man: 'Allegories are always ethical'. The ethical, or what de Man calls, somewhat barbarously, 'ethicity', is not a primary category, but a secondary or in fact tertiary one. 'Ethicity' is necessary and it is not derivative from anything but the laws of language that are all-determining or all-engendering for de Man, but the ethical does not come first. It intervenes, necessarily intervenes, but it occurs at a 'later stage' in a sequence which begins with epistemological error, the error born of aberrant metaphorical naming. One must remember, however, that the sequential unfolding of 'earlier' and 'later' that makes all texts, in de Man's use of the term, 'narratives' is the fictional temporalization of what in fact are simultaneous linguistic operations: aberrant metaphorical naming, the deconstruction of that act of nomination, the allegory of the unreadability of those 'first' two linguistic acts, and so on. Of that allegory of the impossibility of reading 'ethicity' is a necessary dimension, since all allegories are ethical. In this sense ethicity is as first as any other linguistic act. It is unconditionally necessary.

But what does it mean to say that 'allegories are always ethical'? It is clear that the main target of de Man's attack here is Kant's ethical theory. To put this another way, the passage about ethics simultaneously rejects Kant and bends Kantian language to another purpose. In order to make an open space for his own ethical theory, de Man has simultaneously to reject the Kantian theory and appropriate its language to his own uses: 'The ethical category is imperative (i.e., a category rather than a value) to the extent that it is linguistic and not subjective.' In order to argue that ethicity is the product of a purely linguistic necessity de Man has to reject the notion that it has to do with subjectivity, or with freedom as a feature of selfhood, or with interpersonal relations, or with a categorical imperative coming from some transcendental source, whether from subjectivity in the form of the transcendental imagination or from some extrahuman transcendence. 'Ethics', says de Man, 'has nothing to do with the will (thwarted or free) of a subject, nor *a fortiori*, with a relationship between subjects.' And: 'The passage to an ethical tonality does not result from a transcendental imperative.'

Well, if ethics has nothing to do with any of the things it has traditionally been thought to be concerned with, with what then does it have to do? The answer is that ethical judgment and command is a necessary feature of human language. We cannot help making judgments of right and wrong, commanding others to act according to those judgments, condemning them for not doing so, responding ourselves to an ethical demand that will not be the less categorical and imperative for not coming from some transcendent extra-linguistic 'law'.

With the ground cleared of the chief alternative theories of ethics, especially the Kantian one, de Man can assert his own purely linguistic theory. What, in his case, does this mean, and how could an ethical judgment or command founded exclusively on language have the authority necessary in ethics, the 'I *must* do this; I *cannot do otherwise*, and I *ought* not to do otherwise'? The answer is that ethical judgment and command is a necessary part of that narrative of the impossibility of reading that de Man calls allegory. But what, exactly, does *this* mean? The failure to read, the reader will remember, takes the form of a further, secondary or tertiary, narrative superimposed on the first deconstructive narrative. This supplementary narrative shows indirectly, in the form of a story, someone committing again the 'same' linguistic error that the deconstructive narrative has lucidly identified and denounced. Only someone who can *read*, that is, who can interpret the allegory, which seems to say one thing but in fact says something else, will be able to see that what is really being narrated is the failure to read. But that act of reading will no doubt commit another version of the same error of the failure to read, and then again, in a perpetual fugacity of final clarity. In 'Reading (Proust)', an 'earlier' essay in *Allegories of Reading* that anticipates the procedures and formulations of 'Allegory *(Julie)*', de Man expressed this flight of understanding by saying that 'it is forever impossible to read Reading' (*AR*, p. 77). Already in that essay he says that 'any narrative is primarily the allegory of its own reading', and that 'the allegory of reading narrates the impossibility of reading' (*AR*, pp. 76, 77). *A la recherche du temps perdu* is 'read' as an example of the allegory of the failure to read. It is an allegory in the sense that it says one thing and means another. This 'other', in de Man's theory of allegory, is always 'Reading', or rather the impossibility of reading Reading. 'Everything in [Proust's] novel', says de Man,

> signifies something other than what it represents, be it love, consciousness, politics, art, sodomy, or gastronomy: it is always

something else that is intended. It can be shown that the most
adequate term to designate this 'something else' is Reading. But one
must at the same time 'understand' that this word bars access, once
and forever, to a meaning that yet can never cease to call out for its
understanding.

(AR, p. 77)

The category of the ethical or of 'ethicity' intervenes, for de Man, just
at this point where the act of reading bars access to an understanding of
the act of reading. We can do it. We can read, but we cannot understand
what it is we are doing. This means that what we do is always aberrant,
since the only thing worth understanding is Reading itself, the ground
and foundation of the whole of human life, for de Man. The making of
ethical judgments and demands is one necessary feature of this failure to
read.

Just how is this? The answer is that ethical judgments and demands
are one major example of that committing again of the linguistic error
already deconstructed that manifests the failure to read in the form of a
secondary or tertiary narrative. In the 'primary' deconstructive
narrative, says de Man, the 'polarities of truth and falsehood . . . move
parallel with the text they generate. Far from interfering with each other,
the value system and the narrative promote each other's elaboration'
(*AR*, p. 206). The example given of this is the first part of *Julie*, in which
the joy born of the lucid deconstruction of the error of deifying the one
we love generates and sustains the narrative. 'Hence', says de Man, 'the
relative ease of the narrative pattern . . . of the story of passion in the
first part of *Julie* which is said to be "like a live source that flows forever
and that never runs dry"' (*AR*, p. 206). 'In the allegory of unreadability',
however, 'the imperatives of truth and falsehood oppose the narrative
syntax and manifest themselves at its expense. The concatenation of the
categories of truth and falsehood with the values of right and wrong is
disrupted, affecting the economy of the narration in decisive ways' (*AR*,
p. 206). What this means (if I 'understand' it) is that one of the primary
ways that the failure to read manifests itself at the allegorical level is in
the making of value judgments, the uttering of ethical commands and
promises ('You should do so and so'; 'You will be happy if you do so and
so.') for which there is absolutely no foundation in knowledge, that is in
the epistemological realm governed by the category of truth and
falsehood. In fact the lucid understanding of the falsehood in
metaphorical denomination gained at the primary deconstructive level
'ought' to lead to a reading of the ensuing ethical judgments as false,
even though according to the ethical value system they may be 'right'.
That this cognitive 'ought' is always obstructed is the basic
presupposition of de Man's theory of the ethics of reading.

The formulation that 'allegories are always ethical' is therefore completed by a crucial definitional phrase: 'the term ethical designating the structural interference of two distinct value systems' (*AR*, p. 206). If the reader steps back for a moment from the context of de Man's intricate argumentation he or she will probably agree with me that this is an exceedingly odd definition of the term ethical: 'the structural interference of two distinct value systems'! For de Man the categories of truth and falsehood can never be reconciled with the categories of right and wrong, and yet both are values, in the sense of making an unconditional demand for their preservation. Surely one should want to dwell within the truth, and surely one should want to do what is right, but according to de Man it is impossible to respond simultaneously to those two demands. A statement can be true but not right or right but not true, but not both true and right at once.

Why is this? The answer is given in the four sentences that complete the paragraph I have been trying to read:

> The ethical category is imperative (i.e, a category rather than a value) to the extent that it is linguistic and not subjective. Morality is a version of the same language aporia that gave rise to such concepts as 'man' or 'love' or 'self', and not the cause or the consequence of such concepts. The passage to an ethical tonality does not result from a transcendental imperative but is the referential (and therefore unreliable) version of a linguistic confusion. Ethics (or, one should say, ethicity) is a discursive mode among others.
>
> (*AR*, p. 206)

For de Man, as for Kant, the fulfillment of an ethical demand must be necessary. It must be something I *have* to do, regardless of other competing demands. It is in this sense that it is a category rather than a value. A value is a matter of more or less, of differential comparisons according to some measuring yardstick. A categorical obligation is absolute and unconditional. We must do it, whatever the cost. In de Man's case, however, the necessity is linguistic rather than subjective or the effect of a transcendental law. It is a necessity to be in error or at the least confused, as always happens when I attempt to make language referential, and I *must* attempt to make it referential. I cannot do otherwise. In the case of ethics it is a necessity to make judgments, commands, promises about right and wrong which have no verifiable basis in anything outside language. It is in this sense that ethics (or ethicity) is a discursive mode among others. That is, ethics is not just a form of language, but a running or sequential mode of language, in short a story. Ethics is a form of allegory, one form of those apparently referential stories we tell to ourselves and to those around us. De Man's assertion that morality is another version of the same language aporia that generates such concepts as 'man' or 'love' or 'self' tells us what kind of a story ethics tells. The reference of course is to his account of the rise of concepts in the chapter on Rousseau's *Second Discourse* in *Allegories of Reading* and to his demonstration of the way the particular concepts 'man', 'love', and 'self' deconstruct themselves in Rousseau in the chapters on the *Second Discourse, Julie*, and *Pygmalion*, respectively. The reader of 'Metaphor (*Second Discourse*)' will remember de Man's account of the way the spontaneously aberrant metaphor 'giant' is replaced by the deliberately falsifying concept 'man' as the basis of the making equal of men and women, that is necessary to the formation of social order. De Man's reading culminates in a striking formulation:

> The concept ['man'] interprets the metaphor of numerical sameness as if it were a statement of literal fact. Without this literalization, there could be no society. The reader of Rousseau must remember that this literalism is the deceitful misrepresentation of an original blindness. Conceptual language, the foundation of civil society, is also, it appears, a lie superimposed upon an error.
>
> (*AR*, p. 155)

Ethicity too, according to de Man, it would follow, is no more than another version of the same necessary form of lying. It is storytelling in more than one sense. An ethical judgment, command, or promise is like the concept 'man' both in the sense that it has no ground in truth and in the sense that it universalizes without grounds, makes equal the always different moral situations in which men and women find themselves. An ethical command says, 'Thou shalt not ever lie', or 'Thou shalt not ever make promises intending not to keep them', or 'Thou shalt not ever commit adultery.' Or rather, an ethical judgment is a lie but not a lie. It is by no means true, but at the same time it cannot be measured as false by reference to any possible ascertainable true ethical judgment. To it would apply that 'melancholy conclusion' (*trübselige Meinung*) Joseph K. reaches in his discussion with the priest of Kafka's parable, cited as my epigraph for this book: '"No", said the priest, "it is not necessary to accept everything [said by the doorkeeper at the outer gate of the law] as true, one must only accept it as necessary." "A melancholy conclusion", said K. "It turns lying into a universal principle."'

For de Man ethical obligations, demands, and judgments work in the same way as the court system in *The Trial* works, or as the social contract works in Rousseau's theory, that is, as one perpetually unverifiable referential dimension of an irresistible law, in de Man's case a law of language. Ethicity is a region of human life in which lying is necessarily made into a universal principle, in the sense that ethical judgments are necessary but never verifiably true. The failure to read or the impossibility of reading is a universal necessity, one moment of which is that potentially aberrant form of language called ethical judgment or prescription.

It is in this context that we must understand a remarkable series of sentences in de Man's Foreword to Carol Jacobs' *The Dissimulating Harmony*:

> Understanding is not a version of one single and universal Truth that would exist as an essence, a hypostasis. The truth of a text is a much more empirical and literal event. What makes a reading more or less true is simply the predictability, the necessity of its occurrence, regardless of the reader or of the author's wishes. 'Es ereignet sich aber das Wahre' (not *die Wahrheit*) says Hölderlin, which can be freely translated, 'What is true is what is bound to take place.' And, in the case of the reading of a text, what takes place is a necessary understanding. What marks the truth of such an understanding is not some abstract universal but the fact that it has to occur regardless of other considerations. It depends, in other words, on the rigor of the reading as argument. Reading is an argument (which is not necessarily the same as a polemic) because it has to go against the grain of what one would want to happen in the name of what has to happen; this is the same as saying that an understanding is an epistemological event prior to being an ethical or aesthetic value. This does not mean that there can be a true reading, but that no reading is conceivable in which the question of its truth or falsehood is not primarily involved.
>
> It would therefore be naive to make a reading depend on considerations, ethical or aesthetic, that are in fact correlatives of the understanding the reading is able to achieve. Naive, because it is not a matter of choice to omit or to accentuate by paraphrase certain elements in a text at the expense of others. We don't have this choice, since the text imposes its own understanding and shapes the reader's evasions. The more one censors, the more one reveals what is being effaced. A paraphrase is always what we called an analytical reading, that is, it is always susceptible of being made to point out consistently what it was trying to conceal.[4]

This luminous passage is one of the most important formulations de Man made about the ethics of reading and its relation to the epistemological dimension of reading. The understanding of a text is prior to its affirmation as an ethical value, but both are necessary. Both are bound to take place, even though they take place against the grain of the reader's or the author's wishes. 'Take place' is de Man's translation of Hölderlin's *'ereignet sich'*, in the lines from the late hymn, *'Mnemosyne'*, that he cites, wresting them from their context. It is a context, by the way, that is extremely enigmatic and that might take years of study and commentary to begin to 'understand', even though, if de Man is right, the first reading of Hölderlin's poem would cause its understanding to take place as a kind of foreknowledge. A reading 'takes place' as an event in the real world. *Ereignis* is the German word for event. Martin Heidegger has singled out this word in various places for commentary and analysis in relation, precisely, to that notion of *topos* or place. Each event takes place in a place which its occurrence as event makes into a place, as opposed to a vacant space with no meaning or coordinates. The same thing may be said of each act of reading. It takes place as an event in a certain spot and turns that spot in a certain sense into a sacred place, that is, into a place which is inaugural. Reading too turns empty space into a locus where something unique and unforeseen has occurred, has entered into the human world, and where it will have such effects as it will have. An act of reading, moreover, takes place, as something which is bound to happen as it does happen, to a certain person in a certain psychological, interpersonal, historical, political, and institutional situation, for example to a teacher or to a student in a certain university, or to a reader in a public library who happens to have taken the book down from the shelf.

Readings that 'take place' in this way are 'true' in the special sense of being true to an implacable law of language, that is, the law of the failure to read, not truth of correspondence to some transcendent and universal Truth with a capital T. Though de Man's formulation here is in terms of the necessary 'truth' of each reading, and though what he says makes it sound as if reading is a game in which we cannot lose, since we are bound to get it right, however limited we are as readers or however much our presuppositions about what the text is going to mean may seem to foredoom us to get it wrong, the careful reader of de Man, the reader for example of the passage which has been my main focus, will know that what is bound to take place in each act of reading is another exemplification of the law of unreadability. The failure to read takes place inexorably within the text itself. The reader must re-enact this failure in his or her own reading. Getting it right always means being forced to re-enact once more the necessity of getting it wrong. Each reader must repeat the error the text denounces and then commits again. By a strange but entirely cogent reversal which disqualifies the binary opposition between true and false, what de Man calls 'true' (not truth) here is the unavoidable exigency to be true to the obligation to lie, in the special sense de Man gives to lying. It is lying in the sense that one necessary moment in any act of reading is the referential turn which draws ethical conclusions, makes ethical judgments and prescriptions. These are unwarranted but they *must* follow the reading of the text. Both that understanding and the lie of unwarranted ethical affirmations are *bound* to take place, since both are inscribed within the text as its own failure to read itself. The reader in this act of reading must be true to that pattern.

The fact that the relation between ethical statements and the knowledge language gives is always potentially aberrant in no way means that ethical judgments do not work, do not sustain society, are not good in their effects. Ethical judgment, or 'ethicity' in general, works in fact in the same precarious way as the social contract in de Man's description of it. Its working is always threatened by its own lack of ground. It is sustained only by the fact that a group of people can be got to act as if it had a ground, that is, as if there were absolute justice in rewarding people for certain actions, punishing them for others. 'Finally', says de Man:

> the *contractual* pattern of civil government can only be understood against the background of this permanent threat. The social contract is by no means the expression of a transcendental law: it is a complex and purely defensive verbal strategy by means of which the literal world is given some of the consistency of fiction, an intricate set of feints and ruses by means of which the moment is temporarily delayed when fictional seductions will no longer be able to resist transformation into literal acts. The conceptual language of the social contract resembles the subtle interplay between figural and referential discourse in a novel.
>
> (*AR*, p. 159)

Presumably de Man means here that the application of one or another feature of the social contract, for example its codification of ethical judgments into civil law, to actual cases, will be necessarily unjust in the same way as the application of a metaphorically based concept, for example 'man', to the unique case is always unjust. As soon as the metaphorical is applied to the literal, or the moral law applied to the unique individual, we get something like the arrest, prolonged trial, and ultimate execution of Joseph K. for a crime he is not aware of having committed against a law he cannot confront: 'Someone must have been telling lies about Joseph K., for without having done anything wrong he was arrested one fine morning.'[5] Or we get something like what happens to Michael Kohlhaas, in Kleist's story of that name.

What is most precarious about that form of the social contract which takes the form of a general agreement to act according to a given system of ethical judgment is that it has no ascertainable basis outside itself. It has no basis in the universal laws of subjectivity, nor in the 'literal' social or material worlds, nor in some transcendent lawgiving power, though, as de Man observes, the creation of a social order is such a violent and unjustified act that lawgivers always claim, like Moses, divine sanction for their inaugural prescriptions. An ethical judgment is always a baseless positing, always unjust and unjustified, therefore always liable to be displaced by another momentarily stronger or more persuasive but equally baseless positing of a different code of ethics. And yet the imposition of a system of ethics is absolutely necessary. It is necessary in the double sense that it *has* to be made and that there can be no civil society without it.

The example de Man here gives of a shift from *pathos* to *ethos*, the shift from epistemological subtlety to ethical naiveté, is the way Rousseau tells his readers that reading *Julie* will be good for them, that the book contains practical advice for husbands and wives. 'The question', says de Man, 'is not the intrinsic merit or absurdity of these pieces of good advice but rather the fact that they *have to be* uttered, despite the structural discrepancy between their intellectual simplicity and the complexity of the considerations on which they are predicated' (*AR*, p. 207). *Why* do they *have to be* uttered? This, so it seems to me, is just what de Man, on his own terms, is forever barred from making intelligible. Just as, for Kant, the moral law as such is by definition forever inaccessible, though it manifests itself in the necessity, the categorical imperative, of particular moral judgments and acts, so for de Man the linguistic necessity that forces us all to make ethical judgments that have no epistemological basis, that in fact fly in the face of our epistemological insight, can in principle never be understood. We can never read Reading. This means that we can never understand why we cannot read our own epistemological wisdom clearly enough to avoid making ethical statements or telling ethical stories that are contradicted, undermined, and disqualified by that wisdom.

Kant's *Grundlegung zur Metaphysik der Sitten* ends with the following cheerfully positive formulation:

> And so we do not indeed comprehend the practical unconditional necessity of the moral imperative; yet we do comprehend its incomprehensibility, which is all that can be fairly demanded of a philosophy which in its principles strives to reach the limit of human reason.
>
> (Und so begreifen wir zwar nicht die praktische unbedingte Not-wendigkeit des moralischen Imperativs, wir begreifen aber doch seine *Unbegreiflichkeit*, welches alles ist, was billigermaßen von einer Philosophie, die bis zur Grenze der menschlichen Vernunft in Prinzipien strebt, gefodert werden kann.)[6]

The difference between de Man and Kant (and it is quite a difference) is that Kant can have confidence in the ability of language and reason to formulate an understanding of a nonlinguistic impossibility, whereas in de Man's case it is a matter of encountering the limits of the possibility of understanding the laws of language with language.

As Hans-Jost Frey puts this in the sentence I have cited as an epigraph: 'Every construction, every system – that is, every text – has within itself the ignorance of its own exterior as the rupture of its coherence which it cannot account for.' Language cannot think itself or its own laws, just as a man cannot lift himself by his own bootstraps. Nor can language express what is outside language. It can neither know whether or not it has reached and expressed what is outside language, nor can it know whether that 'outside' is a thought, or a thing, or a transcendent spirit, or some linguistic ground of language, or whether it is nothing at all, since for de Man, as for Rousseau, sensation, perception, and thought are not separable from language, cannot occur separate from language. They are permeated by language through and through, or they *are* language. This means that though language cannot help posit its referentiality, it can neither verify nor disqualify that referentiality, though any piece of language necessarily puts in question the validity of its referentiality.

In his reading of Rousseau's *Profession du Foi du Vicaire Savoyard* de Man once more states this basic presupposition of Rousseau's (and of his own) theory of language in its relation to human existence:

> To the extent that judgment is a structure of relationships capable of error, it is also language. As such, it is bound to consist of the very figural structures that can only be put in question by means of the language that produces them. What is then called 'language' clearly has to extend well beyond what is empirically understood as articulated verbal utterance and subsumes, for instance, what is traditionally referred to as perception. . . . The term 'language' thus includes that of perception or sensation, implying that understanding can no longer be modelled on or derived from the experience of the senses. . . . We can conclude that the vicar describes judgment as the power to set up potentially aberrant referential systems that deconstruct the referentiality of their own elaboration. This description warrants the equation of judgment with figural language, extensively conceived.
>
> (*AR*, pp. 234–5)

'Aberrant' here has to be taken in a special sense, as is generally the case with de Man's use of the word. Referential statements, or statements taken referentially, are aberrant not in the sense of wandering away from some ascertainable norm, but in the sense of being a perpetual wandering from beginning to end. They are therefore, strictly speaking, only to be called 'potentially aberrant', since we have no way to measure whether or not they are aberrant. All we can know is that they may be in error.

One of Kafka's aphorisms expresses exactly the human situation for de Man, that is, the predicament of being perpetually within language, spoken by it rather than being able to use it as a tool of power, and condemned by that situation to what de Man consistently calls 'aberrancy'. 'There is a goal but no way', says Kafka; 'what we call the way is only wavering'.[7] Of the laws of language language cannot speak except in language that disqualifies itself as knowledge in the moment that it posits itself as language. Whenever we think we have pushed beyond the borders of language we find that the region we have reached magically reforms itself as still or already included within the borders of language. Though language contains within itself the evidence of its own limitation, the knowledge of that limitation can never be formulated in a way that is wholly reasonable or clear, since any formulation contains the limitation again. This limitation has the double definition of the failure, on the one hand, of language ever to be other than fragmentary, its failure ever to form a complete and completely coherent system, and, on the other hand, the failure of the 'user' of language ever to know for sure whether or not it has validly referred to what is outside language. Among the various forms of that potentially, but never certainly, aberrant referentiality, are those ethical judgments and promises which *have to be made*, though their justice or injustice can never be known for sure, in spite of the fact that they do not jibe with the epistemologically based judgments of truth and falsehood language enables us to make. Even the conspicuous fact that no ethical system has yet brought the millenium of universal justice and peace among men is no proof of the inadequacy of any or all of them, since we can never be sure that the continued sufferings of men and women in society are not the result of a failure to act consistently and totally on the basis of the right one of those systems of ethical judgment. I would even dare to promise that the millenium would come if all men and women became good readers in de Man's sense, though that promise is exceedingly unlikely to have a chance to be tested in practice.

Since 'Reading', for de Man, includes not just reading as such, certainly not just the act of reading works of literature, but sensation, perception, and therefore every human act whatsoever, in this case my apparently limited topic of the ethical dimension of reading would include the necessary but forever potentially aberrant referentiality of what he calls 'ethicity' in human life generally. For de Man the ethical is one (necessary and necessarily potentially aberrant) act of language among others, taking language in the inclusive sense which he gives it in

'Allegory of Reading (*Profession de foi*)'. Kant's concluding formulation in the *Grundlegung* would therefore in de Man's case have to be reformulated in a way that measures the difference, the great gulf, between them. De Man might have said:

> And so we do not indeed comprehend the practical unconditional necessity of the moral imperative; nor do we even comprehend its incomprehensibility, since the moral imperative itself, along with the human reason which strives to comprehend the incomprehensibility of its necessity, are both aspects of language, and it is impossible to use language as a tool with which to comprehend its own limitations.

It is impossible to get outside the limits of language by means of language. Everything we reach that seems outside language, for example sensation and perception, turns out to be more language. To live is to read, or rather to commit again and again the failure to read which is the human lot. We are hard at work trying to fulfill the impossible task of reading from the moment we are born until the moment we die. We struggle to read from the moment we wake in the morning until the moment we fall asleep at night, and what are our dreams but more lessons in the pain of the impossibility of reading, or rather in the pain of having no way whatsoever of knowing whether or not we may have in our discursive wanderings and aberrancies stumbled by accident on the right reading? Far from being 'indeterminate' or 'nihilistic', however, or a matter of wanton free play or arbitrary choice, each reading is, strictly speaking, ethical, in the sense that it *has* to take place, by an implacable necessity, as the response to a categorical demand, and in the sense that the reader *must* take responsibility for it and for its consequences in the personal, social, and political worlds. Reading is one act among others, part, as Henry James says writing itself is, of the conduct of life, however unpredictable and surprising each act of reading may be, since the reader can never know beforehand what it is in this particular case of reading that is bound to take place. Such is the rigor of Paul de Man's affirmation of an ethics of reading. It imposes on the reader the 'impossible' task of reading unreadability, but that does not by any means mean that reading, even 'good' reading, cannot take place and does not have a necessary ethical dimension.

Notes

1. *Allegories of Reading* (New Haven and London: Yale University Press, 1979), p. 206 henceforth *AR*.

2. 'Undecidability', trans. Robert Livingston, *Yale French Studies* **69** (1985): 132.

3. In '"Reading" Part of a Paragraph of *Allegories of Reading'*, forthcoming in *Reading Paul de Man Reading,* a volume of essays on de Man edited by Lindsay Waters.

4. CAROL JACOBS, *The Dissimulating Harmony* (Baltimore and London: Johns Hopkins University Press, 1978), p. xi.

5. FRANZ KAFKA, *The Trial*, trans. Willa and Edwin Muir (Harmondsworth, Middlesex, UK: Penguin Books, 1953), p. 7.

6. IMMANUAL KANT, *Foundations of the Metaphysics of Morals,* trans. Lewis Beck (Indianapolis: Bobbs-Merrill Educational Publishing, 1978), p. 94; *Grundlegung zur Metaphysik der Sitten, Wekausgabe* (Frankfurt am Main: Suhrkamp Verlag, 1982), vol. 7, p. 102.

7. FRANZ KAFKA, *The Great Wall of China* (New York: Schocken Books, 1946), p. 283.

13   Lifting Our Eyes from the Page*

YVES BONNEFOY

To end this collection, Yves Bonnefoy, a well-known critic and translator and one of France's most distinguished contemporary poets, suggests an end to reading – the importance of an *interruption* of reading
constituted in and by reading itself. Arguing directly against the priority given to textuality in structuralism and post-structuralism (see,
for example, the essays by de Man and Miller reprinted above), Bonnefoy expresses reservations about what he sees as a reduction of human experience to a 'game' in what he terms 'the textualist
revolution'. Running through all of the essays in this collection are a
number of crucial, if often implicit, questions concerning the 'truth' or
'faithfulness' of reading: is it possible to be 'true' to a text, or is reading the history of error? Is there a political or ethical imperative to
read 'against the grain', to resist the ideologies or 'truths' of certain
texts? With what kinds of 'truth' do literary texts present readers? Is it
possible to be 'true to oneself' in reading? Does reading approach a
'reality' or 'truth' which goes beyond that reading, beyond language?
And so on. While, in the essay reprinted above, Miller argues that 'it
is impossible to get outside the limits of language by means of language', Bonnefoy insists that 'poetry is what attaches itself . . . to
what cannot be designated by a word of language'. It is for this reason
that Bonnefoy can claim that 'The poet himself . . . hopes that the
reader, at certain moments, will stop reading him'. For Bonnefoy, such
moments, paradoxically, constitute the essence of reading, in an ap-
prehension of what he terms, variously, the 'real', the 'One', 'Presence'. 'True' reading, then, is a form of rupture, of turning away, of
lifting our eyes from the page.

   See also Bonnefoy's collection of essays *The Act and Place of Poetry*
(Chicago: University of Chicago Press, 1989); and see John Naughton,
The Poetics of Yves Bonnefoy (Chicago, University of Chicago Press,
1984). For another writer's impassioned defence of reading in terms
of a movement *away* from the text, see Marcel Proust's eloquent evo-

---

* Reprinted from *Critical Inquiry*, 16 (1990): 794–806. Trans. John Naughton.

cation of childhood reading in his essay 'On Reading', from *On Reading Ruskin* (English translation, 1987).

1

For the past thirty years or so we have witnessed the greatest period – at least for France – in the history of thinking about literature; I want first of all to stress this point, adding, however, that despite this fact problems of fundamental significance still seem to me to have been poorly raised.

Among these is the problem of how to read a work. And yet, it is not as though reading has not been the object of continual attention, from the American fascination after the war with 'close reading' to the work of the deconstructionists: a revolution has taken place that has made reading the very center of its concern. Indeed, today, we think we can recognize in the structure of a text, in the relation between its words, a reality that is much more reliable and tangible than the meaning that runs along the surface, or than the author's intention, or even than the author's very being, the idea of which has been rendered problematical to the point of dissolution by the ambiguities inherent in his simplest utterances. It is not the writer who is real, it is his language – which is neither true nor false, signifying only itself. What is more, it is infinite; its forms and effects are disseminated everywhere in a book without ever being able to be totalized: and because of this, reading has a more clearly creative function than ever before – that is, of course, if readers make themselves attentive to all the levels in the depths of the text and bring them as much as they can into the various networks of their analyses. Reading has become a responsibility, a contribution, equal in its way to writing, and moreover it has now become an end in itself, since those who read need not judge themselves more real, more present in their relation to themselves, than the writer. And so, from this point of view, it would seem difficult to say that the problem of reading has been neglected by contemporary criticism.

But let us be mindful of one or two of the consequences of this way of looking at reading. The first is that reading itself becomes, from the outset, a form of writing, since its duty is to accumulate the observations it is led to make at the most fugitive points of the interaction of the terms, codes, or figures of the text, if it wants to be able to bring about their synthesis. Today, no one can read without a pen in hand, a fact confirmed by the extraordinary abundance of exegeses we see. And in one sense this very fact, this subjection to writing, might seem reassuring to the friends of things literary. They will be able to tell themselves that all forms of writing are personal, even at those moments when one's writing is subordinate to the work of another person; that this writing therefore has its own categories and experiences that interfere with the text; and that a practice thus takes place which remains fundamentally subjective, even in the heart of the most difficult and rigorous deciphering. Thus in addition to disinterested readers – those who seek the laws of the language or simply some truly specific elements of the work they study – other readers, no less knowledgeable but enamored of their freedom, would renew on a higher level than in the past the relationship of irresponsibility – of pleasure – that once united reader to poem.

It remains nonetheless true that readers who write only by extracting from the pages of another and accumulating (for the sake of their own interpretations) simple elements of meaning, or aspects of their stylistic dimension, are thereby condemned to a use of words whose pre-eminently conceptual character – that is to say, abstract and without direct knowledge of the things that are exposed to time and finitude – can only deaden what in Rimbaud's or Artaud's works, or in so many others, was joy or suffering experienced more directly, more violently. The liberty that the textualist revolution gladly allows to those who want it is thus greatly limited; in fact one might fear that it is reduced to nothing so much as a game – a game without any other responsibility than intellectual – whereas the work studied might, on the other hand, have been an experience in the tragedy of life. And so one must worry about a philosophy that moves our modern writing in so massive a fashion toward the use of metalanguages. Doesn't this fact mean that an essential dimension of poetry could cease to be felt when one defines it simply as text?

2

Rimbaud, when he was still at the *lycée* in Charleville, would read the books he borrowed for a night from the bookstore without cutting the pages – which is to say, hastily and only in part. Was this only because he couldn't afford them?

In fact, one can hardly imagine him reading even Baudelaire's *Les Fleurs du mal* with the kind of attention that allows one to detect those sequences inside meaning that involve all the structures of the text. Certain verses overwhelm him, but they only do so by changing the relation of the words of his own most decidedly personal experience. The word *woman*, the word *Paris* will no longer have the same associations for him, the same emotional weight. And precisely because of that revolution that takes place in his mind, but not without being above all determined by the facts of his daily life, we see him distracted from Baudelaire's poem; he ceases to be interested in the details of a work many aspects of which, moreover, seem to him to be of little interest for the poetry of the present moment, for example, the overly aesthetic concerns. Baudelaire, he writes, is 'a true god'; but he adds: 'Even so, the milieu he frequented was too dandified.'[1]

It might be argued that this example hardly bears on the problem of reading, since this kind of relation to a literary work is precisely not a reading at all, but rather a simple way of using, if not of pillaging, the text, justified only by the fact that it is Rimbaud who is doing it. There can only be reading, it will be said, when one stays with a book, remaining as faithful as one can be to what constitutes its own being.

And yet, what do we make of the situation reported by Robert Antelme in his book *L'Espèce humaine*, which records his memories and thoughts about life in a concentration camp? Some of the prisoners organize a recitation of poems in the barracks, 'to be together'. But the weak voice of the person reciting is almost inaudible among so many restless listeners. He says: '"Heureux qui comme Ulysse. . . ."' '"Louder", comes the cry from the back of the room.' Once again much of the text is lost, but should we conclude that even what little the men got from the poem wasn't enough? That what it brought to these suffering human beings wasn't what the poet himself would have considered most essential? And there are those moments in life when, as one commits oneself to a future course of action and shares this decision with others, one cites a few lines from a poem – that is, just a simple fragment – in order to have something complex and mysterious, which one wouldn't know how to say otherwise, directly understood. Should we feel that we have betrayed the work, since clearly we have not taken all of the elements of the text into consideration? In fact, when this kind of reference is made, I am most of all aware of its emotional dimension, I see it as a pledge given spontaneously and without premeditation, and I therefore wonder if the problem of what poetry actually communicates should be raised only with reference to the textual characteristics of the poem.

Furthermore, what exactly is a 'text'? Where does it begin, and where does it end? When Rimbaud stops writing, does he not add something crucial and decisive to his last works, since it is only from the point of view of this all-important sign that we now will read them, even though we might discuss the exact meaning of this decision of silence with the help of this or that element in the late poems, which will appear now under a different light? It is true that Rimbaud could have left only a book to us, and nothing that concerns his life. But at the last lines of *Une Saison en enfer*, completed by 'Solde' or 'Génie', we would always have trouble not imagining the abandonment of poetry, the departure, and so it would be our own life, in everything in it that has no interest in writing, that would relive Rimbaud's renunciation in the text itself.

And when in his poem 'The Swan' Baudelaire indicates that he is 'thinking' of the exiled black woman, of the sailor forgotten on some island, should we say that these are purely textual phenomena, arguing that the black woman or the sailor are indeed only symbolic representations and that this way of 'thinking' only comes to us determined by a textual context from which Baudelaire himself would not really want to withdraw, being, as Rimbaud said of him, 'trop artiste'? It is true that this movement toward others is only a pretense, and this because of a closure inherent in writing. But the black woman and the sailor are nonetheless the representatives in the text of that existence of the other person that dwells beyond its reach: and thus it is that a poem has urged us to turn away from poems.

In fact, *poetry* is what aims at an object – at this being right before us, in its absolute, or at being itself, at the presence of the world, in its unity – even when, in point of fact, no *text* can tell of them. Poetry is what attaches itself – and here is its specific responsibility – to what cannot be designated by a word of language; and this because what is beyond designation is an intensity, a plenitude we need to remember. The One, Presence – poetry can 'think' of them in writing, since the unusual relations that the forms of sonority in verse establish between words break up the codes, neutralize the conceptual significations, and thus open up something like a field for the unknown dwelling beyond. But even in a poem, words formulate; they substitute signification, representation, for this One, this unity faintly perceived, and therefore it is the sense of dissatisfaction that is strongest. Dissatisfaction before this fact of textuality in which the fundamental intuition vanishes, but not without leaving something glittering in its wake.

Poetry is what descends from level to level in its own ever-changing text, going down to the point where, lost in a land without name or road, it decides to go no further, having nevertheless discovered that the essential experience is what still remains hidden, somewhere beyond these unfamiliar places. The text is not poetry's true place; it is only the path it followed a moment earlier, its past. – And if, under these circumstances, someone reads a poem without feeling he must be bound to its text, does this mean that he has betrayed it? Hasn't he rather – and this has been my underlying question from the beginning – been faithful to its most specific concern?

This, it seems to me, is what we have to remember at the present stage of research in criticism. When we read a poet as though absentmindedly, because we are turned by his very words toward something that escapes them, when this intuition of an all-necessary beyond and this impression of something urgent come along – and at the very moment when our sympathy for him is at its most intense – to suspend in us the act of reading, this does not mean that poetry has been slighted; it means that we have become people who – either because they write for themselves, or simply live, but with Presence in mind – will also grow impatient, dissatisfied with their own text, whether this be made of words or of actions; and this is to read on the level where the poem, as poem, has its value, and it is to have done more, for the conception of poetry, than textual analysis: disconnected as the latter is from problems of lived experience by what is neutral and timeless in the words and phrases of the 'accumulative' criticism. In short, it is to rediscover poetry's spirit of responsibility – even if this spirit lacks any means of action – and its quality of hopefulness.

3

And thus it would seem not altogether useless to introduce at this point – and by contrast to the figures, codes, 'anagrams', and other polysemies of critical reading whose fluctuating way of listening keeps the text on the very level where desire builds those networks of words that are pure closure of language – the idea that *interruption* in the reading of a text can have an essential value in the relation of reader to literary work, and even in the relation of the writer to his own work in progress. For interruption is indeed what already takes place the moment the writer perceives that writing essentially means giving oneself over to a few images; it takes place the moment one suspends this dreaming, in order to remember that, outside, there is time, place, chance, choices to make, death – and the richness of a world in all of this as well. Baudelaire is dreaming at the beginning of his poem 'The Swan': this is revealed by his metaphorical use of the 'scaffoldings' and other vague shapes of the Haussmann construction sites, then in perpetual metamorphosis. And he is still dreaming when, in order to signify what is beyond dreaming and the memory of being that is triggered by the actual presence of another person, he imagines Andromache, since she is a literary figure rather than the symbol of the other person as such. But the memory of the real, the acknowledgment of its specific truth never cease growing in him, and the image (of course, it is still only an image) of that homeless and desperate swan, then of the black woman living in exile, results in the fact that the text, while remaining what it is, is nonetheless imbued with a ray of light: that intuition, that illumination sometimes, that religions know, which transcend the systems of representation and myth that are themselves a kind of text. Interruption is already present in the act of creation. It occurs the moment the poem frees itself from the network of its significations and thereby *takes on meaning*: to the extent that these significations, which were nothing but atemporal structures, now see themselves confronted by finitude, thrown into time, claimed by another sort of necessity. In truth, it is as though the words were connected to a current and, because of it, were becoming thousands of lights.

In other words, interruption is a starting point, the true origin of what is specifically poetry in a work, where writing, on the other hand, is already and forever begun, being one of the forms of the activity of the unconscious. And relived by the reader, at some moment of his encounter with the poem, interruption is thus the act by which this reader can find, poetically speaking, his own relation to poetry – and respond, let us remark in passing, to a hope that is in the heart of the poem's text. For every poem is a movement of hopefulness with respect to 'mon semblable, mon frère', as Baudelaire said of his reader: the latter, will he not convert himself to the truth of finitude? – Why, we might ask, is a certain metaphor 'obscure' in some cases? And why does the relation between the things compared thus escape us, wholly or in part? It is because some aspect of the poet's knowledge of the objects compared has not been explicated in the text. The associations he makes are refused to us, though these associations have nothing necessary about them. And yet, this concealment certainly does not mean that the poet is indulging in a soliloquy. It's just the opposite. For what a poet hopes for from words is that they might open to that plenitude that descriptions and formulations cannot reach; and if therefore he writes and even publishes, it is because he hopes that the reader will discover in his own experience the things that he, for his part, has felt he could leave unsaid: in order to accede to the full richness of designation, he asks to be understood *à demi mot*. But doesn't this therefore also mean asking the person who reads to turn away from certain aspects of the text – those roots it has in the author's condition, only half articulated – for the benefit of his own lived experience? Doesn't it mean hoping that readers will only return to the text from the perspective, and in the exigency, of this dialectic of rupture?

The poet himself, then, hopes that the reader, at certain moments, will stop reading him. And this expectation, which is fully justified, is, by the way, what makes possible the poetry that aims at celebration, that is, attests to a quality, to a force – but obviously without being able to prove anything – and therefore only speaks of its object in the most allusive and passionate way. It is only because the reader is ready to leave the text that he can accept and relive its most fundamental proposition, which is that there has been in the poet's experience the emergence of something fully real. But because of this, he does more, since he gives the poet yet another reason to expect his reader to leave his book. Celebrating, in effect, always means substituting some representation controlled and delimited by writing for the authentic experience of the One. Hölderlin's Greece is only a romantic myth; the 'incomparable terre verte douce et funèbre' ['incomparable earth green sweet and funereal'] of Jouve's great poem[2] is only the 'portée du chant', is only the stave that permits the music, as another of the verses says. And the poetry of celebration that takes such risks would therefore be nothing but naïveté if the reader didn't invest it with his own enthusiasm. But this he does, and thus he shows that a great work of poetry is much less the success of one person than the occasion given to others for renewing the same quest. It is not within the poet's scope to reestablish presence. But he can recall that presence is a possible experience, and he can stir up the need for it, keep open the path that leads toward it – after which one will read him and restore to his poem the benefit of that experience it had been unable to completely achieve. Indeed, by the grace of this collective creation, of this truth that will appear only in the midst of the impossible, it is now, despite its delusions, that poetry can set its idle treasures, its chests overflowing with images and mirages, at the feet of that absolute toward which a star has beckoned.

4

In the heart of interruption, communication. In the abandonment of a writer's book, perhaps the only solidarity that can be established with him beyond the misunderstandings of reading. And if I had the time to do it here, I would now try to show how poetry in fact often speaks, and explicitly so, of these moments of rupture that make its reading more richly poetic. I would evoke Georges Seferis who, reading the *Iliad* and running across a quick mention of the king of Asine, suddenly stops reading. It's at the moment when there is the long enumeration of the peoples who have united against Troy and the cataloguing of all their ships.[3] Here poetry becomes more than ever image, marvelous and seductive image. And yet Seferis refuses to continue with it without even knowing exactly why, and this might seem to be a desertion of Homer, betrayal. But let us not forget that the king of Asine, about whom we know nothing more, since he has only survived, if this is the right word, thanks to this line in Homer, is for this very reason one of the possible metaphors of that being marked by finitude, which is poetry's sole object, even at times when, as here, it seems interested only in heroes and demigods. And Seferis, who thus senses in this name the signifier of what is unsignifiable, is therefore less one who betrays a work than the best of all possible readers, since he discerns here an experience that Homer but dimly glimpsed and that Seferis himself will pursue.

And I could also evoke Dante, in one of the most celebrated passages of his *Inferno*,[4] a passage that has become famous for precisely the reasons I have been discussing, though this has hardly been noticed. Paolo and Francesca are reading the poem about Lancelot and Guinevere. But something comes to them from the text that encourages them to turn toward one another, and then 'quel giorno più non vi leggemmo avante', they read no further. Was this reaction the result of the erotic suggestion in the Arthurian romance? Certainly not. It is the result of poetry's own will, which is the force in the words that moves them toward more than words, which is to say, poetry's potential for love, the appeal it throws out to the reader to go further than the poet toward unity, especially when it is right beside him, and even if it is at the expense of the moral conventions and the laws that words organize. In this passage where Dante's own emotion bursts forth, he has represented, 'en abîme', the essence of poetry, except that he betrays it later, as every poet always does, by reducing this fundamental intuition of the other into devotion to a kind of icon. In *The Divine Comedy*, Beatrice is a symbolic figure, the keystone of meaning, but not the passionate look or the trembling hand. What Dante would need would be another Seferis to both read him and leave him.

5

And yet, in fact, how many alterations, how many distortions, barely perceptible and yet fatal, menace – and from within the very working of the poem – these interruptions whose aim, at every moment, should be to set free what poetry tries to point out! And how many others of the same sort also ruin reading, at the very moment when reading could seem to be an impatience seeking to rejuvenate the spirit of poetry. From which it follows that it might be a good idea to mention a few of these dangers, since one might think that, in essence, I am suggesting that the reader read in whatever way he wants and even take pride in doing so.

One of the 'bad' ways to break off reading is the one that is sometimes demanded in the name of freedom, 'spontaneity', the right to be one's self. It is easy to convince oneself that poets as well as philosophers – not to mention those who hold social or political power – repress or colonize an 'instinct' that would be our only access to 'true life'. But this is to fail to recognize that there is no reality, even in the most ecstatic expenditure of oneself, that isn't constructed by language, and that trying to do without the words that are elaborated in the text one reads can only mean giving oneself over, without realizing it, to the tyranny of other words that are in fact much more impoverished, being only an even more partial and therefore abstract approach to things. One needs to leave the text, it's true, but one also needs to have gone into and crossed through it as well; one needs to have made a place for oneself here and there in the text for a more panoramic view of that world outside that it breaks up and that we must unify. And let's not try to make Rimbaud the patron saint of this kind of escapism, since he never sought to distinguish his search for pure sensation from his proposal of new values. Presence never emerges from these undialectical refusals that are secretly ideological. Presence asks us to listen, and to make even our impatience a form of empathy.

I would not want, furthermore, to appear to be suggesting that I support the romantic idea of a poet whose capacity to read differently than the ordinary critic would somehow place him or her above the condition we all share. To grow impatient with the effects produced by a text certainly does not mean that one can escape from the laws that govern the use of the words and always postpone the poetic intuition. And to delight in believing such a thing, and then to give in to mirages of the mind that in fact are nothing so much as one more closed set of signs, once again means losing the benefit that language can be when it is made the place where everything it pretends to say can and will be brought into question. The only authentic chance of epiphany is when the projections into one's own poem of one's personal desires, for instance, have at least been recognized as such and so relativized. And to find this kind of transparency in words, it will indeed be useful (for the person who wants to read himself or others with 'impatience') to apply himself patiently to the observations that have been made by critical reading – the kind of reading that knows how to dismantle the pretense at many levels of speech, through its thoughtful recourse to semiology or to Freudian categories. Poetry has nothing to fear from the study of signifiers, provided that this science is not coupled with an unconscious ideology or metaphysics. It has only to put this science on guard against yet another way of interrupting reading, one which has its place at the very core of textual analysis: the idea suggested by Roland Barthes in his first lecture after assuming a chair in 'literary semiology' at the Collège de France. Barthes proposed that the writer evade the authority of the structure of the texts he reads – that is, that he submits to – but he asked him to refuse this power only by means of 'digressions' and 'excursions' that would keep him among notions and essences, among verbal representations, however unstable or impressionistic he may have wished that these representations be. Barthes wanted to know nothing of 'l'aigrette de vent', of the light pencil strokes of wind around our temples that, as Breton said, a line of poetry can be, calling us to pass from representation to a more direct intuition of presence.

To conclude, I would like to stop for a moment at those lines, at those passages in a poem, that more often than others capture the reader, and at the same time restore him to what he is, in his own life, quite apart from the book he had taken up and that he now puts aside.

Even for those who want to think in terms of deep structures and of effects that tighten all the verbal material, is there not, in these moments of intensity, of beauty, of a suddenly stronger sense of evidence, the clear indication that writing is marked by a certain heterogeneity? And should we be surprised at these openings among the clouds, at these sudden bursts of light, when the experience of what is, in its appeal to what is beyond language, is only made up of moments of rising and of falling: moments of enthusiasm – when a certain configuration of circumstances permits it, unsettling the relation between words – followed by moments of waiting in vain? This fundamental unevenness in lived experience cannot be inscribed in a continuity of text unless the ambition that maintains this experience is given up; otherwise it gives the writing over to breaks, to renewals at different moments and by chance, after which the book that one consents to publish will be nothing but a juxtaposition of various parts where the experienced eye will know how to make out the fissures – those verses that are sometimes more intense than the others – that run between the plates that retain the traces of earlier upheavals.

In short, a poem, if at the outset it does not limit itself simply to a few verses, can only be an aggregate in which the fortuitous element of the various moments of its conception is never transcended or even abolished – and from this point of view, Mallarmé's idea of the book, which presupposes the notion of a perfectly homogeneous writing, and furthermore would have the reader disappear in it, seems to me to be less the first serious principle of a modern science of writing than the manifesto of a certain way of thinking – the one that seeks to reduce a poem to purely interverbal relations, because the world itself is seen only as an architecture of timeless essences, destined by their birth into the region of the Intelligible to be named by words that are as stable and transparent, in their mutual relations, as the constellations in the heavens. To think that a text of poetry owes its significance and its reason for being to its structure implies the existence of this universe in simple reflection – like the 'septet' of Mallarmé's sonnet in yx – in the mirror of language. And once one has decided, with today's followers of Mallarmé, to trace the workings of the signifier against the structure, the movement from one text to another, the discontinuities of their codes, but this without ever calling into question the authority of language as such on these successive particular languages, it will be useless to try, as Barthes did, to put movement back into the house of Ideas, since one will not have gotten rid of the utopian notion of a reality outside time:

the words kept within the horizon of a language – that is atemporal as system – are too ignorant of death.

The criticism of our time, with all it has learned from linguistics, has had to recognize the multiplicity of codes in the act of speech, the pluralities in the signification, in the representation: that is to say, the problematical, heterogeneous, and contradictory character of this world of our experience that Mallarmé still reduced to Nature – to which, as he said, 'nothing can be added'. In writing itself, we have also had to see that the transgressions, the disseminations, the activity of the signifier in the words seeking meaning are like those rifts just mentioned that take place in lived experience, and we have even had to wonder if they don't activate them, innervate them, as a way for desire, for instance, desire that has countless ties with chance and with death even when its reverie refuses them. As a result of these discoveries, it is less easy than before to consider writing an atemporal experience, an escape from finitude, and the same thing could be said of reading. Every exegesis should lead us to the truth of existence, which is alienated by the verbal play of form. But if, in one's attention to the various significations, one fails to go beyond the aspect in them that is form, that is to say, the ways in which they are articulated, added to one another, engendered by the sound of the word, the way in which they become beautiful tropes; if one spends all one's time seeking laws or admiring styles; if, in short – and this is the 'pleasure of the text' – one gives priority to the play of the signifier and not to the meaning of the signified, one still might be able, it's true, to postpone the moment of bringing to consciousness the being-in-time that we are. And this is why 'textual' analysis is a way of censoring, despite the exploring it does among the facts of existence, an even more serious form of censoring than before – because of its moments of possible absorption in the arid and impersonal scientific work, followed by other moments that are just playing. Whereas reading, as Rimbaud read, reading while knowing that it is our right to stop reading, means wanting to recognize the nature of existence, which is tragic and certainly not playful.

I'm looking over the pages that announced this project of a special issue of the *Nouvelle Revue de Psychanalyse* on reading.[5] That Proust never speaks of 'texts' goes along perfectly with what I have been trying to say, but so does the way in which he associates so spontaneously his memories of books he has read with the places he has read them in, with the things and the people in these places. To sum up my idea of the kind of reading that tends toward poetry, I might have said that it asks us to lift our eyes from the page and to contemplate the world, that is always so unknown, always so virginal, so full of life – 'vierge et vivace', as Mallarmé would say[6] – and that written forms interpret but thereby conceal beneath the play of possibilities that each time are less than the world is. And I might have added that the sense of a text can only begin to have meaning for us after the verification that consists – quite instinctively – in giving new life to its words with our memories or present experiments. How can we read about 'forgotten woods' over which 'somber winter' passes without going into woods that are our own, where we can either find or lose ourselves?[7] And here we can see one of the secret connections between poetry and painting. What demands more attention, when we risk being caught in the spell of words, is what in sensory experience is more than they suggest, and this is where painting begins – often to evoke in a direct way, and through means that are non-verbal, that unity that words destroy. 'To stop reading' therefore means becoming a painter, or at least asking painting to be of some help, as for instance through its practice of landscape: which is what the West has done, at certain of the great moments of its awakening to poetry – those that Wordsworth and Constable, for example, represent.

Notes*

Bonnefoy's text 'Lever les yeux de son livre' ('Lifting Our Eyes from the Page') was first published in a special issue of the *Nouvelle Revue de Psychanalyse* entitled 'Reading'. The issue was published in spring 1988.

1. Rimbaud to Paul Demeny, 15 May 1871, *Oeuvres de Rimbaud*, ed. Suzanne Bernard (Paris, 1960), p. 349: 'Baudelaire est le premier voyant, roi des poètes, *un vrai Dieu*. Encore a-t-il vécu dans un milieu trop artiste; et la forme si vantée en lui est mesquine.'

2. The reference is to a line in Pierre Jean Jouve's poem 'La Femme noire', in his book *Sueur de sang, Oeuvre*, ed. Jean Starobinski, 2 vols (Paris, 1987), 1: 239.

3. Homer, *Iliad*, 2, 560.

4. Dante, *Inferno*, 5, 138.

5. The reference is to the call for texts on the problematics of reading sent out by the editors of the *Nouvelle Revue de Psychanalyse*. In it, the editors contrast the contemporary obsession with deciphering and decoding 'texts' with Proust's evocation of reading as an experience enriched by its associations with places and people. 'Do we still read', asks the announcement, 'to open ourselves to the unknown or simply to master more data?'

6. The allusion is to Mallarmé's sonnet that begins: 'Le vierge, le vivace et le bel aujourd'hui.'

7. Bonnefoy is alluding to another sonnet by Mallarmé, which begins 'Sur les bois oubliés quand passe l'hiver sombre.'

---

* These notes have been added by the translator, John Naughton.

Key Concepts

ACTUAL READER   The individual subject in the act of reading a particular text, supposedly available to examination by empirical means (also **real reader**).

AFFECTIVE FALLACY   Term used by W.K. Wimsatt and Monroe Beardsley to designate what they see as the error of attending to the subjective responses (cognitive or emotional) of readers as criteria for interpretive, critical, or aesthetic judgements.

AFFECTIVE STYLISTICS   Stanley Fish's term for the study of the way in which a reader's response to a text can be plotted as the reader moves through the text in time.

APORIA   In deconstruction, a logical contradiction or paradox, the necessary cohabitation of two or more contradictory codes, 'messages' or 'meanings' within one text, passage or sentence which produces an impasse or site of undecidability as a result of which the reader is said to be unable to decide on a particular reading. See also **indeterminacy, unreadability.**

AUDIENCE   Peter J. Rabinowitz distinguishes between the 'actual audience', the various 'flesh and blood' people who read; the 'authorial audience', a hypothetical group of readers towards whom the author directs his work; and the 'narrative audience', which is 'a role which the text forces the reader to take on' (*Before Reading* (1987), p. 95).

CLOSE READING   Attention to 'the words on the page' rather than the historical context, the biography or intentions of the author, theories of aesthetics, politics, and so on: close reading, despite its name, brackets questions of readers and reading as arbitrary and irrelevant to the text as an artifact (see **affective fallacy**), and argues that the function of reading and criticism is simply to read carefully what is already 'there' in the text.

COMPETENCE, READERS' Term borrowed from the linguist Noam Chomsky to designate the reader's capacity to make sense of a text through the internalized system of rules and interpretive strategies or conventions of literature and of reading that he or she has assimilated.

CONCRETIZATION Wolfgang Iser borrows this term from the phenomenology of Roman Ingarden to describe the process by which a text is 'completed' in reading: the text's 'gaps' or 'blanks' are said to be 'filled' by the reader in the act of reading to produce a 'virtual' work.

EMBEDDED READER The 'figure' or 'representation' of a reader or reading situation within a text. It has been suggested by critics such as Ross Chambers and Lucien Dällenbach that attention to the embedded reader allows insight into strategies of reading presupposed by the text itself, into how reading is constructed or imagined by the individual text. Also **inscribed reader;** see also *mise-en-abyme*.

HERMENEUTICS Formerly a term used to designate attempts to establish a set of rules governing the interpretation of the Bible in the nineteenth century; in the context of reading theory, the term refers to theories of interpretation more generally.

HEURISTIC READING Michael Riffaterre's term for the first reading in which the reader deciphers the linear surface of the text and during which the meaning is apprehended in a general sense: this is followed by **retroactive reading.**

HORIZON OF EXPECTATIONS Hans Robert Jauss's term for the various concerns, presuppositions, assumptions and knowledge of readers at any given historical time: these are said to combine to delimit readers' expectations about how texts come to mean. According to Jauss, such horizons of expectations change over time.

IDEAL READER Hypothetical reader who would be best equipped to extract the maximum potential from a particular text – equipped in terms of knowledge, sympathies and prejudices, strategies of reading, previous experience of reading, and so on. Also referred to as the 'optimal reader'.

IMPLIED READER Wolfgang Iser uses this term to denote a hypothetical reader towards whom the text is directed: thus the implied reader has certain expectations and employs certain reading strategies in order to get the most out of a particular text. The implied reader is to be distinguished both from the **real reader** and from the **narratee.** Like the narratee, the implied reader is inscribed in the text. Unlike the narratee, however, the implied reader is not the addressee of the narrator: rather, he or she is the addressee of the so-called 'implied author'.

INDETERMINACY   Term used by Wolfgang Iser to refer to an ambiguity or uncertainty which must be decided on by the reader – a space (or 'blank' or 'gap') left open for the reader's input. The term is used rather differently in deconstruction, however, to refer to questions which cannot be decided due to the absence of any final arbiter to judge on the validity of different readings (also **undecidability**).

INFORMED READER   Stanley Fish's term for a construct, an idealized reader, who would possess not only a 'mature' grasp of the language of the text but also of the conventions of the literary tradition, and would be able to make the appropriate choices concerning possible connotations, implications, suggestions, and so on.

INSCRIBED READER   See **embedded reader.**

INTENDED READER   Reader for whom the author writes – whether it be a particular individual, a specific group of readers, or a hypothetical or generalized type of reader.

INTERPRETATION   Usually understood to involve an attempt to define the meaning or meanings of a specific text, with the assumption that a text has a limited set of meanings authorized either by the words of the text itself or by the intentions of the author.

INTERPRETIVE COMMUNITY   Stanley Fish's term used to refer to groups of people sharing 'interpretive strategies': in his work of the late 1970s, it is Fish's view that the interpretive strategies of such (interpretive) communities determine the way texts are read, as opposed to the view that the text governs its own reading (also **reading community**).

MISE-EN-ABYME   Term borrowed from heraldry and used to refer to the way in which a text may be represented within itself by a part of itself – the internal repetition of a whole in a part: the narrator in 'The Yellow Wallpaper', for example, in 'reading' the wallpaper, may be seen as a repetition of the reader of the story as a whole. See Lucien Dällenbach, *The Mirror in the Text* (1989).

MISREADING   Harold Bloom uses this term (together with the term 'misprision') to designate a defensive reaction of one poet to another by which the earlier poet is distorted or misrepresented by the later poet.

But Bloom also suggests that *any* reading may be termed 'misreading': according to Bloom, every reading is a distortion of the text as a defensive reaction against it. More generally, deconstruction has suggested ways in which misreading might be fundamental to and inescapable in reading.

MODEL READER   In *The Role of the Reader* (1979), Umberto Eco suggests that in order to communicate, the author assumes that his or her potential or hypothetical reader – what Eco calls the model reader – interprets in a manner which accords with the kinds of interpretive strategies that the text requires. While no actual reader need read in this particular way, this model reader is said to act as, precisely, a model for readers.

NARRATEE   Term used by Gerald Prince to refer to the fictional character whom the narrator addresses. As such, and like the narrator, the narratee is a fictional construct, a part of the text. The narratee should be distinguished from both the **real** reader and the **implied reader** (the addressee of the 'implied author').

OPPOSITIONAL READING   This term is used by various critics to denote a reading which actively opposes the strategies of reading and interpretation apparently presupposed by the text. See **resisting reader**.

READERLY TEXT   In *S/Z* (English translation, 1974), Roland Barthes uses the term 'readerly' or 'readable' (in French, *lisible*) to refer to those texts which are 'closed' and simply available for passive consumption by readers, by contrast with 'writerly' (*scriptible*) texts, which challenge readers to respond to the open play of textuality, where readers become more active producers (co-writers) of the text.

READER-RESPONSE CRITICISM; READER-ORIENTED CRITICISM   General terms covering criticism and theory concerned as much with how readers read as with establishing authority for interpretation within texts themselves. Specifically associated with work by, for example, Wolfgang Iser, Jonathan Culler, Michael Riffaterre, Stanley Fish, in the 1970s and early 1980s.

READING COMMUNITY   See **interpretive community**

READING FORMATION   Tony Bennett's term for 'a set of intersecting discourses that productively activate a given body of texts and the relations between them in a specific way' ('Texts, Readers, Reading Formations' (1989), p. 208): Bennett proposes to use the concept to study ways in which, in particular, reading is determined by social and political discourses, rather than by an individual text or an individual reader.

REAL READER   See **actual reader.**

RECEPTION THEORY   Study of ways in which a text is disseminated, read and responded to at any particular historical moment. In particular, reception theory is closely associated with the *Rezeptionsästhetik* of the Constance school.

RESISTING READER   Various critics have suggested that reading should involve a resistance to dominant or hegemonic structures of power inscribed in and potentially reproduced by the text. Thus Judith Fetterley, for example, argues that women should read classic American Literature against the grain in order to avoid 'immasculation', to avoid 'reading as a man'. See **oppositional reading.**

RETROACTIVE READING   Michael Riffatterre's term for the secondary stage of reading – after **heuristic reading** – in which ideas, themes, and so on are 'grasped together' in an attempt to make sense of the text as a whole – also **hermeneutic reading** (see *Semiotics of Poetry*, 1978).

REZEPTIONSÄSTHETIK   Term particularly associated with the Constance school in Germany, amongst whom Hans Robert Jauss is the most prominent. For Jauss, a literary text is produced within a context of certain **'horizons of expectations',** the parameters by which readers expect a literary text to function and within which they expect to read and understand. For Jauss, therefore, criticism should be concerned with attempts to establish the historically specific horizons of readers' expectations, knowledge, and presuppositions. For Jauss, too, the meaning of a work will change over time with changing expectations.

SUPER-READER   Michael Riffaterre's term for a hypothetical reader who has all possible knowledge of the text and its interpretations at his or her disposal, collected from other readers' analyses, editorial comments and information, students' and colleagues' interpretations, etc. The **super-reader** (inevitably someone like Riffaterre himself) is a construct, a kind of magpie-effect produced by reading not only the text but all available interpretations; compare **ideal reader.**

TRANSCENDENT READING   Jacques Derrida's term for a reading which attempts to go beyond language itself in the search for the 'meaning'.

UNDECIDABLE   See **indeterminacy.**

UNREADABILITY   Paul de Man uses the term **unreadability** to designate the irreducible conflict of grammar and rhetoric, of the literal and the figurative, or of propositional and performative aspects of language. For de Man, such conflicts produce logical **aporias** within which reading is literally impossible and the text unreadable due to the impossibility of deciding between one reading and another.

Further Reading

This is a selective list which focuses on work published in the 1980s and 1990s: for more detailed information on work published before 1980, see the bibliographies in Suleiman and Crosman (eds), and Tompkins (ed.).

1 Collections

BENNETT, ANDREW (ed.) *Reading Reading: Essays on the Theory and Practice of Reading*. Tampere, Finland: University of Tampere, 1993. (Includes essays by Michael Riffaterre, Ross Chambers, Timothy Clark, Nicholas Royle and others.)

DAVIDSON, CATHY N. (ed.) *Reading in America: Literature and Social History*. Baltimore: The Johns Hopkins University Press, 1989. (Essays, historical and sociological, on literacy, book production, book history, and empirical audience / reader research; includes essays by Darnton and Radway.)

FLYNN, ELIZABETH A. and PATROCINIO P. SCHWEICKART (eds) *Gender and Reading: Essays on Readers, Texts, and Contexts*. Baltimore: The Johns Hopkins University Press, 1986. (Important collection of essays from a variety of perspectives: includes bibliography for feminism and reader-response criticism.)

GARVIN, HARRY R. (ed.) *Theories of Reading, Looking, Listening*. Lewisburg: Bucknell University Press, 1981. (Essays by, amongst others, Louise Rosenblatt, David Bleich, Wolfgang Iser, Peter J. Rabinowitz.)

HOFFMANN, GERARD (ed.) *Making Sense: The Role of the Reader in Contemporary American Fiction*. München: Wilhelm Fink, 1989. (Includes essays by Barbara Herrnstein Smith, Steven Mailloux, Frank Lentricchia, Isab Hassan.)

HUNTER, G.K. and C.J. RAWSON (eds) *Literature and its Audience, I: Special Number, The Yearbook of English Studies*, **10** (1980). (Essays on the relationship between texts and historical audiences.)

MACHOR, JAMES L. (ed.) *Readers in History: Nineteenth-Century American Literature and the Contexts of Response.* Baltimore: The Johns Hopkins University Press, 1993. (Important collection of essays on the relationship between reading and history.)

MILLS, SARA (ed.) *Gendering the Reader.* Hemel Hempstead: Harvester Wheatsheaf, 1994. (Interdisciplinary collection of essays from perspectives including those of ethnography, sociolinguistics, literary and film theory – on reading novels, TV, pop songs, magazines, etc.)

SCOLINCOV, HANNA and PETER HOLLAND (eds) *Reading Plays: Interpretation and Reception.* Cambridge: Cambridge University Press, 1991.

SPOLSKY, ELLEN (ed.) *The Uses of Adversity: Failure and Accommodation in Reader Response.* Lewisburg, PA: Bucknell University Press, 1990. (Variable collection of essays on aspects of reading.)

SULEIMAN SUSAN R. and INGE CROSMAN (eds) *The Reader in the Text: Essays on Audience and Interpretation.* New Jersey: Princeton University Press, 1980. (Influential collection of original essays on various aspects of reading and reader-response criticism – essays by Jonathan Culler, Gerald Prince, Wolfgang Iser, and others: includes comprehensive bibliography of the field.)

TOMPKINS, JANE P. (ed.) *Reader-Response Criticism: from Formalism to Post-Structuralism.* Baltimore: The Johns Hopkins University Press, 1980. (Important collection of previously published essays in reader-response criticism, including work by Stanley Fish, Georges Poulet, Wolfgang Iser and Tompkins: includes useful annotated bibliography.)

WATERS, LINDSAY and WLAD GODZICH (eds) *Reading de Man Reading.* Minneapolis: University of Minnesota press, 1989.

2   Reader-response criticism

BERG, TEMMA F. 'Psychologies of Reading'. In Joseph Natoli (ed.) *Tracing Literary Theory.* Urbana: University of Illinois Press, 1987, pp. 248–77. (Despite its title, this essay is a standard summary of the reading theory of I.A. Richards, Louise Rosenblatt, Fish, Iser, Jauss, Holland, Bleich, and Bloom.)

BLEICH, DAVID 'Intersubjective Reading'. *New Literary History* **17** (1986): 401–21.

CALINESCU, MATEI *Rereading*. New Haven: Yale University Press, 1993.

DÄLLENBACH, LUCIEN 'Reflexivity and Reading'. *New Literary History* **11** (1980): 435–49.

— *The Mirror in the Text*. Trans. Jeremy Whiteley. Cambridge: Polity, 1989.

EAGLETON, TERRY *Literary Theory: an Introduction*. Oxford: Basil Blackwell, 1983. (See Chapter 2 on reader-response criticism.)

ECO, UMBERTO *The Role of the Reader: Explorations in the Semiotics of Texts*. Bloomington: Indiana University Press, 1979.

— *The Limits of Interpretation*. Bloomington: Indiana University Press, 1990.

FISH, STANLEY *Is There A Text in This Class? The Authority of Interpretive Communities*. Cambridge, Mass.: Harvard University Press, 1980.

FREUND, ELIZABETH *The Return of the Reader: Reader-Response Criticism*. London: Methuen, 1987. (Excellent introduction to the field.)

ISER, WOLFGANG *The Implied Reader: Patterns of Communication in Prose Fiction from Bunyan to Beckett*. Baltimore: The Johns Hopkins University Press, 1974.

— *The Act of Reading: A Theory of Aesthetic Response*. Baltimore: The Johns Hopkins University Press, 1978. (Iser's major elaboration of his influential reading theory.)

— *Prospecting: From Reader Response to Literary Anthropology*. Baltimore: The Johns Hopkins University Press, 1989.

— *The Fictive and the Imaginary: Charting Literary Anthropology*. Baltimore: The Johns Hopkins University Press, 1993.

LOTMAN, YURY M. 'The Text and the Structure of its Audience'. *New Literary History* **14** (1982): 81–7.

McCORMICK, KATHLEEN 'Swimming Upstream with Stanley Fish'. *Journal of Aesthetics and Art Criticism* **44** (1985): 67–76. (Account of Fish's changing theories of reading in the 1970s; critique of Fish's notion of interpretive communities for its restrictive conception of reading.)

NEWTON, K.M. 'Reception Theory and Reader-Response Criticism'. Chapter 7 in *Interpreting the Text: A Critical Introduction to the Theory and Practice of Literary Interpretation*. Hemel Hempstead: Harvester Wheatsheaf, 1990. (Survey/introduction to the field.)

OXENHANDLER, NEAL 'The Changing Concept of Literary Emotion: A Selective History'. *New Literary History* 20 (1988): 105–21. (On emotion/affect and reader-response criticism.)

POULET, GEORGES 'Criticism and the Experience of Interiority'. In Tompkins (ed.) *Reader-Response Criticism*, pp. 41–9.

PRATT, MARY LOUISE 'Interpretive Strategies/Strategic Interpretations: On Anglo-American Reader Response Criticism'. *Boundary 2*, 11 (1982–83): 201–31. (Critique of reader-response criticism – especially on Prince, Culler, and Fish – as apolitical and formalist.)

PRINCE, GERALD 'Notes on the Text as Reader'. In Suleiman and Crosman (eds) *The Reader in the Text*.

— 'Introduction to the Study of the Narratee'. In Tompkins (ed.) *Reader-Response Criticism*, pp. 7–25.

RABINOWITZ, PETER J. *Before Reading: Narrative Conventions and the Politics of Interpretation*. Ithaca: Cornell University Press, 1987.

— 'Whirl Without End: Audience-Oriented Criticism'. In Douglas G. Atkins and Laura Morrow (eds) *Contemporary Literary Theory*. London: Macmillan, 1989, pp. 81–100. (Survey of reader-response criticism, defining two major types of reader – 'hypothetical' and 'real'; includes brief annotated bibliography.)

RAY, WILLIAM *Literary Meaning: From Phenomenology to Deconstruction*. Oxford: Basil Blackwell, 1984.

RIFFATERRE, MICHAEL *Semiotics of Poetry*. Bloomington: Indiana University Press, 1978.

— 'The Making of the Text'. In Mario J. Valdés and Owen Miller (eds) *Identity of the Literary Text*. Toronto: University of Toronto Press, 1985, pp. 54–70.

— 'Compelling Reader Responses'. In Bennett (ed.) *Reading Reading*, pp. 85–106.

SCHOLES, ROBERT *Protocols of Reading*. New Haven: Yale University Press, 1989.

SHEPHERD, DAVID 'The Authority of Meanings and the Meanings of Authority: Some Problems in the Theory of Reading'. *Poetics Today*, 7 (1986): 129–45.

STIERLE, KARLHEINZ 'Studium: Perspectives on Institutional Modes of Reading'. *New Literary History* 22 (1991): 115–27. (On study as a mode of reading.)

TODOROV, TZVETAN 'Reading as Construction'. Chapter 4 in *Genres in Discourse*. Trans. Catherine Porter. Cambridge: Cambridge University Press, 1990. (On the question, 'How does a [classic, fictional] text lead us to the construction of an imaginary universe?')

WEBER, SAMUEL 'Caught in the Act of Reading'. In Samuel Weber (ed.) *Glyph Textual Studies I: Demarcating the Disciplines*. Minneapolis: University of Minnesota Press, 1986, pp. 181–214. (On Iser's reading theory.)

WILSON, DANIEL W. 'Readers in Texts'. *PMLA*, **96** (1981): 848–63.

WIMMERS, INGE CROSMAN *Poetics of Reading: Approaches to the Novel*. New Jersey: Princeton University Press, 1988.

3   Historical, sociological and political approaches

ALTICK, RICHARD D. *The English Common Reader: A Social History of the Mass Reading Public, 1800–1900*. Illinois: University of Chicago Press, 1957. (Seminal historical study of nineteenth-century readerships and the book trade.)

BAYM, NINA *Novels, Readers, and Reviewers: Responses to Fiction in Antebellum America*. Ithaca: Cornell University Press, 1984. (Historical study of presuppositions governing book reviews in nineteenth-century America.)

BEERS, TERRY 'Reading Reading Constraints: Conventions, Schemata, and Literary Interpretation'. *Diacritics* **18** (1988): 82–93. (On Mailloux's *Interpretive Conventions*.)

BELT, DEBRA 'The Poetics of Hostile Response, 1575–1610'. *Criticism* **33** (1991): 419–59.

BENNETT, TONY 'Texts in HIstory: the Determinations of Readings and their Texts'. In Derek Attridge et al. (eds) *Post-Structuralism and the Question of History*. Cambridge: Cambridge University Press, 1987, pp. 63–81.

— 'Text, Readers, Reading Formations'. In Philip Rice and Patricia Waugh (eds) *Modern Literary Theory: A Reader*. London: Edward Arnold, 1989, pp. 206–20.

BOURDIEU, PIERRE 'Reading, Readers, The Literant, Literature'. Chapter 6 in *In Other Words: Essays Towards a Reflexive Sociology*. Trans. Matthew Adamson. Cambridge: Polity, 1990.

CHAMBERS, ROSS 'Narrative Point'. *Southern Review*, **16** (1983): 60–73.

— *Story and Situation: Narrative Seduction and the Power of Fiction*. Manchester: Manchester University Press, 1984.

— *Room For Maneuver: Reading (the) Oppositional (in) Narrative*. Illinois: University of Chicago Press, 1991.

— 'Reading and Being Read: Irony and Critical Practice in Cultural Studies'. In Bennett (ed.) *Reading Reading*, pp. 15–43.

CHARTIER, ROGER 'Frenchness in the History of the Book: From the History of Publishing to the History of Reading'. *Proceedings of the American Antiquarian Society*, **97**: 2 (1988): 299–329.

— *The Cultural Uses of Print in Early Modern France*. Trans. Lydia G. Cochrane. New Jersey: Princeton University Press, 1987.

— 'The Practical Impact of Writing'. In Chartier (ed.) *Passions of the Renaissance*. Vol. 3 of Philippe Ariès and Georges Duby (eds) *A History of Private Life*. Cambridge, Mass.: Harvard University Press, 1989, pp. 111–59.

— 'Leisure and Sociability: Reading Aloud in Early Modern Europe'. Trans. Carol Mossman. In Susan Zimmerman and Ronald F. E. Weissman (eds) *Urban Life in the Renaissance*. Newark: University of Delaware Pres, 1989, pp. 103–20.

DARNTON, ROBERT 'Reading, Writing, and Publishing'. Chapter 6 in *The Literary Underground of the Old Regime*. Cambridge, Mass.: Harvard University Press, 1982.

— 'Readers Respond to Rousseau: The Fabrication of Romantic Sensitivity'. Chapter 6 in *The Great Cat Massacre and Other Essays in Cultural History*. New York: Basic Books, 1984.

— 'What is the History of Books' and 'First Steps Toward a History of Reading'. Chapters 7 and 9 in *The Kiss of Lamourette: Reflections in Cultural History*. London: Faber & Faber, 1990.

DAVIDSON, CATHY N. *Revolution and the World: The Rise of the Novel in America*. Oxford: Oxford University Press, 1986. (A combination of book history, reader-response criticism, and *Rezeptionsästhetik*; together with the history and sociology of reading and reception.)

DE BOLLA, PETER *The Discourse of the Sublime: Readings in History, Aesthetics and the Subject*. Oxford: Basil Blackwell, 1989. (See Chapter 10, for a discussion of eighteenth-century reading theory and practice.)

FROW, JOHN *Marxism and Literary History* (Oxford: Basil Blackwell, 1986). (See Chapter 8, 'Limits: The Politics of Reading'.)

FURET, FRANÇOIS and JACQUES OZOUF *Reading and Writing: Literacy in France from Calvin to Jules Ferry*. Cambridge: Cambridge University Press, 1982. (A history of literacy up to the twentieth century.)

HOLUB, ROBERT C. *Reception Theory: a Critical Introduction*. London: Methuen, 1984.

— *Crossing Borders: Reception Theory, Post-structuralism, Deconstruction*. Madison: University of Wisconsin Press, 1992. (On German reception theory, and a polemical attack on Anglo-American ignorance of *Rezeptionsästhetik*.)

JACK, IAN *The Poet and His Audience*. Cambridge: Cambridge University Press, 1984.

JAUSS, HANS ROBERT *Toward an Aesthetic of Reception*. Trans. Timothy Bahti (Brighton: Harvester, 1982).

— 'The Identity of the Poetic Text in the Changing Horizon of Understanding'. In Mario J. Valdés and Owen Miller (eds) *Identity of the Literary Text*. Toronto: University of Toronto Press, 1985, pp. 146–74.

— 'The Theory of Reception: a Retrospective of its Unrecognized Prehistory'. In Peter Collier and Helger Geyer-Ryan (eds) *Literary Theory Today*. Cambridge: Polity, 1990, pp. 53–73. (On the precursors of reception theory – including theology, law, philosophy.)

KITTLER, FRIEDRICH A. *Discourse Networks, 1800/1900*. Trans. Michael Metteer. California: Stanford University Press, 1990.

KLANCHER, JON P. *The Making of English Reading Audiences, 1790–1832*. Madison: University of Wisconsin Press, 1987.

McALEER, JOSEPH *Popular Reading and Publishing in Britain, 1914–1950* Oxford: Oxford University Press, 1992. (Sociological study of popular reading habits, publishing, etc.)

McGANN, JEROME J. *The Beauty of Inflections: Literary Investigations in Historical Method and Theory*. Oxford: Oxford University Press, 1985.

— *Social Values and Poetic Acts: the Historical Judgment of Literary Work*. Cambridge, Mass.: Harvard University Press, 1988.

MAILLOUX, STEVEN J. *Interpretive Conventions: the Reader in the Study of American Fiction*. Ithaca: Cornell University Press, 1982.

— *Rhetorical Power*. Ithaca: Cornell University Press, 1989.

RAJAN, TILOTTAMA *The Supplement of Reading: Figures of Understanding in Romantic Theory and Practice*. Ithaca: Cornell University Press, 1990.

ROSE, JONATHAN 'Rereading the English Common Reader: A Preface to a History of Audiences'. *Journal of the History of Ideas* **53** (1992): 47–70.

SHEPHERD, DAVID 'Bakhtin and the Reader'. In Ken Kirschkop and David Shepherd (eds) *Bakhtin and Cultural Theory*. Manchester: Manchester University Press, 1989. (On Bakhtin and reader-response criticism: seeks to elaborate similarities and dissimilarities.)

SLAWIŃSKI, JANUSZ 'Reading and Reader in the Literary Historical Process'. *New Literary History* **19** (1988): 521–39.

TROTTER, DAVID *The Making of the Reader: Language and Subjectivity in Modern American, English and Irish Poetry*. London: Macmillan, 1984.

4   Poststructuralist and psychoanalytic approaches

ALCORN, MARSHALL W. and MARK BRACHER 'Literature, Psychoanalysis, and the Re-Formation of the Self: A New Direction for Reader-Response Theory'. *PMLA*, **100** (1985): 342–54.

BARTHES, ROLAND *S/Z*. Trans. Richard Miller. 1974. Oxford: Basil Blackwell, 1990.

— *The Pleasure of the Text*. Trans. Richard Miller. New York: Farrar, Straus & Giroux, 1975.

— 'Theory of the Text'. In Robert Young (ed.) *Untying the Text: A Post-Structuralist Reader*. London: Routledge & Kegan Paul, 1981, pp. 32–47.

— 'On Reading'. In *The Rustle of Language*. Trans. Richard Howard. Oxford: Basil Blackwell, 1986.

BENNETT, ANDREW 'On Not Reading: Reading Theory'. In Bennett (ed.) *Reading Reading*, pp. 221–37.

BERG, TEMMA F. '*La Carte Postale*: Reading (Derrida) Reading'. *Criticism*, **28** (1986): 323–40.

BLANCHOT, MAURICE *The Space of Literature*. Trans. Ann Smock. Lincoln: University of Nebraska Press, 1982.

BROOKS, PETER *Reading for the Plot: Design and Intention in Narrative*. Oxford: Oxford University Press, 1984. (Influential elaboration of the desires and impulsions of narrative, or plot, in reading: based on post-Freudian theories of desire.)

CLARK, TIMOTHY 'Reading in Blanchot'. In Bennett (ed.) *Reading Reading*, pp. 183–99.

CORNIS-POPE, MARCEL *Hermeneutic Desire and Critical Rewriting: Narrative Interpretation in the Wake of Poststructuralism*. London: Macmillan, 1992. (Elaborate presentation of theories of reader-response criticism and deconstruction (especially de Man); based on a reading of Henry James's 'The Figure in the Carpet'.)

CULLER, JONATHAN *The Pursuit of Signs: Semiotics, Literature, Deconstruction*. London: Routledge & Kegan Paul, 1981. (Includes chapters on 'Semiotics as a Theory of Reading', on Riffaterre and on Fish.)

— *On Deconstruction: Theory and Criticism After Structuralism*. London: Routledge & Kegan Paul, 1983. (Includes extensive discussions of reading theory, including chapter on 'Reading as a Woman'.)

— *Allegories of Reading: Figural Language in Rousseau, Nietzsche, Rilke, and Proust*. New Haven: Yale University Press, 1979.

DE MAN, PAUL *Blindness and Insight: Essays in the Rhetoric of Contemporary Criticism*. 2nd edn; London: Methuen, 1983.

— *The Resistance to Theory*. Manchester: Manchester University Press, 1986.

DERRIDA, JACQUES *Of Grammatology*. Trans. Gayatri Chakravorty Spivak (Baltimore: The Johns Hopkins University Press, 1976). (See especially 'The Exorbitant Question of Method', pp. 157–64.)

— *Acts of Literature*, ed. Derek Attridge. New York: Routledge, 1992. (See especially '"This Strange Institution Called Literature": An Interview with Jacques Derrida', pp. 33–75.)

FELMAN, SHOSHANA 'Turning the Screw of Interpretation'. *Yale French Studies*, **55/56** (1977): 94–207.

— 'On Reading Poetry: Reflections on the Limits and Possibilities of Psychoanalytical Approaches'. In Joseph H. Smith (ed.) *The Literary Freud: Mechanisms of Defense and the Poetic Will*. Psychiatry and the Humanities, vol. 4. New Haven: Yale University Press, 1980, pp. 119–48.

HAMACHER, WERNER 'LECTIO: de Man's Imperative'. In Waters and Godzich (eds) *Reading de Man Reading*.

HOLLAND, NORMAN 'Unity Identity Text Self'. In Tompkins (ed.)
Reader-Response Criticism.

KENNEDY, ALAN *Reading Resistance Value: Deconstructive Practice and the
Politics of Literary Critical Encounters.* London: Macmillan, 1990.

MILLER, J. HILLIS *The Ethics of Reading: Kant, de Man, Eliot, Trollope, James,
and Benjamin.* New York: Columbia University Press, 1987.

— *Versions of Pygmalion.* Cambridge, Mass.: Harvard University Press,
1990.

PLATZ, NORBERT H. 'Analyzing the Reader: A Critical Survey of Recent
Psychoanalytical Theories of Reading'. In Graham McGregor and
R.S. White (eds) *The Art of Listening.* London: Croom Helm, 1986,
pp. 87–101. (Summaries of the work of, especially, Holland and Bleich;
includes brief bibliography.)

REDFIELD, MARC W. 'De Man, Schiller, and the Politics of Reception'. In
William Flesch (ed.) *Aesthetic Ideology: De Man and Politics.* Detroit:
Wayne State University Press, 1990.

ROUSTANG, FRANÇOIS. 'On Reading Again'. In Thomas M. Kavanagh (ed.)
The Limits of Theory. California: Stanford University Press, 1989.

ROYLE, NICHOLAS *Telepathy and Literature: Essays on the Reading Mind.*
Oxford: Basil Blackwell, 1991.

— 'On Not Reading: Derrida and Beckett'. In Bennett (ed.) *Reading
Reading*, pp. 201–19.

SCHRIFT, ALAN D. *Nietzsche and the Question of Interpretation: Between
Hermeneutics and Deconstruction.* New York: Routledge, 1990.

STEWART, GARRETT *Reading Voices: Literature and the Phonotext.* Berkeley:
University of California Press, 1990. (On the relationship between
(silent) reading and voicing.)

WARMINSKI, ANDREZEJ 'Dreadful Reading: Blanchot on Hegel'. *Yale French
Studies,* **69** (1985): 267–75.

WEBER, SAMUEL *Institution and Interpretation.* Minneapolis: University of
Minnesota Press, 1987. (Including essays on Fish's *Is There a Text in This
Class?*, and On Derrida and reading.)

WRIGHT, ELIZABETH 'The Reader in Analysis'. In James Donald (ed.)
Psychoanalysis and Cultural Theory: Thresholds. London: Macmillan, 1991,
pp. 158–68.

5 Feminist approaches

ABEL, ELIZABETH 'Black Writing, White Reading: Race and the Politics of Feminist Interpretation'. *Critical Inquiry*, **19** (1993): 470–98.

CAUGHIE, PAMELA L. 'Women Reading/Reading Women: a Review of Some Recent Books on Gender and Reading'. *Papers on Language and Literature*, **24** (1988): 317–35.

COMLEY, NANCY R. 'Reading and Writing Genders'. In Bruce Henricksen and Thais E. Morgan (eds) *Reorientations: Critical Theories and Pedagogies*. Urbana: University of Illinois Press, 1990, pp. 179–92.

FELMAN, SHOSHANA *What Does a Woman Want? Reading and Sexual Difference*. Baltimore: The Johns Hopkins University Press, 1993.

FETTERLEY, JUDITH *The Resisting Reader: a Feminist Approach to American Fiction*. Bloomington: Indiana University Press, 1978. (Influential early elaboration of feminist reading theory, plotting the 'immasculation' of women readers.)

FLINT, KATE *The Woman Reader, 1837–1914*. Oxford: Oxford University Press, 1993. (Important consideration of the relationship between gender and representations of reading in the nineteenth century.)

JACOBUS, MARY *Reading Woman: Essays in Feminist Criticism*. London: Methuen, 1986.

KOLODNY, ANNETTE 'A Map for Rereading: Or, Gender and the Interpretation of Literary Texts'. *New Literary History* **11** (1980): 451–67.

MILLER, D.A. '"*Cage aux folles*": Sensation and Gender in Wilkie Collins's *The Woman in White*'. In *Speaking of Gender*, ed. Elaine Showalter. New York: Routledge, 1989, pp. 187–215.

MILLER, NANCY K. 'Rereading as a Woman: the Body in Practice'. *Poetics Today*, **6** (1985): 291–9.

MULVEY, LAURA 'Visual Pleasure and Narrative Cinema'. *Screen*, **16**: 3 (1975): 6–18. (On the identification of audiences with male characters in Hollywood movies, as 'movers' of the action, as opposed to screen women, who are the object of the gaze.)

PETERSON, CARLA L. *The Determined Reader: Gender and Culture in the Novel from Napoleon to Victoria*. New Brunswick: Rutgers University Press, 1986. (Study of 'reader-protagonists' in nineteenth-century English and French novels.)

RADWAY, JANICE A. *Reading the Romance: Women, Patriarchy, and Popular Literature*. Chapel Hill: University of North Carolina Press, 1984.

SCHOLES, ROBERT 'Reading Like a Man'. In Alice Jardine and Paul Smith (eds) *Men In Feminism*. New York: Methuen, 1987, pp. 204–18. (Critique of deconstruction, especially of Culler's section on 'Reading as a Woman' in *On Deconstruction*.)

SEGAL, NAOMI *The Unintended Reader: Feminism and 'Manon Lescaut'*. Cambridge: Cambridge University Press, 1986. (Argues that the alienation of women from 'masculine' texts allows the woman a position of privilege, in that 'the text's refusal of her can be construed as an invitation to seek its unconscious meaning, the initial, repressed impulse' from which it emerges (p. xiii).)

WYATT, JEAN *Reconstructing Desire: The Role of the Unconscious in Women's Reading and Writing*. University of North Carolina Press, 1990.

6 Other approaches

APPLEYARD, J.A. *Becoming a Reader: The Experience of Fiction from Childhood to Adulthood*. Cambridge: Cambridge University Press, 1990.

HARKER, W. JOHN 'Information Processing and the Reading of Literary Texts'. *New Literary History* **20** (1989): 465–81.

KENNEDY, ALAN *The Psychology of Reading*. London: Methuen, 1984. (Approach from the perspective of clinical psychology.)

LAW, JULES DAVID 'Reading with Wittgenstein and Derrida'. In Reed Way Dasenbrock (ed.) *Redrawing the Lines: Analytic Philosophy, Deconstruction, and Literary Theory*. Minneapolis: Minnesota University Press, 1989.

PEREC, GEORGES 'Lire: esquisse socio-physiologique', *Esprit* (January 1976): 9–20. (On the reading body.)

PROUST, MARCEL *On Reading Ruskin*. Trans. Jean Autret et al. New Haven: Yale University Press, 1987.

RICOEUR, PAUL *Time and Narrative*. Vol. 3. Trans. Kathleen Blamey and David Pellauer, Illinois: University of Chicago Press, 1988. (See Chapter 7, 'The World of the Text and the World of the Reader'.)

— 'World of the Text, World of the Reader' (interview with Paul Ricoeur by Joël Roman), in Mario J. Valdés (ed.) *A Ricoeur Reader: Reflection and Imagination* (Hemel Hempstead: Harvester Wheatsheaf, 1991).

SMITH, FRANK *Understanding Reading: a Psycholinguistic Analysis of Reading and Learning to Read*. 2nd edn; New York: Holt, Rinehart and Winston, 1978.

— *Reading*. 2nd edn; Cambridge: Cambridge University Press, 1985.

Notes on Authors

MAURICE BLANCHOT is a French novelist and critic, of whose many works a number have been translated into English, including *Death Sentence* (New York: Station Hill, 1978), *The Space of Literature* (Lincoln: University of Nebraska Press, 1982), *Writing of the Disaster* (Lincoln: University of Nebraska Press, 1986), and *The Gaze of Orpheus and Other Literary Essays* (New York: Station Hill, 1981).

YVES BONNEFOY is Professor of Comparative Poetics at the Collège de France and is one of France's most respected living poets. He is the author of a number of books of poetry, including *Du mouvement et de l'immobilité de Douve* (1953), *Pierre écrite* (1965), *Dans le leurre du seuil* (1975), *Ce qui fut sans lumière* (1987). Bonnefoy is also a translator of Shakespeare and has published numerous critical essays on the visual arts, Shakespeare, and poetry. A collection of his essays has been translated into English by John Naughton as *The Act and Place of Poetry: Selected Essays* (Chicago: University of Chicago Press, 1989).

ROGER CHARTIER is Director of Studies at the Centre for Historical Research at the Ecole des Hautes Etudes en Sciences Sociales, in Paris. He has been visiting professor at Yale University and the University of California, Berkeley. Professor Chartier is the author of a number of books, including *The Cultural Uses of Print in Early Modern France* (1987), *Cultural History: Between Practices and Representations* (Ithaca: Cornell University Press, 1988), and *The Cultural Origins of the French Revolution* (Durham: Duke University Press, 1991).

MICHEL DE CERTEAU was, at the time of his death in 1986, Directeur d'Etudes in the Historical Anthropology of Beliefs at the Ecole des Hautes Etudes en Sciences Sociales, Paris. He is the author of a number of books which cross disciplinary fields, including *The Practice of Everyday Life* (Berkeley: University of California Press, 1984), *Heterologies: Discourse on the Other* (Minneapolis: University of Minnesota Press, 1986), *The Writing of History* (New York: Columbia University Press, 1988), and *The Mystic Fable: The Sixteenth and Seventeenth Centuries* (Chicago: University of Chicago Press, 1992).

PAUL DE MAN was, until his death in 1983, Sterling Professor of the Humanities at Yale University. He is the author of a number of books, including *Blindness and Insight: Essays in the Rhetoric of Contemporary Criticism* (1983), *Allegories of Reading: Figural Language in Rousseau, Nietzsche, Rilke, and Proust* (1979), and *The Resistance to Theory* (1986).

WAI-CHEE DIMOCK is associate professor of literature at Brandeis University. Professor Dimock is the author of *Empire for Liberty: Melville and the Poetics of Individualism* (New Jersey: Princeton University Press, 1989), and of *Symbolic Equality: American Literature, Law, Political Culture* (forthcoming).

SHOSHANA FELMAN is Thomas E. Donnelley Professor of French and Comparative Literature at Yale University. Professor Felman is the author of a number of books concerning feminism and psychoanalysis, including *Writing and Madness* (Ithaca: Cornell University Press, 1985), *The Literary Speech Act: Don Juan with J.L. Austin, or Seduction in Two Languages* (Ithaca: Cornell University Press, 1983), and *What Does a Woman Want? Reading and Sexual Difference* (1993).

WOLFGANG ISER is Professor of English and Comparative Literature at the University of Constance and Professor of English at the University of California, Irvine. Professor Iser's books include *The Implied Reader: Patterns of Communication in Prose Fiction from Bunyan to Beckett* (1974), *The Act of Reading: A Theory of Aesthetic Response* (1978), *Prospecting: From Reader Response to Literary Anthropology* (1989), and *The Fictive and the Imaginary: Charting Literary Anthropology* (1993).

MARY JACOBUS is John Wendell Anderson Professor of English at Cornell University. In addition to two books on Wordsworth, Professor Jacobus has published a number of books in the fields of feminism and psychoanalysis, including *Women Writing and Writing about Women* (editor; New York: Harper and Row, 1979), *Reading Woman: Essays in Feminist Criticism* (1986), *Body/Politics: Women and the Discourses of Science* (co-editor; London: Routledge, 1989), and *First Things: Reading the Maternal Imaginary* (forthcoming).

WAYNE KOESTENBAUM is Associate Professor of English at Yale University. Professor Koestenbaum is the author of *Double Talk: The Erotics of Male Literary Collaboration* (London: Routledge, 1989), and *The Queen's Throat: Opera, Homosexuality and the Mystery of Desire* (New York: Simon and Schuster, 1993), and of two volumes of poetry, *Ode to Anna Moffo and Other Poems* (Persea Books, 1990) and *Rhapsodies of a Repeat Offender* (New York: Persea Books, 1994).

VINCENT B. LEITCH is Professor of English at Purdue University. He is the author of *Deconstructive Criticism: An Advanced Introduction* (New York:

Columbia University Press, 1983) and *Cultural Criticism, Literary Theory, Poststructuralism* (New York: Columbia University Press, 1992).

J. HILLIS MILLER is Distinguished Professor of English and Comparative Literature at the University of California at Irvine. Professor Miller is the author of many books, including *Fiction and Repetition: Seven English Novels* (Oxford: Basil Blackwell, 1982), *The Ethics of Reading* (1987), *Versions of Pygmalion* (1990), *Tropes, Parables, Performatives: Essays on Twentieth-Century Literature* (Durham: Duke University Press, 1990), *Victorian Subjects* (Durham: Duke University Press, 1990), *Hawthorne and History: Defacing It* (Oxford: Basil Blackwell, 1991), *Ariadne's Thread* (New Haven: Yale University Press, 1992), and *Illustration* (Cambridge, Mass.: Harvard University Press, 1992).

PATROCINIO P. SCHWEICKART is Professor of English and Women's Studies at the University of New Hampshire. Professor Schweickart is co-editor of *Gender and Reading: Essays on Readers, Texts, and Contexts* (1986) and editor of the *NWSA Journal*, the scholarly journal of the National Women's Studies Association.

Index